# My Secret Self:

*SERIES - BOOK TWO*

*Questioning Life
in Marriage*

**Christine U. Cowin**

**My Secret Self: Questioning Life in Marriage**
First published in Australia by Christine U. Cowin 2019
www.christineucowinwriter.com
www.amazon.com/author/christineucowinwriter

Prepublication Data Service details available from
The National Library of Australia
ISBN: 978-0-6484013-2-2 (pbk)
ISBN: 978-0-6484013-3-9 (ebk)

Typesetting and design by Publicious Book Publishing
Published in collaboration with Publicious Book Publishing
www.publicious.com.au

# Dedication

I dedicate my book to all those who have crossed my path, offering me a chance to learn what I needed to learn. This story is my truth and there is no intention on my part to ever hurt or harm anybody, I just want to tell my true story. Thank you to all who have been a part of my life. Our journey together has enabled me to understand life and grow as a person. And for that I love you and appreciate you.

# Acknowledging

Each side will have their own story to tell and their reasons for what they did and why they did it. It's our conditionings that separate us all and the fact that each feels they are right. Maybe none of us are right.

## Other Book by Christine U. Cowin

*My Secret Self: Book 1 - Trials and Tribulations of an Innocent*, published in, September 2018

My website contains my Bio, links to
purchase my books and reviews:
Website: www.christineucowinwriter.com
Email address: christine@christineucowinwriter.com
Amazon Central Authors Page:
www.amazon.com/author/christineucowinwriter

# She Is Ready

She is ready,
Steady, steady she must go,
Don't despair,
Your turn will come for the curtain to lift,
Trust your heart,
Live and wait,
Study don't hesitate,
Life and knowledge will open doors to you,
Your journey is long,
The time is near to bring forth your true self.

Christine U. Cowin

# Mysterious Me

I am a mystery to me; because I was never allowed to be me,
I succumbed to the whims of others and allowed them
to squash me,
My heart grew wiser and started to question,
Caught in the illusion was a hidden self, an unsure self,
Who am I?
What is this all about?
Seek to reveal.

Christine U. Cowin

# Introduction

How deceived we are in life. I am sure we're dancing to the tune of some author directing his play of mischief and mystery.

I had left school and was embarking on a job that I didn't want to be in. This was it for a woman. Marriage was the only avenue left to escape my life with my parents. From a teenager, destiny told me I'd marry a person from overseas, and fate, or the director of the play, organised that.

This will prove to be not in line with me, nonetheless it was done. There were two children born from this union. I had to bring changes in for them. I didn't want my children to follow in the footsteps of my life or my husband's life.

How could I ensure those changes would be brought forth and family patterns wouldn't carry through to them? Trust was all I had and my mind was determined enough to do it. I knew what I wanted and didn't want. Only I could make those changes happen.

The families of both sides would be a challenge for me; as time moved forward, bigger questions would invade my mind. I'd discover an aspect of myself: a seeker of knowledge. I bided my time.

I wanted to read books; this new aspect was causing my husband concern. I knew reading was a normal thing to do, but not in his eyes. He was thinking I may develop ideas around romanticism, which was the furthest thing from my mind. I would bide my time and grow silently as I waited out my chance for change.

We all carry a secret self within, and until we unlock those secret parts of ourselves, life will push us to seek out those hidden parts.

# A Thought

I was born to experience life and my experiences in life have created this book. Without those experiences, how would I have grown as a person to find my true self out of the lie I thought I was?

Life is to be lived and experienced to develop and grow as a person. When we deny our Self this opportunity, we deny our Self the experiences of life.

Live your life, whether it is good, bad, or indifferent, until you conquer the falsehood holding you a prisoner of your mind.

Just take the reins of life and go for it, allowing your Spirit to be your horse as you ride through the plays of your journeys.

So don't hold back on those reins; you'll never know if you don't take the plunge, to answer what you need to do.

## Phrase:

Look beyond the dramas of your life to see the wisdom in your life.

## Quote

All I encounter are mere characters of me, for I am the creator of my own play, I am the storyteller unfolding the story.

> – Christine U. Cowin

# Chapter 1

# My First Job Interview

In the new year of 1969, I wanted to train as a metallurgist. My parents took me to one of our regional mining companies for a job interview. I put on my lovely blue A-line dress, a mature look for the job interview. In this dress my whole sense of being changed. I wasn't the wild girl I'd so far been. I became the serious, proper girl. The drive down to Dawson Hill was quiet; my parents didn't have much to say to me or each other, especially when Dad was in our company. Mum had been connecting with me and we seemed to be hitting it off away from him. I just admired the scenery as we travelled along, wondering how long it would be before all the vacant land between Dawson Hill and Hastings Crossing would be filled with houses.

I felt old, and ready for something. I wasn't sure what it was, but there was a change in the air. I sensed it. It had been good going out with Carmel, and I was so glad I'd met Brook. I pondered on how nice it was, but he'd gone to Jacksonville. I had to be more serious. What would have made me happier would have been if I could have gone on to fifth and sixth year.

We arrived at the head office. I didn't know anything about metallurgy but I loved geography, and metals and metal compounds in science. There was some connection I had with these subjects, but I was not sure what or where from.

I felt things from somewhere deep inside me. It was like there was an outer layer of me and a hidden layer.

Dad asked a passerby for the main office block, and the gentleman indicated with a nod of his head and a smile. At the receptionist's desk, the lady smiled politely and ushered us into a waiting room, telling us she'd inform Mr Bentley. The waiting room was plain and drab, with no feeling or welcoming furniture. Mum picked up a magazine, browsing. I glanced over at Dad; he was reading the notice board. I sat on my chair and scanned the room. I felt a bit nervous and numb because I didn't know what to expect. An unknown feeling grabbed me just as this short, middle-aged man with grey, receding hair walked in. He was wearing brown-rimmed glasses. He seemed impatient as he adjusted his glasses. All eyes on him, we stood as he edged in closer to us.

'Yes, how can I help you?' he impolitely asked. Straight away I knew he didn't like what he saw.

My father spoke up. 'My daughter wants to be a metallurgist.'

The man leaned around Dad to get a better view. I could feel his contempt and his thoughts; how could she think she'd get a job here? Not commenting, he turned back to my parents, coldly stating, 'Take her to the typing pool; she'll be married in two years.'

My parents were stunned speechless. The man walked out, leaving us all dumbfounded. There was nothing we could do.

Dad asked me, 'What do you want to do?'

Disappointed, I said, 'I want to go home.'

We drove home in silence. I sat on the back seat thinking, I'll be married in two years? How does he know that? I haven't even got a boyfriend, or even thought that I wanted to marry. I had no intention of marrying until I was at least twenty-eight. Annoyed with myself, and the man, I remembered I'd marry a person from overseas anyway.

My first job interview was disastrous but life goes on. Dad pulled into the driveway at the top gate. I got out of the car and opened the gate. He drove through and I gently closed the gate, looking at the neighbours' houses across the road, wondering how Sherry was in Rosemount. How lucky she was to have a bigger sister to help her move out of the country life. I loved here and I loved the farm, however it was time for a change. I wanted a new life. Now Aunty Connie was preoccupied with her husband, there was no way she could help me to move to Rosemount. I walked to the next gate, opened and closed it, and walked to the house. Nothing was said, and life continued without any change.

# Chapter 2

# My Car Has To Be Replaced

I eventually found a job vacancy at Bolt Steel Fabrications in the industrial section of Hastings Crossing. I was given an interview for 10am with the manager, Mr Leif Nordstrom, on 7th January. I wore my mature A-line again. Mum and I arrived at the main gate at 9.45am. I parked the car on the road so Mum could see me walk into the complex.

Mum had said she'd come in with me to the office. I said nicely, 'Mum, I want to do this by myself.' She could see from my face I needed to do this alone, so she agreed to wait. I breathed a sigh of relief because I didn't want to look like a little girl, especially after the last interview. I think having my parents with me may have lost me that job.

I went over to a demountable building on the right. I knocked and waited.

A young woman in her twenties opened the door. 'Can I help you?'

'Yes. Hello, ah, um, my name is Christine Kinread and I have an appointment with Mr Nordstrom.'

I followed her to a room. 'Take a seat. I'll let him know you're here.' She smiled and I smiled back. After a while, she re-entered the room and said, 'You can go in now.'

'Thanks.'

He was sitting behind a large desk and never stood up, only indicated with a nod for me to sit. I sat and waited for him to respond, thinking what an unusual-looking man. There was a moment's silence. He was finishing up some paperwork. He fascinated me because I'd never seen anyone with a body his shape. He had a big belly, the back of his head was flat, and his face was a bit like a hound dog. I could see he wasn't old, probably in his thirties, but he looked old with his big stomach. He was almost lying on the table as he worked, and he didn't look at me much. Then he sat up straight and asked for my school score.

I handed him my school certificate. Impatiently, he asked me to write my name and address as quickly as I could. I sprawled my name and address over the paper, not being careful or neat, but fast.

He checked it and said, 'Call me this afternoon around 3pm.'

I knew that was the end of our interview, so I got up, said thank you, and left. In the car, Mum asked me how I went. I told her I wasn't sure but he'd told me to call at 3pm. We went to Grandma Owen's house and sat there until three, when I called Mr Nordstrom and was given the job at Bolt Steel Fabrications. Now I was set: a new job, my own car, and money I earned.

My job started the following week. On my first day I was formally introduced to the secretary, Charlene, and she was so lovely, very helpful, and explained to me what I had to do, letting me know I could come to her at any time for help. I got to know the other staff members; many men in their twenties and thirties worked in the main office. There were engineers, designers and supervisors, and leading hands. Each had their own personalities and funny ways. All seemed to have a good sense of humor and liked to joke around. I was very shy around these men and it was hard for me to break free of it. Mr Nordstrom was the same; he didn't say much to us women. He seemed to be more at ease with the men. My role was very basic. I filled in order forms and invoices, and often went driving up the street on errands for Mr Nordstrom.

At the end of January, school started for my sister and brother, and they had to walk the long dirt road to catch the school bus. This was Maxine's last year at high school and she told me about her fear of Derek. After the flood had washed away the bridge we used to cross to walk the track to the road nearer to Lachlan's Pit, he had been picking us up in his jeep at our top gate and driving us to the alternative bus stop off Spencer Shire.

It wasn't arranged, but if he was on the road, he stopped and picked us up. Most days he'd arrive as we reached the road. If he didn't, we'd walk to the bus stop. Maxine became more frightened of Derek, especially if Barton didn't go to school, which was hardly ever. She became a bit closer to me; I understood her anguish. Even though we fought like cats and dogs, I wouldn't let her feel afraid. Despite how she was unkind to me in our early days, I never held that against her.

Often she'd come with me and it was fun. With my newfound freedom, I became more outgoing and loved to show off in the car. Going to work one day with Maxine, I was showing off, but it got out of hand and we nearly ended up in a dried-up creek bed. I was fish-tailing down the road and caught some really loose gravel and spun the car one-eighty degrees. For me, it was fun, and I had the car under control. We ended up facing home again. I looked over at Maxine, who was holding on tightly still, and I laughed. Her eyes narrowed.

She said not too angrily, 'That wasn't funny.' She knew she needed me, and as far as I was concerned, she could have blasted me. I didn't care. We still had our differences, but time would heal them. Neither of us had the opportunity to go further at school. My parents never encouraged us to think of an educated life, and to be truthful, I don't think they realised the importance of education. The distance between our home, town, school and work was an issue. Dad didn't want to be paying for my petrol as well as his own, and I guess as soon as we got jobs, that took that worry and responsibility away from him.

One of my father's problems was being responsible. He'd had it too easy all his life, living with his mother, where he never had to pay rent or utility bills. Still, he and Mum never saved any money between them. Mum was saving. She'd confided in me how she had this secret bank account and I wasn't to tell anyone about it. She knew I could keep a secret, and she knew she could tell me anything and it would stay with me. My parents had money for themselves, but not us kids for our further education. How I would have loved to have gone on to university. I felt mine and my siblings' lives would have been so different if we'd lived in town, moving away from Grandma's house and her influence. In town, us kids would have had more opportunities. We could have played sports, been involved in arts, and mixed more with other children. Our parents would have seen how important it was for children to have a good education, because they'd have got to see how other families encouraged their children to study further. Sometimes I don't think they saw us; they were too tied up in their own lives.

Later on, my Standard 10 car developed lots of mechanical problems. Without asking me, Dad decided I needed a new car. He asked Grandma to lend me some money to buy a better car. I had to pay her back a certain amount of money each week out of my pay. Dad arranged all of this for me, and next I knew, I had a debt of twelve hundred dollars. My wages didn't stretch far enough for that debt and the lifestyle I was starting to enjoy. Twenty-seven dollars a week; I had my pay spent before I got it. This was one of the worst times of my life. I'd be telling my grandma I'd pay her some money next week, but next week came and I didn't have the money. I guess she resolved she wouldn't be getting her money back, and she didn't, but I didn't ask for that debt.

My new job gave me a sense of newfound power. I was starting to buy lovely clothes. Now I had this flash car, a Falcon 1966, a relatively late model car in March 1969. I didn't know that what goes around comes around, and some of us must experience similar issues to understand others' dilemmas. I was totally irresponsible and should have said no to my father's suggestion and gone for a car I could afford and been responsible for payments that were in proportion to my wages. The problem for me was seeing such a large debt and a small wage. It just didn't match.

My girlfriend Carmel and I had lots of good times in that car. We would go to the discos around town. It was good that there was no set time for me to come home. My parents never placed a curfew on me and I was never answerable to them. Most times I spent my weekends at my friend's house, which I'd been doing for years.

Driving home along the old dirt road was never an issue. I had no fears in this period of my life. All my fears of the unknown were gone. Now I wasn't scared. Many times I'd come home around twelve, or into the early morning hours.

One night it was really late, about 1am, and I pulled into the top gate, parking the car on the top of the little sloping hill that rolled down into our property. I got out of the car and went to open the gate. As I was removing the heavy chain, I heard a noise. Quickly I turned around. My car was running towards me. My reflexes were fast. I put my hands out to stop the full force of the car rolling onto me and was pinned at my pelvic area, jammed between the car and the gate. I tried to push the car off me, up the little hill, but I wasn't strong enough. The only thing left to do was to start screaming out. 'Mum, Mum,' I screamed, and continued to scream until she came running up behind me. So did the neighbours, Todd and his mum, from across the road. Todd got into the car and drove it back off me. I righted myself and Mum came through the gate, asking me if I was alright. Todd and his mum were doing likewise. He told me his mother had heard my screams and she woke him. I looked at Mrs Dawes' toothless face and thanked her. I was so glad Todd had been home, because if not, Mum would have had to go back and get Dad. Mum was good and I felt her concern for me. She constantly asked was I alright.

'Yes, Mum, just stunned, and it scared me a bit when I turned and saw the car coming towards me. I couldn't get out of its way.' I laughed.

She said, 'I thought I was dreaming and hearing your calls, then I woke completely and realised they weren't in a dream.'

'Well, I'm glad you heard me or I could have been pinned there until morning.'

# Chapter 3

# Grandma Owens, But Use Henderson

I'd never had much to do with my Grandma Owens, as I knew her, on my mother's side of the family. It was her birthday and I decided to buy her a gift. Our relationship wasn't the same as with Dad's mum. We only visited her now and then with Mum. Grandma was a quiet, distant, secretive woman. She seemed unusual to me. She was very guarded; you could never get to close to her, but she always intrigued me. This confused me at times. I'd question Mum about Grandma Owens and Mum would tell me that the man Grandma was married to, Mum's father, was from a wealthy family and this family disowned him when he married Grandma because she was poor. That seemed very harsh to me. Mum told me that her father died when she was two-and-a-half years old, killed on the railway tracks. She disclosed that he was an alcoholic, and he fell onto the rail tracks and was run over by a passing train. With quick calculations, I realised my Aunty Kay was in the womb when he died, because there was three years between Mum and Kay. So Aunty Kay didn't know her dad, like my father didn't know his dad. And there were the two names: Owens and Henderson. I knew Grandma used Owens, and so did my mum, and I did know about these two names because, I'd heard them mentioned. When I got my birth certificate, on it I read Henderson as Mum's name. Mum had always called herself Carol Owens and didn't want to talk about the names too much, or maybe she didn't have an answer as to why, and just said Grandma used the name Owens, which was the name of the man who had left Grandma the house she lived in after his death. I accepted Mum's answer and was told, if I had to fill in any legal papers, I had to put Henderson down as my mother's maiden name.

I felt it was time to get to know this Grandma without my Mum around. I was so excited. I'd gone present-hunting and found her the perfect gift, spending my whole week's pay on her. I loved to buy gifts, and best of all, I loved people's reactions to the gifts I'd bought them. It gave me a lot of pleasure.

Grandma was home on her birthday, and on entering her house through the back door, I went up to her and said, 'Happy birthday, Grandma,' and handed her my gift. Her face was serious, but she was always like that. 'I know I've never bought you anything before, but now I'm working, I can.'

'Do you want a cup of tea?' she asked.

I sat down and she made our tea and we talked about my work. I could see our worlds were different. Grandma lived a very poor existence and only had the basic necessities in her house. Her homemade stocking rugs scattered the floors over old, worn-out linoleum, but you could see she was extremely clean.

She opened her gift, but there was no reaction or appreciation. She said, 'they're nice, Christine,' putting them aside.

'I am glad you like them, Grandma,' I said, smiling slightly.

We sipped our tea and she asked me, 'How's your mother?'

Openly, I replied, 'She's good, but she's always complaining about something and it's hard to listen to her complaints.'

Grandma asked, 'What does she complain about?'

I looked at her with surprise, thinking she must know. 'Dad,' I said, pausing as I watched her face. 'Mum's always telling me about her problems with him.'

'Maybe she has lots of worries with him,' Grandma suggested.

'Yes, but I get sick of hearing about him from her.' I was not usually this talkative with her, or other people, for that matter. I really opened up to her and became very comfortable as I confided my feelings about Mum to her.

She sighed and stared at me, asking, 'Do you want another cup of tea?'

'No, thank you,' I said. Not sure what to say, I said, 'Grandma, you've been working in your garden again, I've noticed, and you put in new plants.'

'Yes.'

'You love gardening, don't you?' I asked, feeling awkward I'd said too much about Mum and she wasn't happy about it.

She didn't answer me and I felt it was time to go.

Standing up, I said, 'Well, I'd better go, and happy birthday again, Grandma, and I hope you enjoy the rest of your day.'

She walked with me to her front door and I kissed her goodbye. Her face was weathered, and she had distinctive Chinese features, especially around her eyes, which were small and tired from years of loss and suffering.

Leaving her at her front door, I walked down her hand-made cement path, bricked flower beds laid out on either side filled with pansies. There was an array of newly planted flowers in a circular plot made with bricks. She'd probably found these bricks and carried them back home to use as garden borders. I turned one more time and waved goodbye. She was leaning on the side of the front door, and even though Grandma was partially blind, she stayed there until she heard my car go.

At my car I sang out, 'Bye, Grandma, see you again.'

'Bye, Christine.'

As I drove down her street, I thought on how difficult it was to be with her. She was like a stranger to me. I had thought she'd be so delighted with my gift. I shrugged. 'Oh well, we are all different.' Not long after that visit, Mum and I had a disagreement. She told me she knew how I felt about her. I stopped and looked at Mum and instantly knew who had told her. Again, my trust was betrayed by a woman.

# Chapter 4

# Meeting Javier

I decided to take on two courses to help me in my new job, a blueprint tracing course and a touch typing course. Not that I liked the idea of typing, but I didn't mind the tracing course suggested by my boss. The course was in Dawson Hill on Monday and Wednesday nights, so straight after work, I drove down to the TAFE where the course was held. On Tuesdays I went into Wentworth for the typing course, so these two courses took up three nights a week after work. Due to the nature of the industry, I got to meet lots of police officers. Being a steel fabrication plant, we had the contract to build most of the steel structures used on the Bryson site. These had to be transported from Hastings Crossing to the Bryson site, with police escort, to Bryson Power Station, near the town of Cloverbrook. It was the Denver Shire police branch we dealt with. Many times I had to drive escort for these loads with the police and truck driver, or just the truck driver. It depended on the size and width of the load. I knew them all well, or I thought I did, until one time I came home late after my tracing course in Dawson Hill.

I was so tired, and leaving the Fordham Bridge, I started to put my foot down, hitting eighty miles an hour. Not thinking about police, I came tearing over the bridge that connected to the Ashford turn-off on my immediate right. After descending the bridge, I flashed past the turn-off. Lights shone, and looking in my rear-vision mirror, I saw a Mini Minor police car pulling out of the road. For some reason, I floored my accelerator and increased speed, thinking I could outrun the Mini with my Falcon 66. Unfortunately I got caught behind a petrol tanker going up a hill. Not wanting to pass on a hill crescent, I had to stay behind the tanker. The police car was still way back, but the tanker was so slow that the police caught up with me. If I hadn't got caught behind the tanker, they'd never have caught me. I found out from the officer booking me that the tail light over my number plate was out. The officer must have been new at the station, and so was his offsider. The police knew me, and if it had been someone I knew, I'm sure they would've just fined me, not recording my speed, but because I'd gone so fast, I had to go to court.

I was lucky Mr Nordstrom somehow arranged for a light penalty of one week's suspension of my licence and a twenty-dollar fine. It was a big fine for me; it took my whole pay, almost. Our speeding penalties were high and I could have lost my licence for much longer, especially trying to outrun a police car, which I never admitted to. I used the excuse that I didn't see the police car. That was my first taste of a courtroom and it was nerve-wracking. I couldn't drive for one week and Charlene had to do my driving jobs at work. I was lucky

I could stay at my girlfriend Carmel's house until the suspension was over.

Around August, 1969, I was coming out of my shyness and starting to show an open side of me. I was talkative with the men in the office. I started to love working there and all the men in the office joked a lot. It was great fun. My confidence was coming through and I did a complete change around from being conservative in my dress to wearing the latest fashion at work - the mini skirt - and so did Charlene. Before, I was so self-conscious of my body and didn't want to expose it, but now I wasn't so guarded. I was happy being in such a well-developed body. My confidence wasn't about attracting men, because I wasn't interested in going out with men. The older men in the office never made a pass at me and showed me a lot of respect, and I was much younger than them. Compliments on my new dress sense were given, and maybe I was too immature to notice their looks and see what was really going on with the men.

Charlene and I got on so well and she invited me to go to Rosemont with her. We had a fun time and I bought some really beautiful dresses. Charlene knew where all the fashionable shops were and we ate lunch out. This was a world I really liked.

My sister was cranky with me because she was in her last year at school and wasn't able to buy new clothes. Sometimes I'd buy clothes and later didn't like them. Rather than take them back, I asked her if she wanted to buy them.

She quickly said, 'I'll buy it for half price.'

Indignant, I replied, 'No. I haven't even worn it.' Or I may have only worn it once.

She snapped, 'It's secondhand.'

Shocked by her words, I told her my clothes weren't secondhand.

'Well, I won't buy it, and you can take it to the shop.'

I couldn't because I had maybe worn it once so I couldn't return it. She had an edge over me and if I didn't like something, I wouldn't wear it, so she usually won out and got the dress for half price, with Mum paying for it.

I even started to make my own dresses, not that I knew how to sew, but Maxine could, and she had a sewing machine. I watched her a few times cutting out from patterns. I couldn't work off a pattern, so I created my own styles, cutting the garments out from just watching her. Because we were still in the sister-rivalry stage of our lives, Maxine never did anything for me, so I tried sewing my cut-out clothes, and I did it. I was so happy with the end results and at work, the men started calling me thoroughly Modern Millie.

7th September 1969 was a normal day at work, and some of the staff members were having lunch together in the staff room: Neil, Mitchell, Todd, Charlene and I. We were all being entertained by Neil. He had us in stitches, laughing at one of his sly remarks with a double meaning. Sometimes I didn't get what he meant, and to not look too silly, I laughed along with them. There was a knock at the door, and because I was the junior, I was sent to answer it.

This dark-skinned Mediterranean man stood before me. He had a mass of jet black hair and thick glasses. In his accent, he said something I couldn't understand, but

I got that he wanted to talk to Neil. I was a bit puzzled and thought I needed more information.

Frowning, I said, 'What?'

He muttered something else.

I said, 'Wait here.' Going into the staff room, I announced, 'Neil, there's a guy out there and I can't understand a word he's saying, but I heard your name.'

Neil's eyes lit up and he grinned with his usual cocky expression. Drinking his tea, he said, 'Yeah, I know who it is. That'll be Javier. Does he have a mass of hair?'

I nodded.

He got up, said something to Mitchell, and walked out to see this guy. I sat back down to finish my lunch. Neil returned about twenty minutes later.

He stared at me, asking, 'Well, what do you think of him?' I felt a bit taken aback, what with the smirk on his face that stretched from ear to ear.

Casually I said, 'I've seen better looking men,' and walked off to my room.

Neil was grinning at me as if he knew something I didn't.

The leading hand, Todd, had asked me to go out on a date with his brother, Johnny. I really wasn't interested in men, other than just having a laugh with them and a bit of banter. There'd been no one in my life since Brook left to go travelling. Todd convinced me to date his brother, telling me his brother was a really lovely guy, and it was arranged for Saturday night. I told Todd I could meet Johnny in town because I lived so far out, but he wouldn't hear of it, so I gave Todd my address and the road directions to my house. Mum and Dad knew about Johnny coming. I'd not met him yet.

Saturday came, and Johnny came out to our house, all the way from Wentworth to pick me up. I thought it was a long drive for him. There was a knock on our kitchen door and Mum answered. She invited in this tall, quiet man with fair hair and skin like peaches and cream. He immediately introduced himself to my parents and stared at me. Shyly, I put my head down.

'Hello, I'm Johnny.'

I half-smiled. 'Hi, I'm Christine.' By the look on my parents' faces, I could instantly see they liked him.

Well-mannered and polite, Johnny spoke to both my parents. He reassured them he'd have me back safe and sound. We went out to his car, a clean, well-kept Holden, and he opened my door. This lovely man was so kind and friendly. He kept speaking as we drove into Wentworth and he took me to a very nice Chinese restaurant. Whenever I got out of or in the car, he'd open the door for me; he was just perfect. I was not used to such kindness. In Wentworth, when he tried to hold my hand or lean on my shoulder, I pulled away. He drove me home, walked me to my kitchen door, and leaned forward to kiss me goodnight. I couldn't allow him to touch me and I pulled away. He was not being forward; he just wanted to kiss my cheek. He looked puzzled and tried to kiss my cheek again, and I pulled away again.

I stood in the doorway and said, 'I don't want to see you again.' I closed the door and rushed into my bedroom. Fear grappled at my senses. I told myself this was not what I wanted.

The next morning Mum and Dad asked me how last night went. I told them, 'I am not seeing him again.' They were both shocked.

Mum asked, 'Why not?'

I said, 'He's too quiet.'

Dad was truly annoyed with me. They both looked at me strangely and I cowered away from their looks. I could see they both liked Johnny, but I didn't, and they weren't going to tell me who to go out with. They could see his qualities where I couldn't, and on return to work, Todd and his other brother, Hayden, were very disappointed in me. Todd asked me what had gone wrong. I told him I just didn't feel anything for his brother. My relationship with Todd was not as strong after that incident, and actually the atmosphere in the office in general changed.

# Chapter 5

# Javier

Javier started working on the site the next day after he'd spoken with Neil. Charlene became chatty with Javier and he asked her and I out. So we'd both go out with Javier the Espanola, as we called him. The week after he started work there, we three became friends. For some reason, my wild side started to emerge. Slowly Javier and his dark Mediterranean looks began to interest me. Even though he wore thick-rimmed glasses, he was handsome, and there was something in his looks that captured me, an alluring look that drew me in. I didn't recognise it, but he was familiar without me knowing it. Javier's English was terrible; it fascinated me. The three of us went on day trips to Rosemont and had lots of fun.

Javier had an accident in his brand new car and it ended up being a write-off. His insurance company wiped him because he had been drinking when the accident happened. So even though he didn't have a car, we girls drove him around. There was no competition between us for favouritism from Javier. I liked Javier, but that was it. Even so, I think Charlene really liked him more than me. He'd take Charlene and I out to nightclubs in Dawson Hill. I will never forget our very first date at a nightclub with him. He went to the bar to get us a drink. The drinks were in tall glasses and each had a small paper umbrella. Charlene and I looked at each other and shrugged.

Sipping the drink together, we both said, 'Yuk!' pushing the drinks aside.

Javier's face dropped and he asked us why we'd pushed the drinks away.

We pulled faces and Charlene said, 'It tastes terrible.'

He told us it was a gin sling. Unfortunately both Charlene and I didn't drink alcohol, so his fancy drinks sat on the table untouched.

There was no evidence of romance between any of us, as far as I could see. Javier started to just want to see me, separately to Charlene, but I wanted the three of us to remain friends and I didn't have any romantic attraction to Javier. I liked him because he was different. He favoured me more and more. After my eighteenth birthday, Javier and I began to go out without Charlene.

He started to open my eyes to the other side of life. Javier took me to all these weird places and I'd never seen such places, people or goings on. It was what I'd read about in Dad's hidden Pix and People magazines when I was fourteen. I saw drug users, sex workers, transvestites, and the most unusual people ever. This was so intriguing for a sheltered, naïve farm girl who'd just turned eighteen. Javier dragged me into the seedy world of the darker elements of life. I was going to bars I never knew or dreamed existed, especially in a place like Dawson Hill. The underworld I'd read about was in my own backyard.

It was the Capricorn Bar. There were blackjack tables, gambling wheels, and, most interesting to me, was this stunning prostitute with a rich, ethnic guy, who was a well-to-do businessman. There were men dressed as women, and there were men with boobs and a couple of day's facial growth. When I questioned Javier about these men, he told me some of the men had sex operations and were women now. My eyes widened as I looked around the room, wondering which were the men who dressed up as women, and which were the real women. I tried to be discreet about it, being the polite child I was. Javier told me there were lots of mafia people as well. The place was full of mainly ethnics. I was so fascinated and loved this new world I was exposed to, so we dated more often and he took me to places I never thought existed in real life.

In November, Mr Nordstrom called me into his office. I had my pen and paper ready to take his instruction.

'Christine, sit down.' I sat down and he stared at me, probably not knowing where to start or how to start. 'You're going out with one of the ground staff here?'

'Yes, I am going out with Javier.'

He diverted his eyes. 'You can't do that.'

'Why?'

'You can't go out with people who work outside of this office. You understand me, don't you?'

'No.'

He paused and leant his unusual frame on his desk.

I broke the silence. 'Why?'

'Because we have important documents in this office and you can't mix with people outside of the office staff,' he growled.

Then I was mad.

He saw my reaction and restlessness as I twisted in my seat. 'If you continue to see Javier, you will have to leave our company.'

I was furious. 'Well, you're not my father and you can't tell me what to do, and I quit.' I stood up.

He looked at me. 'Are you sure?'

'Yes, I am.'

'Okay, then.' Calling in Charlene, he told her, 'Finalise Christine's pay; she's leaving us.'

Charlene looked at me and I looked at her and back at Mr Nordstrom, saying, 'Thank you for having me here, but I want to go.'

He said, disappointed, 'It's your choice.'

I went with Charlene to her office. Concerned, she asked me, 'Chris, are you sure?'

I nodded.

'You can change your mind now.'

Smiling, I said, 'No, Charlene. I like Javier and I like going out with him and we even went out together for a while, so why should this be a problem? I never know what's going on here in this office, and Javier and I never talk about work.'

'Sorry, Chris.'

She prepared my final pay. I said goodbye and thanked her for all the good times we'd shared together. We smiled at each other and I left. In the yard, there was no one in sight and looking around, I sighed. It was good there and I liked working there, although it hadn't been easy in the office since I'd turned down Johnny's offer to date me. Both his brothers had become cool to me and all our fun times vanished. It had been so much fun with them until Javier came on the scene. I got into my car and drove out of the yard for the last time.

I knew Mum was in town visiting Grandma Owens, so I went over to Fenton. Driving up the street to Grandma's house, I drove onto the footpath across the road, made a wide U-turn and parked alongside the house. Out the front, I could see everything was quiet. Mum and Grandma would be in the kitchen. Sitting in my car for a moment, I knew it wouldn't matter if I quit my job anyway.

I made my way down the left side of her house, passing her big fig tree, her old laundry, to the back door.

'Grandma,' I called as I grabbed the handle of the back door.

'Carol, that's Christine,' I heard Grandma say.

When I came in, Mum said, 'Christine, what are you doing here?'

I could see they'd consumed a pot of tea and they'd been quietly chatting. Casually I said, 'Well, I just quit my job.'

Mum asked, 'Why?'

'Mr. Nordstrom told me I couldn't see Javier and work there as well, so I quit,' I said confidently.

Mum couldn't understand it and thought it was ridiculous. Explaining it, I declared, 'If I work in the office and he's out in the yard as a site worker, then me being a staff member, we can't mix out of hours because there are important documents in the office. So I was told I can't see him, and if I want to see him, I can't stay there. So I left.'

Grandma said, 'I've never heard of anything as silly as that.'

I agreed with her. Mum told me it was my decision and whatever I thought was best, to do it.

'Do you want a cup of tea?' asked Grandma. I sat and joined them and they chatted about general everyday stuff. I watched the two women as they interacted. My Grandma never had much to say to us grandchildren. She was also quiet with my mum, but because Mum did all the talking, she probably didn't notice Grandma was just nodding and responding in short sentences. It was interesting to watch them and I didn't have much to say anyway. While they chatted, I thought I would go and see Javier later and tell him what had happened. Dad would pick up Mum later on, so I didn't have to take her home.

I checked my watch. Javier would be home by now. 'Mum, I'm going to see Javier and I will see you at home.'

She stared up at me. 'Alright, then.'

I kissed them both and drove over to Ella and Mitchell's house, where Javier was boarding, wondering what he'd say. From the verandah, I heard her children fighting as I knocked on the front door. Her kids came screaming to the door and then she came from a room, holding her head, and told me she had a migraine headache. She screamed at her kids and threw one against the wall as she was separating them. The kids laughed and she screamed at them to get.

In between I asked, 'Is Javier in?'

'Javier,' she yelled.

'What?' I heard coming from his room.

'It's Christine.'

I stood on the verandah and he came out a bit dazed, saying he'd been resting.

I told him what happened and what Mr Nordstrom said about the documents in the office. Javier moved out of the house and he didn't argue or disagree, or say anything.

I asked, 'What do you think, Javier?'

'Nothing. What can you do? You can only leave.'

I needed more of a response from him. 'But it's not fair that because I want to see you, I either have to leave you or the job.'

'Well, that's it.' He shrugged.

I wondered was I in love with Javier. We were going out often enough to be seen as a couple.

We cuddled, and he stroked my face and said, 'You're so beautiful, Chris.' This wasn't solving my inner need to know how he felt about the situation. I thought on it and realised he'd never been a great conversationalist. I guess he didn't want to leave his job.

By the end of November I'd found another job. Jobs were easy to get back then. I got a job in Wentworth with an electrical appliance firm, Barkers Electrical, working in the office. I liked the job, sharing the work with two men, Don and Peter. They were very helpful and didn't mind training me or answering my numerous questions. It was more enjoyable because I got to meet different people in the community.

Javier and I grew closer. I started to become infatuated with him and liked being in his company. I can't say I loved him but I was accepting him as a partner. Other men never interested me and there was no man who had held my attention as much as he did. He wasn't putting any pressure on me at this stage of our relationship; we were only kissing and cuddling. If he tried anything, I'd stop him, telling him I wanted to be married as a virgin.

Christmas was around the corner and I lay-byed my gift for him, a peridot ring and an Omega watch. At Christmas we planned to announce our engagement, and I picked the ring I wanted him to buy me, a diamond set in two gold arms, just not touching on either side, on an eighteen-carat gold band.

# Chapter 6

# Meeting The In-Laws

I will never forget the day he took me to meet his family in Newbridge, a suburb of Dawson Hill. At the Newbridge railway crossing, Javier drove up to the next street and turned right into it. He drove a very short distance and then turned into another street on our left, making a U-turn and turning back on to the street from the railway crossing, down the road we'd just come down. He parked the car outside this big, old, wooden, rambling house painted army green.

'Chris, wait here. I'll be back.'

I smiled at him and nodded. While waiting, my attention took me to a moment at the far end of the dark street ahead of me. As we'd turned into this street, I'd noticed a big, old pub on the corner. Someone had come out of it and I became lost in that moment. It was the only sign of life on the street and it caught my eye. As I sat there, suddenly I sensed something at the window. Turning, I saw these two children with their faces pressed up against the car window. I jumped and locked the door. They stood staring at me like I was on show. They looked like little urchins in the black of the night, with their eyes peering in at me. I hadn't heard them. They were accompanied by a wild, scary-looking woman; big, fat, and dressed in black. As she stood there, gaping at me and smiling, I could see her teeth had been neglected and she had one tooth filled with a gold filling. I was still unable to move from the initial shock. The children just grinned at me.

They motioned for me to open the car door. I hesitated. They kept motioning to lift the lock and they pulled at the door handle. I unlocked the door in trepidation and slowly opened it. The warm, humid air of the night hit me and I felt its heaviness. They immediately grabbed my hand and led me to the front gate of this dark, big, old house. As I looked up its front steps, it seemed to loom over me. Next I was dragged up seven or eight steps, and as I climbed them, there was an uneasy feeling coming from the front door of the house.

The children were asking me questions: 'What's your name? I'm Gema. How long have you been seeing Javier?' The other one rushed in, stating he was Jules.

I hesitated on the top step, looking at the old house and its heavy green paint. Glancing down at the floorboards on the verandah, I could see they were well-weathered and it was not a clean house.

The children spoke Spanish to each other, but my mind was elsewhere. I felt this house had even greater secrets than the house I lived in. On hearing, 'Come, come, come,' I came back to myself. They were all smiles and speaking amongst themselves. I smiled back at them. We stopped and the children turned. I could hear the woman calling to Jules. He ran down the steps and dragged the overweight woman up the steps.

The girl and I waited as he helped her and I looked in through the house and saw a wide, open hallway. I felt like I was being dragged into a different, but somehow familiar place.

Stepping over the threshold and down through the wide hallway, I glanced at each doorway, large bedrooms on either side, like our large bedrooms at my house. These were so dark: even the bed coverings were dark. There was an odour emanating out of these bedrooms, a smell of being locked up; a musky smell. The whole house had a dark feel and the bare wooden floors under our feet made an echoing sound as we walked. A buzz of chatter came from the end of the hallway.

We hit a wall and I was turned to the right to pass through a small walkway into a brightly lit kitchen. Released from the grip of the two children, I moved over to Javier and he introduced me to all his family members. As I greeted each individual, I could feel some approved of me and others were questioning me. The two children and his mother seemed to be the ones who accepted me the most. They kept smiling at me. Again I was seized by Gema and Jules and they took me into the lounge room. Not having any younger children in our family, I found them overbearing. These two were aged around ten and eleven. We sat on the sofa and they chatted incessantly, asking me many questions. They grew on me and I liked Jules' name and I told him so. He was so pleased. I thought, I love Julian as a name, but his name is so beautiful, it's a name I'd love to call one of my sons one day. We were joined by Bianca, Vince and Alexandre, who were also firing a hundred and one questions at me. Bernat, who was my age, and

Pia, a year older, joined us, but sat back making their assessments of me.

As they nattered, I changed my mind about giving my children family names, because I felt they could be affected by having a family name, and they could carry on living that family member's life. Not fully understanding, but somehow I didn't want to inflict my children with others' histories.

Little did I know that this was going to be my place in the house - in the lounge room with the children - and I would be one of the children and not be allowed to join the adult circle. These children had no concept of taking turns and I was answering two or three people's questions at once. Javier had ten brothers and sisters. I was yet to meet his two older brothers, Juan - who they called John - and Dante, who were living in Cloverbrook. I noticed the younger ones and the older sister were of the same mind frame as me: childish. I mixed well with the younger ones that night.

My relationship would be with them, rather than with my future husband, while in this house. Time showed me another side to this family. I wasn't encouraged to learn Spanish because the true family history was well hidden in the language, and my inability to understand the language, clinched the history in secrecy. The walk down that wide hallway changed my whole life.

# Chapter 7

# Getting Closer

Javier and I grew closer and I took him out to the farm to meet Mum and Dad. It wasn't easy for Dad, knowing how he felt about foreigners. Javier won my mum over straight away by calling her Mum. With time, they got used to him. Javier became a regular for dinner and after dinner I'd drive him back home to Hastings Crossing because he couldn't stay at our house overnight.

On a particular evening when Javier came for dinner, Mum said, 'You've got a letter, Christine,' as she attended the food on the stove.

'Oh, good.' I beamed excitedly, knowing it was from Brook. Months ago, he had informed me he'd left Australia for overseas and I never thought I'd hear from him again. I surmised there'd be no commitment between us, so I'd allowed Javier in.

I rushed into the dining room, picked up the letter and studied the handwriting on the envelope. I forgot about Javier.

'Who's that from?'

Smiling, I said, 'Brook. He's away overseas and he writes to me.'

Javier had a stern look on his face. I knew he wasn't happy about it and he soon deflated my happiness, squashing it completely by insisting, 'Next time you write to him, tell him you won't be writing to him again.'

'But Javier, he's just a friend,' I defended.

'If you write to him, we're finished.'

I looked at him and he walked off to Grandma's door to say hello to her. The joy of reading my letter left me and I put it back down on the table. In the background, I could hear him talking to Grandma, asking her how she was. I felt there was something not quite right with Javier's demands. I listened to him talking to Grandma. He was buttering her up.

After this incident, I looked at Javier differently. He had a dark side he wasn't fully showing me. I didn't realise the full extent of his nature, but I was seeing he had a slippery tongue and he used that on others to give them the impression he was a great person. I was too naïve to see through him. When I wrote to Brook, I told him I wouldn't be writing to him anymore. It was hard to write those words to a nice guy like Brook; however, Javier was here, and Brook and I had never made any agreements.

After that letter, I never heard from Brook again. I had a shoe box full of love letters in my secret drawer from admirers: beautiful love letters with beautiful words. I didn't understand the true meaning of and what these men were trying to convey to me. Brook wasn't the only one. From the age of fourteen, I'd had many letters from many admirers. Unfortunately I couldn't feel or understand what these men, Alex, Peter, Ryan, and Brook, saw in me. I didn't understand their love for me or see that they loved me. I had so many admirers but I was too shy to see them. I questioned why I was allowing Javier to win me over when others couldn't.

After Javier learnt about my letters from Brook, he wanted to touch me more. I'd kept him away from me for a long time, and he was happy about me being a virgin, saying it was good.

I asked him, 'Have you slept with other women, Javier?'

Not looking at me, he answered, 'No, I haven't. I'm a virgin too.' Then he cuddled me, but I felt it wasn't true. It didn't bother me if he'd had other girlfriends. I just stared at him, wondering why he had to lie to me.

When I brought him out for dinner in the evening, he wouldn't just get out of the car and go inside. He insisted on us kissing before we went into the house. This made me feel pressured, and to be truthful, I was not ready for sex at all.

My biggest embarrassment was when Dad came out to the car. I didn't see him, but heard him when he roared out, 'Come on, you two, get in the house now.'

His voice startled me. I pulled away from Javier and sat up. I stared out the window, watching Dad walk back into the house, and coldly stated, 'Javier, now I'm embarrassed to go into the house.'

Javier didn't seem to worry about it and he went to cuddle me again.

'No, and in future I don't want to do this here at my house,' I said in a cranky voice. I was totally cranky at myself for allowing this to go as far as it had.

Javier sat back, saying coolly, 'Alright.'

We waited until I'd reclaimed myself to go inside.

Javier wanted sex and I didn't. One afternoon, on meeting him after work down near the railway track, he was very cranky at me, ignoring me.

Puzzled at his behavior, I asked him, 'What's wrong? Why are you ignoring me?'

Not answering, he moved away.

I tried to touch his arm. 'Javier.'

He pulled away. 'I have to go and I don't want to see you today.'

'Why?' I asked, feeling pain I'd never felt before with him.

He walked off.

'Javier.' Tears were surfacing as I followed him, but he kept walking. 'Javier, stop and speak to me.'

'I don't want to talk, and you know what I want, and you won't give it to me, so I don't want to see you again,' he proclaimed.

I freaked out and suddenly started to scream uncontrollably, forgetting where I was, 'Javier, no! Don't leave me. Please.'

He turned and looked at me, saying softly, 'Stop screaming. I won't leave you.'

I was sobbing like a child. He had played with my emotions and put me in a position I'd never dreamed I'd ever be in, and he was using threats to get me to have sex with him.

Seeing my despair, he said, 'Chris, we've been going out together for a while now and I want to sleep with you, and if you don't, I will have to leave you.'

Still crying, I said, 'Okay, I will do it.'

The thought of having sex before marrying was painful. On the other hand, and for some unknown reason, he was the one to enter my life. I had to allow him to have sex with me.

We walked back to my car. His friends, Kelvin and Pete, pulled up in their car. Kelvin asked, 'What's wrong?'

Javier says, 'Nothing. It's alright.'

Kelvin looked at me. I was so embarrassed because I knew Kelvin well. When I had worked at the Bolt Steel Fabrication firm, we'd done wide-load trips and had lunch together. He had fixed the clutch pad on my car a month ago.

Gently, Kelvin asked me, 'Are you alright, Chris?'

'Yes I am.'

'You like him?'

Now I was really embarrassed, knowing that they'd probably heard everything at the Rolland's Steel Fabrication plant where he was working. 'I do,' I answered, looking straight at Javier.

Kelvin put his foot on the accelerator and drove off. 'Let's go to Mitchell's place,' I heard.

Fear grabbed me. I hated the thought of doing it in their house. What if they came back? I wasn't ready for sex. I felt like a timid lamb.

At Mitchell's house, we walked into his room and he closed the door, then took me in his arms and kissed me, rubbing his hands all over my body.

It didn't feel right and I cried out, 'Javier.'

'What?' he snapped at me.

'It's too early for me.' I lowered my eyes.

He moved in on me again. I felt cold and awkward and not sure of what I was to do or what to expect. He pushed me onto the bed and climbed on me. I heard him unzip his zip and he pulled aside my underwear and tried to enter me.

I was too tense and I got scared as he forced me a little. I pushed him away, saying, 'Javier, don't stop.'

He kept on trying, and did a little. I felt all this warm liquid run down my bottom. He rolled off and looked away from me. We lay there on the bed and I felt as if I was in shock. It was not a loving or good experience and I didn't like it at all. It was nothing. There were no feelings of warmth or love, only emptiness. I cried as we lay there.

He asked, 'Are you alright?'

'No.'

He got out of the bed. 'Did you bleed?'

Bewildered by his question and not understanding what he meant exactly, I looked at him, puzzled.

He realised I had no idea what he was talking about. 'Are you bleeding below, between your legs?'

I stood up off the bed and checked between my legs for blood. 'No.'

He seemed cold towards me.

There was a second time he tried to have sex with me. It was close on Christmas time and he took me to meet his friend, Mike. Mike's flat was at Glenrock Bay, and for some strange reason Javier had a key to his flat. We arrived to find he wasn't home. Javier opened the door, telling me Mike had given him a key to his flat ages ago, and he was able to stay there anytime he wanted to. He told me Mike was probably still at work, and we had some time before Mike returned. I knew what he meant. He wanted sex again.

'Chris, I want to try again.'

'No, Javier. Please, let's wait,' I said calmly.

'I can't wait, Chris. I want it now.'

'Not here - what if your friend comes?' I would try any tactic to escape the ordeal.

'He won't,' Javier said.

He took me to the bedroom. We didn't lie down on the bed. He unzipped and pulled my pants down. He was already fully erect. He grabbed me and kissed me, pushing into me while I was against the wall. He penetrated me this time, broke my virginity, and I bled. It stung me. He was all excited when he saw the blood.

I was horrified and told him, 'Quick, we must clean it up before your friend comes back.'

'You were a virgin,' he stated.

I'd lost my virginity, but I was more worried about being caught; falling pregnant never entered my head. We cleaned up the mess and Javier was so happy with me. Cleaned up, I felt safe. Mike would never know what Javier had just done in his flat. We sat on the lounge and waited for Mike to return.

He arrived about an hour later. I was introduced to him and acted as if nothing had happened. He was a really nice guy, if a bit over-active.

'Javier, how about you and Chris coming to the club with me?' He was rummaging in his bedroom.

Javier looked at me. I smiled and nodded yes.

'Okay,' Javier said.

An un-ironed shirt in his hand, Mike said he didn't have an ironed shirt and had to iron one.

I asked, 'Oh, can I do that for you?' I stood up to take the shirt from him.

Javier said sternly, 'No, you can't.'

'What?'

He glared at me. I seemed to know without knowing that I had to tell Mike I couldn't iron his shirt.

Mike looked at both of us and he got out the ironing board and ironed his own shirt. My sexual experience proved to be a bad experience, even on the second attempt. Javier became more possessive and kept me under deeper scrutiny.

Not long afterwards, when I woke up, I had to run outside to vomit. I couldn't control the vomiting. Dad and Mum followed me out of the house.

Disgusted, Dad said, 'Carol, you'd better get her to the doctors. You know what's up with her.'

They may have known, but I had no idea. Back on the verandah, Dad jumped at me and told me to go and get dressed to go into town. His sharp eyes showed me his disapproval. I sheepishly walked off, fearing my father might hit me.

I put on my mature blue dress I hadn't worn for a long time, that conservative dress. I'd been wearing short miniskirts up around my undies. Now I felt the need to cover up. Mum and I walked to my car. I was still vomiting.

Dad was so angry that his whole body shook as he belted out, 'You know she's pregnant.'

Hearing those words, I was horrified, thinking, no, I couldn't be.

Mum didn't say a word in response. I stopped vomiting, got into my car and we drove to the doctors.

At the surgery we were told Dr Jones was on duty. Immediately I said to Mum, 'No, I don't want to see him.' This time Mum allowed me my choice of doctor, his wife, Dr Judy.

The receptionist told us she was busy and we'd have to wait. I thought of how lovely Dr Judy was. She was so kind when Mum had brought me to her to explain periods to me. She never made me feel judged. Mum hadn't told me about such things. I'd felt comfortable with her, even though I didn't retain anything she said.

We had a consultation and she wasn't sure if I was pregnant, so she gave me a test and I had to call back for confirmation in the afternoon. Mum and I went to Grandma Owens' house. Every time there was a crisis in my life, we seemed to go to Grandma's house. Now I was older, I didn't wait for that sixpence or threepence to run up to the shop and spend on lollies. Now I joined in the adult conversation while we drank cups of tea, but there wasn't much to say. Things hadn't changed in that respect. Grandma still had little to say to me.

The two women talked about everyday life, and later on Mum started whining. I couldn't be bothered listening to her complaints, so I finished my tea, excused myself and went into the lounge room. I looked at all of Grandma's bits and pieces. I did love her comfortable old lounge chairs and it was relaxing sitting there. I stroked the pile of the chair in the opposite direction and admired her handiwork of plaited stocking floor rugs. The lounge room was so dark; no natural light entered the house. I could see into her bedroom. It was tidy: just a few things lying over the back of the bed. Feeling comfortable, I closed my eyes and wondered what would happen next in my life. I couldn't imagine myself pregnant. It's like a story, I told myself. I couldn't feel anything in my body, only sick. Slowly I drifted off to sleep until it was time to go back to Doctor Judy's office.

We went to the surgery and were ushered in to Dr Judy's office, and as we went there Dr Jones, her husband, came out of his room. I faltered as I looked at him guiltily. I froze and stared at him for so long, I felt I couldn't break it, thinking now he'll know I'm pregnant and I'm a bad person.

All smiles, Mother broke the strain. 'Hello, Dr Jones.' I knew she thought highly of him.

He casually asked her, 'How are you, Carol?'

'I'm well.'

I was wishing she'd hurry up and leave him, and then Dr Judy appeared and we went into her room. It was confirmed; I was pregnant.

Before we went home, Mum insisted we go over to see Javier. I didn't want to go to him; not now. Pulling up out front of the house, I got out and walked to the door. As I was about to knock, through the fly-screened door I saw Ella coming down the hallway. She'd seen me and had come to open the door.

'Hello. Come in. And how are you?'

I told her I was looking for Javier, as I followed her into the house.

I was so quiet, she asked, 'Are you alright?'

'Yes.'

'He's in his room.'

He was lying on his bed, sleeping. I edged over to him and gently touched him. 'Javier, Javier.'

On opening his eyes and seeing me, he said 'Chris, come.' He indicated to lie with him, touching my face, and I could see he was pleased to see me.

'Javier, I have something to tell you.'

He asked sweetly, 'What?'

'I've just been to the doctors and I am pregnant,' I announced.

He looked at me and he said nothing.

'Mum's in the car. You'd better come and see her.'

He sat on the edge of the bed, put his face in his hands and rubbed his face as if to wake himself completely. 'Chris.'

'Yes.'

He came over to me and we smiled at each other slightly. Then he embraced me and told me how beautiful I was, but I had no feelings, and just allowed him to hold me. We walked out of the house together, and as soon as Javier got close to the car, Mum wound down the window and said in her sharp voice, 'You'll have to marry her.'

I looked at Mum and at Javier.

He said, 'I will, Mum.'

I was disgusted with Mum and thought she was rude. Mum was angry with me and taking it out on Javier wasn't fair. Javier seemed like a lamb near her. He didn't say much.

Mum snapped, 'Come on, we have to get home to your father.'

I looked at Javier. Both of us were bewildered. I moved slowly to the driver's side and as I looked over the roof of the car, I could see he too was in shock. I left him standing there as I drove off down the road and all I could hear was my mother ramming down my neck the seriousness of this situation. Looking in the rear view mirror, I saw him walking back into the house.

The drive home was long. By the time we'd driven to the edge of town, Mum got out of her system what she wanted to say. The rest of the trip home was in peace and I found myself in a trance, not here nor there, and I was left wondering where it all would lead me. At this age, I wasn't prepared for marriage, and had never wanted to marry until I was at least twenty-eight. I sighed as the reality hit me; I was going to have to marry Javier.

We arrived at the top gate. Mum got out of the car and opened the gate. I stretched my body and prepared for Dad, because he would be angry. I drove through, she got into the car, and her eyes were cold as steel. I couldn't talk to her in case I said something wrong.

Dad was suddenly out the front gate of the house; he must have heard the car. As I drove through the second gate, fear rose up inside me. I knew he couldn't do anything to me, but he could hate me for being pregnant. We pulled up at Dad's side. Mum got out.

'She's pregnant.'

He was very angry, and he started to twist and sway on the spot, saying, 'God bugger me.'

I was so empty, I didn't know what to say in my own defence.

'That bloody wog,' he said.

This made me crouch. I knew he had an issue around ethnics, but I didn't; I saw everyone as just people. His outrage was so great that he and Mum walked off, talking between themselves. I was left standing there, in fear of what would happen to me, and my parents didn't seem to see me or care about how I was feeling. They were worried over their predicament I'd got them into. I followed them into the house.

Dad said, 'We'll have to arrange a wedding and tell everyone it's just a quick decision on their part to marry.' He was growling in his usual bear-like manner and shouted out, 'We'll have to sell a cow to pay for this wedding.'

Mum didn't say too much, just agreed with him by nodding. They both talked around me about arranging my wedding day and never thought to include me or let me have a say in it.

Again I watched as my life was being played out for me. It was like I couldn't feel anything. Pregnant, I held my belly, and the whole time no one was looking my way. I could feel their shame at me.

When my sister came home and we told her I was pregnant, she laughed and smirked at me, as if I'd disgraced myself for her benefit. I didn't know why she didn't like me. I wondered if Maxine had ever experienced the same things I'd experienced in this family. I felt she hadn't because she was the accepted one. Maxine had been given more opportunities than me. She would never have any idea of what my life was like and what I'd had to endure in that house, and for that matter, I had no idea of her life experiences or anyone else's lives in that house. I only knew how my mother felt due to her bitching to me about Dad's infidelities. Other than that, nothing else seemed real.

Now that we were going to get married, Javier said he wanted me to meet his two older brothers, John and Dante. He told me John was in a boxing tournament and we'd go and see him box. I was excited because I'd never been to a boxing match before. The weekend came and I wanted to dress up really nicely to meet his brothers. I wore high heels and my crimson mini-dress with its pleated front, diamantes on the short sleeves.

When Javier saw me, I knew he approved. He was always complimenting me on how I looked.

We went up to Cloverbrook. It was a long drive there. We were both very happy, and he held my hand and kissed me as he drove. I was feeling some love for Javier, happy with him at last. In Cloverbrook, we went straight to Dante's house to meet him and his wife, Nita. Javier had explained to me why we had to see Dante first; if not, he'd be very jealous. I looked at Javier as he was checking the numbers of the houses. He slowed the car right down when he found the house and parked the car on the roadside.

'Are you ready?' he said, smiling.

I shrugged. 'Yes. Why not?' Before we got out, I questioned Javier. 'You're joking about Dante being the jealous type?'

He laughed, whispering, 'You don't know Dante. He's jealous, I tell you, very jealous.'

We walked up the long, bare, dry front lawn. I was staring around the area and it was quiet. I guess most people were inside, out of the heat. This over-excitable woman was at the door, speaking Spanish, welcoming Javier and I in. We were taken to their lounge room and there was Dante. I stepped back and thought, my goodness me, he is so handsome. I was introduced and they seemed pleased with me. I met their two children, Peter and Iberia. Nita was the real little housewife and fluttered around the house, all smiles. She seemed immensely happy and brought us tea and cakes. Later we had lunch with them, and she truly was a good cook. They really seemed very happy: Dante was praising her, and she was smiling at him. Her eyes were always lighting up, and she had this permanent Cheshire cat smile, and she'd blink her eyes and nod as she answered his questions. Later on we left Nita and the children and went to meet John at the hall where the boxing match was held. It was all amateur.

Walking into the hall was amazing; the atmosphere was ripe and loud, and there was the ring and action going on. People were singing out and throwing their own punches in the air. Silence, and then the crowd roared and screamed as the favorite scored a punch. I couldn't stop looking around. Javier was oblivious to it all, probably used to it. He was talking to Dante. There weren't many women there, only a few, and I started to notice the men staring at me, so I shyly looked away.

Javier said, 'There's John.'

I stretched to see where and Javier told me over near the ring. 'Oh yes, is that him; the guy in the yellow boxing clothes?'

'Yes. Come.' Javier dragged me over to John. Standing close by him, I could see John was getting himself worked up to go on next. Javier said, 'John.' He didn't hear and Javier tried again. 'John.' He turned, the crowd roared, and everyone was standing up, some singing out abuse, others cheering, as one of the boxers lay cold on the floor. The ref was doing the countdown.

I felt a tug.

'Chris, this is John.'

I smiled at him and said, 'Hi.'

He winked and started to box the air and get prepared. I turned back to the ring to see the boxer in the red trunks, his hand raised, being declared the winner. Boos and cheers mixed in the air. Over near the ring, John was anticipating how he would fair. Then it was his turn to go into the ring. He jumped into the ring and bounced around. His opponent was also in there, a taller, fair-haired man wearing blue trunks. We watched the match and Javier sang out to his brother. Some supported him, and some didn't, and some were saying 'Kill the Spaniard,' - it was pretty gruesome. The crowd roared at certain blows by each of the boxers, but alas, John was defeated.

After John cleaned up, we were introduced properly and I found him interesting. Then Dante, John, Javier and I went to the local club, and after settling there, I went to the toilet, taking my time. Coming back to the table, the three of them were staring at me.

I felt it and John sensed it and said, 'How's he treating you?'

Looking at Javier, I said, 'Good.'

Dante seemed a bit cheesed off and didn't stay too long. Later on, Alexandria, John's girlfriend, came to the club and I was introduced to her. She seemed a very quiet and serious girl. As the night went on, I saw that John could be a volcano if erupted, and I noticed Alexandria flinch sometimes as he sparred with her jokingly. As the night went on, John came over close to me and cuddled me around my shoulders, and announced I was his favourite sister-in law to be.

I looked at Javier and shyly smiled.

I was still working at Barkers Electrical, and on some mornings, I wasn't feeling very well. I wanted to stay at work because I'd lay-byed these Christmas gifts for Javier. Later on, before Christmas, thinking about where we were up to in our lives, I thought it'd be better to cancel one of my gifts to Javier, either the watch or the ring. Instead of getting him a gift, I could buy our wedding bands. I discussed it with him and he agreed it was a good idea. We'd looked at an engagement ring for me before this happened, and I'd found the one I liked, but he never bought it for me.

On the day I went and cancelled one of his gifts, I decided on the watch. Javier wouldn't come with me to buy our wedding bands, so I picked them for us. His mum and dad were fine about us having a baby. I think they were pleased he was going to marry me.

On Christmas morning, Javier and I exchanged our gifts. He'd bought me a beautiful gold watch and a gold bracelet like the bracelet Grandma Kinread was given by my grandfather when they had their first child. It was uncanny to receive the same gift from my future husband that my grandma had received from her husband. Javier had both of these pieces of jewelry engraved, declaring his love for me. I gave him his present: the peridot ring. I had engraved on the ring, 'forever yours'. Javier loved his gift and placed the ring on his finger.

He said, 'I love you, Chris, and you're so beautiful,' staring as he told me he'll buy me an engagement ring another time.

Excitedly, I showed him our wedding bands and he liked them. We did have some nice times together and Javier was always telling me how beautiful I was.

# Chapter 8

# The Stranger

Something strange happened. Javier must have been living in Dawson Hill at one stage. After he wrote his car off, he lived with Mitchell and Ella in Hastings Crossing. He told me he had to pick up his clothes at a place in Dawson Hill. He had no car, so we drove down to Dawson Hill. It was in the suburb of Leighton. I remember the day clearly. I'd seen the Leighton address recorded at work when he'd first applied for his job at the Bolt Steel Fabrication firm. On the day, Javier had parked my car around the corner from this street and told me not to get out of the car and to wait for him, so I did. I never questioned him. The street was very quiet and there was no one around. It was a hot day and I wound down the car window to allow the breeze to enter. I was feeling overwhelmed by the heat, and I looked up and saw Javier coming towards me, almost running to the car, and looking over his shoulder as he fled something. He got into the car puffing and tried to catch his breath. His eyes were intense and dark. We drove off.

Nothing was ever discussed. Not long after, Javier got a letter. He couldn't read so I had to read it to him. It said he had to go to the District Court House. He turned white and silent.

I looked at him and asked, 'Why?' He didn't answer, and I read out the letter, saying, 'There's an order on you to go to the Leighton Court.'

'Why?'

I read further into the letter and told him there was a woman putting a court order on him. Innocently, I asked him what this was all about, and he told me how this woman was saying she had his baby.

'Javier?' I squirmed.

'No, listen, it's not true.' He swore to me it wasn't his child and I believed him.

The day came when he had to go to court and his two older brothers came down from Cloverbrook to accompany him.

On our arrival at the district court, both brothers greeted us. 'Hello, Chris,' John said. He gave me a quick smile and Dante smiled at me as well. I was still shy with them because I'd only met them once. They started to talk in Spanish.

This didn't bother me. I stood there not knowing what was happening.

John said, 'How's my favorite sister-in-law-to-be,' and he put his arm around my shoulder.

'I am fine.' I smiled in my innocence, and my innocence was so great, and so was my trust.

Again, Javier told me to wait outside the court and he wouldn't be long. I sat on a seat under the cool of a shaded tree and waited. I watched the crowds come and go. I was not familiar with courthouses; I'd been to one once when I was caught speeding and lost my licence for seven days.

I started to reminisce on how lucky I was when that happened and working for that firm had helped me because I needed my licence to do that job, accompanying wide loads to Bryson Power Station, or to take documents to the Bryson office. Mr Nordstrom was good about me losing my licence, and I think he arranged my small punishment. I'd stayed at Carmel's place for the seven days. At that time things were changing between Carmel and me, because she had a boyfriend and she was more interested in him. We had been drifting apart, but she was still great and allowed me to stay at her parents' house.

I checked my watch, noticing they'd been in the courthouse for a long time, and I became restless. Javier had told me to wait and I thought if I moved, they could come. I twiddled my foot in the loose dirt and waited and waited.

I went back to my day in the courthouse as I looked across to the doorway of this one, and I thought how nervous I'd been and how silly of me it was to speed. It taught me a big lesson and I didn't speed again. I smiled, thinking of the great police guys I'd worked with. Sometimes I was the front-runner for the wide loads going to Bryson. On the way back to Hastings Crossing, the police would tell me to speed, but no way. I went at the proper speed for P-plate drivers. I'd learnt well and quickly through my mistakes. Well, sometimes, I thought.

Time marched on and I was truly getting restless. I stood up and walked around, and walked to the end of the street. Then I saw the three of them moving out of the courthouse. I went to where they'd huddled in a bunch, talking.

'Hi,' I said, but they were too busy.

Then John said, 'Sorry for the long wait, but it took longer than we thought.'

Dante was really aggravated. 'We'll go. See you, Chris.'

'Yes, bye,' I said. 'What happened in there, Javier?'

'It's not good. She said it's my child and I said it's not. I told them it could be anyone's because she worked on the docks.'

'Javier, how did she know you?'

'I don't know. I think she's probably got me mixed up with one of my brothers.'

'Well, tell them that,' I demanded.

'No, I can't do that.'

'Why not? If it's one of your brother's kids, they should take responsibility for it, not you,' I reasoned.

'I can't, and I have to pay six dollars a week until the child's sixteen.'

'Javier, that's not fair if it's not your child.'

'Well, if it's my brother's, then it's in the family,' he rationalised.

I couldn't rationalise it that easily; the subject was closed, and I paid the six dollars until the child turned sixteen. If I didn't pay it, I am sure Javier would never have paid it. The truth always comes out in the end, and so will the truth around this be revealed eventually, in the far off future, with some startling information.

# Chapter 9

# The Plans

Plans were under the way for the wedding. Our first visit to the church I'd chosen to be married in, the minister, Father Peterson, had questions and advice to impart to us before we got married. He informed us we should wait until we were married before having sex. I thought too late for that, and looked away as an unexplained feeling of dirtiness overtook me. I was already pregnant; how silly of me to give in to Javier, and most of all for not going on the pill. My reason for that was even more stupid: to not hurt my parents. Here I was in church making arrangements to marry someone I hardly knew, due to not wanting to hurt other people that hurt me continuously. Worst of all, I was marrying someone I wasn't even sure I loved. My childhood was so sheltered; no one had talked about sex. I had to sneak in to the forbidden areas to find out things by looking at Dad's hidden magazines in the cellar of Barton's room and checking out the dictionary on sex. It didn't give me any understanding of sex. When Dad wasn't at home, I'd followed Mum into their bedroom and seen his *Playboy* magazines lying around.

Those had also fascinated me, but I'd had to wait to read those ones until both Mum and Dad had gone out and we had stayed home with Grandma.

Mother couldn't talk to us about sex or periods, and the day I questioned her about periods, it was a shock to her. She acted as if it was a life-threatening disease. I was made to feel like a child by her taking me to the doctor to have the doctor explain it all to me. My mother should have been supporting me and explaining all these facts of life to me. We got taught no life skills or given any instructions on how to deal with life. We just existed.

I planned for my children to be instructed in life skills and have all the opportunity I could offer them. I swore I was going to make an effort to change the role of parent and not do the same things with my children that my parents did with us. I would do it completely differently to my parents, raising my children with love, playing with them, allowing them to be educated and go to university. I wouldn't make the same mistakes they did. My children would play sports, learn music, and I would be there for them. They would always see me in the house, not as a hidden mum.

It was a bit of a shame to be pregnant and getting married, but I wasn't the only one in our town in the 1970s having to get married. There were quite a few people caught out and getting pregnant. Funny, though, the ones who didn't have to get married were all pointing their fingers at us, and it seemed to be the nicest girls who got caught out. I guess the others were wiser and on the pill.

Father Peterson was a lovely man, and his advice and instructions were good. He tried to explain to us that in marriage there will always be ups and downs, and the best way to handle these was through good communication. Javier and I had to go and visit him a couple of times before we were married, and we also had to have a practice night. On my practice night, I got a fit of the giggles. I think it was pre-nerves. At work I was becoming a little bit sicker. I didn't want to give up my job yet, so I held in there.

My wedding day was completely organised by Dad. He didn't consult me on what I'd like for my wedding. The only thing I was asked was if I wanted corned meat or ham, and I was told the corned meat was cheaper. In other words, I still wasn't having any say in the preparations.

On the day of my wedding, I called into the hall to see how the preparations were going, and I nearly died. There was Dad, pouring wine into Coca-Cola bottles from a container of bulk wine. I turned to my mother for help. 'Mum, look what Dad's doing.'

I thought she'd help me but she told me, 'You know what your father's like,' and turned her head from me as if to say we can't question him.

I watched him as he chatted to the person behind the bar. They were laughing as he poured the wine into the bottles. I was so embarrassed because my dad did everything on the cheap. I'd been to other weddings and no one did what he was doing. Again I turned to Mum for support.

'Mum!' I frowned, my face full of anguish.

She replied, 'You know what your father's like.' So that was that. At 2pm on the 7th February 1970, Dad drove my sister and I to the church. I only had my sister as my bridesmaid and I was lucky to be able to wear my Aunty Connie's wedding dress. Maxine wore the bridesmaid dress she wore to Aunty's wedding. This was the first time in years that Dad and I weren't actually supervised by my mother, but my sister was with me.

The trip in was solemn, which was normal because Maxine and I didn't always see eye-to-eye. Dad seemed happier. He seemed to be accepting Javier all of a sudden. I knew Dad could be two-faced: nice to your face and awful behind your back.

At the church, I saw my Aunty Kimberly and my cousin Charlene coming down the footpath. Charlene was adjusting her big hat and I could almost hear her words as she leant in to Aunty Kimberly and whispered in her ear. I felt she knew my secret, but I knew she was pregnant, but lost her baby, before she got married. After that she never tried to have children - or wanted any. I wondered what everybody really thought, especially with Javier being a foreigner. I hesitated in the car and had second thoughts. What am I doing here? As I thought this, my photo was being taken by my cousin, Henry. Walking down the aisle, I saw both sides of our families and friends. There was a vast difference between the people. Looking down at the altar, I saw Javier standing with his brother, John, his best man. Javier also seemed nervous. I smiled and realised we were both embarking on a journey not really knowing anything about each other. Our wedding ceremony seemed so long and it took ages to go through the sermon. I even started to tire. Dante was thumping around the church taking photos and breaking our boredom. Finally, after long speeches, we were pronounced husband and wife.

Our reception turned out really well, everyone had great fun, and the wine in the Coca-Cola bottles wasn't even mentioned. It was so good having all the family members together.

My cousin Henry had been a surprise entrant to our family. A few weeks before my wedding, he'd turned up out of the blue saying he was my Aunty Betty's son. None of us knew about him but my mother. Henry and my cousin Kelvin, who I knew and who was supposed to be my Aunty Betty's first child, shared the same surname. So Henry and Kelvin were brothers. Henry was fully accepted into the family and we needed a photographer for my wedding day. Good fortune supplied Henry.

Apparently my Aunty Betty had been married twice. We just were never told, or about her son, Henry. Even her children never knew about Henry. I only saw Henry for about a month after our wedding. He had done a good job with our photos, but as quickly as he appeared, he disappeared, and he never returned again. Nothing was ever questioned; it just was.

# Chapter 10

# In The Beginning
# Of Our Marriage

For our honeymoon, we went to my Grandma Kinread's house on the waterfront at Sandy Lake. Our honeymoon only lasted two days, because Javier hadn't been at work a year to accumulate annual leave, so he had to go back to work. On our honeymoon night, Javier showed me how he too was a virgin when we'd had our first real sexual experience, showing me he'd bled on the back of his penis. I had no idea of such things and I had to believe him. After the honeymoon, we went and lived in the house of Javier's friends, Mitchell and Ella. They'd gone to Dawson Hill to live for about a month. At this time I became very sick at work, vomiting excessively, and sometimes Don, my boss, caught me out in the backyard toilet vomiting. He actually advised me to think about leaving work. He was right. I'd be in the middle of helping a customer and I'd have to run out to the toilet, so I left work. It was a bit sad because I'd got on so well with Don and Peter.

Being married to Javier was difficult. We'd fought before we got married: living with him was worse. It was so hard to make him understand me. His mind didn't think the same way as mine. I had a totally different perspective on married life than him. He wanted to go out drinking with his workmates after work and he was going to leave me alone in the house. I'd been alone all week while he was working and I demanded his company.

A month into our marriage, we had a really big fight. It was a Friday, close on him coming home, so I got dressed up, hoping we could do something together and make it the beginning of a good weekend. On Fridays he usually came home early, and he did. His workmates dropped him off and left. I was on the verandah waiting to greet him. I smiled at him and kissed him hello. We went inside and he informed me he was going out and this time I wasn't going to stop him.

My face dropped and I saw red. There was no way he was going to do that. Calmly I asked, 'Javier, why are you going out?'

'Because I want to and the boys are waiting for me in the pub.' He went into the kitchen, dropping his workbag on a chair.

'But I've been here all week on my own and I thought we could do something together.' I remained calm, hoping to win him over.

He went into our bedroom to get out some clothes.

I grabbed his hand to stop him. 'You're not going out.'

He pushed me, screwed up his face and got his clothes out.

I screamed, 'You're a bastard, you are.'

This stopped him. His eyes were wild. He scared me and I walked out of the room. He followed me, pulling me by my arm, spinning me around to make me face him. He told me his mother was married when his oldest brother was born and no one in his family was a bastard.

He threw me out of his grip and went back into the bedroom.

I sang out, 'You are a bastard.'

'You bitch,' he yelled, and rushed at me.

I screamed, 'Help,' and ran into the bathroom, throwing the door shut, but he threw it back open and cornered me. I had to act quickly. 'This is not a bad word to an Australian. I'm not saying anything about your mother.' He raised his hand and I screamed and fell to the floor, out of his way. He just glared down at me and I kept trying to tell him it was nothing to do with his mother. Sitting on the floor, I realised Javier was unapproachable and he would never understand me. That night neither of us went anywhere, and there was no talking. I learnt Javier would always be misinterpreting the meaning of my words. Over time it was so hard to cope with his inability to understand me, and this caused me a lot of pain.

In our silence, I had time to ponder on events, and realised what was happening to me. My first realisation was that I'd married a man I was not in love with, only infatuated with. The only time he showed me any affection was before he wanted sex. I got to know his behaviour and gradually I lost all feelings for him, and for our sexual relationship. It became so repetitious and I was never satisfied. He never took the time to stimulate me; it was as if I had to be just ready for him to take what he wanted. After the sex, he'd roll over. I already had problems dealing with my body. I knew nothing about the physical body and sex. My body was a mystery to me and sex was a greater mystery.

I was married and there was a child coming. Even though I didn't want to get married until I was much older, I was married and so I really wanted to be happy in my marriage. Marriage to me was sacred and I'd almost kept my virginity. I don't know why. Maybe it was because it's a sacred union.

Strange, though. When Javier had seen my letter from Brook, that's when he started to put pressure on me to have sex. I wondered if he didn't trust me. Did he think I was tricking him in saying I was a virgin?

After our fight, he started taking me to his mother's place on the weekends. I guess this was the only way he knew to entertain me. There he'd leave me with his younger brothers and sisters. I hardly saw him while we were at his mother's and I wasn't sure where he went.

He told me how he bragged to his brothers I was a virgin and how he loved telling them and rubbing it in their faces, mainly because Dante's wife wasn't. I thought, what's the big deal; we all have a choice to have sex when we want it. Sex for me was not an issue or desire, and I had no sexual feelings within me at all. I've never felt sexually aroused.

With time I started to see through his family for what they were. Never before in my life had I encountered a family like theirs. The sisters were always talking badly about each other, or two sisters were back-stabbing one sister, and the sister who was talked about didn't know she was being stabbed in the back. When my sister and I fought, we'd say to each other what we thought about each other. We didn't talk about each other behind each other's back. Our arguments were over petty things - clothes, lollies - or even because we were angry at ourselves or another person in the house. In Javier's family, it was all because of jealousy around looks, money, or because one had something the other hadn't: happiness, good luck, a good marriage, a new car. I'd never seen such goings on and I was always happy for other people's good fortune, good looks or success.

My soft nature made me a target for their verbal abuse and games, and their jealousies, because they were under the impression Javier and I had the perfect marriage. Not long into my marriage, I came under attack and that lasted for a long time. I never knew how to deal with their mean behaviour. I didn't know what was happening and or why one sister in particular was so nasty to me when I was always nice and gentle to her.

Pia would gradually make innuendos about me and drag me down with her cruel words, lowering my self-esteem. Between her and Javier, they were doing a good job at demeaning me. She made unrealistic remarks about my body, picking on my nose and telling me it was so big. The torments ate at me and tore me to pieces. Jealousy, judgments and criticism were family traits and I was the scapegoat. This behaviour seemed to engulf my very being.

# Chapter 11

# Move To The Lake And Then Back To The Farm

Mitchell and Ella returned to their home, so Javier and I went to Sandy Lake to live in Grandma Kinread's house. This was the only property my grandma kept after the death of my grandfather. Sandy Lake is a quiet coastal hamlet even lonelier than our farmhouse. I was surrounded by old people who never ventured out of their houses, hiding behind closed doors. Looking down from the main road, an elderly man lived in the house on the right. Growing up on a farm and never having neighbours in close proximity, I wasn't used to seeing people walking around their yards. The neighbours on my left stayed hidden. The elderly man came out of his house when I was in the bathroom, which was separate to the main house. He began to frighten me. I was afraid he was looking in on me.

I told Javier what was happening. He brushed it off as nothing, saying it was normal that people walked around their houses. I told him I wanted to leave but he wouldn't because he didn't want to pay rent. Although I was used to being alone as a child, there it was too lonely. On the farm I'd had my pets to play with and I was missing my pets. I could always go to them and they'd never reject me, and they'd tolerate my demands. I spent my days sitting in the house waiting for Javier to return from work. Sometimes I'd go to the small shop across the road and I'd buy a chocolate Heart ice cream. I started to crave them. The owner of the shop would talk to me but I was too shy to talk to him. I found it too hard to strike up a conversation.

I finally got to meet the neighbours on my left, Mr and Mrs Adams. They told me they weren't always in the house. They often went to visit their daughter and stayed with her. This made me more fearful because I was sometimes totally alone.

It was May and getting cold. The wind blew more often. There were places where it whistled through the boards. It got dark so quickly and Javier came home so late. I became more frightened.

One weekend, when visiting Mum and Dad, I was so upset I had to tell them how I was scared to live in the house down at the lake, and how cold it was there. I saw them both look at each other.

I knew my sister was still at home and there was no space in the house for us, even though my brother, Barton, had been away in a boy's home for the past two months. Not long after Javier and I were married, Barton and his mate, Patty, decided to steal a car and go for a joy ride. Even with Barton away, his room wasn't appropriate for us and a new baby. My mum's always been an emotionally nervous woman, and the incident with Barton had nearly pushed her over the edge, along with Dad's behavior; she thought Dad was cheating on her with their friend, Hilary. Mum's emotions and fears had become worse, making it even harder to live with her and tolerate her pain and anguish. I needed to feel safe now I was pregnant and not cause my baby too much stress.

Nothing was said to me on that visit and we returned to the lake house, but on our next visit they told both Javier and I we could stay. They'd spoken to Grandma and she'd agreed, but we had to use the bottom bedroom past the archway, the room that freaked me out as a child. I had to face my fears around that bedroom or stay at the lake. When we were told we could come back, I felt a sense of not being part of this old farm house; I felt the house had separated itself from me. But there was nowhere else to go, because Javier would never stay full-time at his mother's, so the farm house won out. I didn't want to live at the lake house all alone. I thanked Grandma for letting us stay and she was happy to have us there.

My biggest dread was facing that bedroom. On my first day back, May of 1970, I was taking my belongings to the bedroom. I stopped in the living room and gazed at the archway that took you into a different world. Terror seized me, but I couldn't say anything to my parents. I stood holding some of my clothes, staring and waiting for I don't know what to appear. I felt eyes were upon me, waiting for me to place my foot over the threshold to gobble me up and drag me into their dark, hidden world.

'Chris,' I heard, and I almost threw the clothes out of my hands.

'Yes. What is it?'

'Why haven't you put those clothes away?' Javier asked.

'I was just thinking,' I lied.

'Well, stop thinking and come on.'

I watched him and thought he mustn't feel anything down there. I walked into the wide hallway and glanced quickly across to the formal lounge room. In the bedroom, Javier had placed the bags on the bed and he was opening the French doors onto the verandah, which let in an amazing amount of light, making the room seem a bit better.

I placed my clothes on the bed and turned to look at the bedroom door and across the way into the formal lounge room. Slowly I raised my eyes up to the wedding photo of my grandparents. I could feel my grandfather's presence in the room and his eyes seemed to be transfixed on mine. I loved him, not knowing him, and feared him. I felt he had me where he wanted me - in his presence.

Javier had busied himself looking at all the wonderful old bits and pieces decorating the room. 'Chris, some of this stuff is so old.'

I relaxed. 'Yes, most of it was bought when Grandma was married and nothing ever got replaced.'

'This furniture is beautiful. I like this bed.'

'Yes, it's a poster bed. Come and look at this.' I showed him the white porcelain cylinders decorated with seventeenth century figures.

Javier liked the room, and of course it was a grand room. He told me his family was once rich, so rich that they threw coins down the road. They'd had an army contract to make saddles, but everything was lost when the horse infantry died off and motorisation came in. We were well off once. I looked at my grandfather and sighed.

I had to get used to living in that room. I'd often come out of the bedroom and run up the hallway into the living room. I'd look back at the hallway. Whatever was there only came as far as the archway. As soon as I ran into the living room, there was no chilly feeling. After a couple of months in the room, I asked Javier, one night when we were in bed, did he feel anything down there?

He saw my face and asked, 'Like what?'

I knew he didn't, but I had to continue what I'd started. 'It's colder down here.'

As if to check the temperature, he looked around and said, 'No, it's the same as the rest of the house.'

I lay back on the bed and felt being home was different. The atmosphere seemed strange and I'd really have liked to have moved into town and rented a house. Dad seemed to be the only one overjoyed by our move back home. I'd soon find out why.

# Chapter 12

# Buying Our Land

I was happy for a while, living with Mum and Dad, and my sister was still home. She was working, had her own car, and was still going out with Collin, her high-school boyfriend. Mum and I were home most of the time, but I'd often drive Javier to work so we'd have the car and could go out for the day. Grandma was bed-ridden, but many times she was sent to hospital. Even if she was home, Mum would make her lunch, place a jug of water near her bed, and we'd go out. Dad was also home more often these days, and he and Javier would go into town to the pub for a drink. I tolerated it.

When we first got married, we didn't go house-hunting because we'd married with only fifty-four dollars, his weekly wage, and I hadn't saved a penny while working. He also had a debt, the brand new car he'd written off, so the first few months of our marriage we'd concentrated on trying to clear his debt. I kept reminding him I wanted my own house. He agreed. Most weekends, Dad, Mum, Javier and I would go house-hunting. This was disastrous because the houses were so small, old and run-down. I wasn't happy with any of the houses we'd seen. I couldn't go from our big, grand old home to a small house like a box that would have fitted twice into the house on the farm.

Javier was cranky with me because I wouldn't accept any of the houses we looked at. He told me he'd be happy to live in a shack.

Shocked at his words, I said disappointedly, 'Well, I am not.'

It was getting closer to having the baby and I really wanted to move into our own home. Some of Javier's work mates told him about some exhibition houses, so we looked at them. Straight away I liked what I saw. We changed our plans from buying an established house to buying a block of land. We ended up finding a block near Hastings Crossing swimming pool; not the best part of town, but a nice area - and affordable. There was a problem; we didn't have any money to buy it. When we told Dad about the land, how much it cost and where it was, he wondered if it was part of the land my grandfather had owned. Apparently, Grandfather had owned a big slice of land at the back of Hastings Crossing, near to Southampton, and he had accumulated lots of wealth, but it was lost after his death. It mysteriously disappeared. Dad felt Grandma had given it away to her relatives and he was very annoyed by that thought.

The only thing we owned of any value was my car, the Falcon 66, and I hadn't paid what I owed on that back to Grandma, but Dad agreed it was my car and what I did with it was up to me. He also stated that when she died, it wouldn't matter. So in June, we sold the Falcon and bought an old Vauxhall. It was a big, awkward car, but we had a good deposit for our land. On purchasing the land and inspecting the deeds, Grandfather's name wasn't on them. With the land purchased, we went to see the builders, Fenton Brothers. We picked a deluxe house and they advised us to go and see the Dawson Hill credit union about a house loan. We made an appointment and the manager informed us that as soon as we'd paid off our land, we could get a housing loan with one hundred dollars deposit. Now I knew we could get our own home, a lovely home, and I knew what was required of us to do that. With our land bought and everything in order, motherly feelings kicked in very strongly. I needed to mother; I wanted to get a puppy. Javier agreed to buying a puppy. I called it Lucky, because I felt it was so lucky to have been picked by me. I mothered that pup so much. I actually treated it like a baby, much to Mum's horror.

'Oh, Christine, it's just a dog,' she snapped as she caught me burping it.

'I know, Mum, but I love it so much and I feel like it's a baby.'

She laughed at me and walked off as I cleaned its face after I'd fed and burped it. I was feeling so maternal.

# Chapter 13

# My Sister And I Were Both Pregnant

One afternoon in August, Maxine and Collin came home. They stood on the verandah as if waiting for something. Dad wasn't home. There was only Mum and I there. In her sharp tongue, as if to say don't jump on me, Maxine announced she's pregnant. I smiled and happily said we could share having a baby together.

She snapped, 'Don't laugh, Christine; it's not funny.'

I looked at her puzzled because she'd read me wrong. She wasn't happy and continued to glare at me. In my defense I said, 'No. It's not like that. I'm happy for you both and we'll be having our babies close together.'

She'd misinterpreted my smile. I wasn't being malicious towards her. It's not my nature to be nasty. I was happy for them and happy I could share our baby times together. There seemed like there was a small feeling of payback reflected on her from me, from when I'd fallen pregnant and she'd smirked.

Collin didn't say much. He normally didn't. Maxine did all the talking, telling us how worried she was because Collin was still doing his apprenticeship and he wanted to complete his trade. I could have completed my blueprint tracing course if I'd not met Javier. Dad was also doing his electrician's apprenticeship when Mum got pregnant with me and he'd had to leave it to go into a better paying job, and Mum and Dad had agreed to stay with Grandma for two years after they'd married. They were still here with her after twenty-one years. No way did I want to repeat that scenario. All our lives were being disrupted.

Now that we were both pregnant, my sister and I seemed to get on better. She was still living with the family until they got married in October. Mum and Dad had gone out for the day to see Barton in Cloverbrook and Grandma was in hospital. Maxine and I could actually get on for the first time in our lives. We talked to each other with no sibling issues. We seemed to grow up: having a mutual issue drew us closer. We talked about our lives and what we wanted for our new families. We spoke about our likes and dislikes, and we got to know each other better, something we'd never done before. We talked about our mum, trying to understand her. We both agreed we couldn't reason why Mum took sedatives or why she couldn't cope in her life. We were both coping with what we had to face in our lives and we wondered why she couldn't cope. Maxine and I vowed we'd never take any form of drugs to sedate ourselves and we'd cope naturally.

We discussed how we felt about having a baby. We both would have liked to have waited, but were resigned to the idea. We talked about baby names. I told her I already had my first son's name picked years ago.

'How?'

'Well, firstly I don't want to ever have a girl.'

'Why?'

'I just don't. I just want boys and my first son's name will be Julian, after the model Sophia's boyfriend's name. When I first read that name I said, there and then, when I have a boy, that is what I'm going to call him.'

'Well, it's too early yet, and Collin and I haven't thought of names,' she admitted. 'Are you scared having a child?'

'No, but I don't know what to expect.'

'Me either,' she said pensively.

'But I do know one thing; no one else will be caring for my baby, I promise you that; and I will care for my own children.'

We heard a knock at the front door. We looked at each other; I was not expecting anyone. We went together to investigate. At the front door was a tramp. The last one I'd seen was when I was about twelve. For many years my grandma had helped these people.

Maxine jumped out onto the verandah and asked him questions. 'What do you want?'

'I'm cold, and I was caught in the rain last night, and can I get some dry clothes?'

We looked at each other and our hearts went out to the man.

'There are some old clothes hanging up in the laundry, Maxine,' I suggested.

I asked her to go and get them because my tummy was too big to stretch up and pull them down. She brought out an array of old clothes and the tramp happily searched through them.

'Have you any spare shoes?' he asked.

'Yes, there're some old shoes in this box here.' I pointed to the box on the verandah.

He pulled off the lid and rummaged through the old shoes, pulled out two pairs with a grin and indicated, by lifting the shoes up and down, if he could take both.

'Sure,' Maxine said.

'Sit on the shoes box,' I said, pointing to it, 'and try them on.'

He looked at us and the box.

I said, 'Put the lid down on it and we'll make you some tea and sandwiches.'

He did that and sat and looked at us both, noticing I was pregnant. He smiled and I touched my stomach. He seemed a kind type of man. I was still glad Maxine was with me.

Maxine suggested I stay with him while she went inside and made his tea and sandwiches. I went into the laundry and did another search for any other old clothes Maxine may have missed. As I did this, he was sitting quietly, watching us going about our missions. I came out with a thick coat and offered it to him. He inspected it and accepted it. While he waited, he slipped off his old, worn-out shoes and put on one of the pairs of shoes he'd retrieved from the box.

Maxine brought out the tea and sandwiches and he wolfed them down. We watched him like fascinated children, glancing at each other.

She said, 'I'll go and make you some more to take with you.'

I nodded. She later came out with a parcel of sandwiches. He was so grateful and thanked us as he ate.

Maxine said, 'It's okay.'

We didn't ask him too many questions as we were too intrigued, but we also kept an eye on him.

After eating his food, he picked up his newly acquired items and said, 'Thanks, girls, and I saw some oranges on the tree. Can I pick some?'

We both nodded and smiled at him.

He walked off. We ran into the house, locked the kitchen door, ran to the side of the house and watched him to make sure he left. He took some oranges off the orange tree and stuffed them into his bag. He walked passed the lemon tree and headed to the mystery fruit tree, glancing back towards the house, as if he felt us staring at him. He hurriedly filled his bag with mystery fruit. My sister and I giggled - holding our hands over our mouths, trying not to make a loud noise - because we knew tonight, when he went to eat those mystery fruits, he'd have a nasty shock. Finally he left the house yard, headed down the paddock, and we saw him making his way along the road.

# Chapter 14

# Birth Of Julian

I had to go into hospital three days before the birth of my child. I'd developed toxemia and needed to be watched. The doctor had calculated I'd be having my baby on the 31/8/70. I wasn't happy in hospital. Javier and Mum visited me really late in the evening, because of Javier's work, and they only stayed for a short time. Around 6pm, on the 31st August, I developed bad pains. I was told by the sister I was going into labor. I was watched all night. The following day, around 1pm, the pain got very bad, so they wheeled me up into a quieter room away from the other patients. There I lay all alone waiting for my baby to move further down the birth canal. I had no idea of what to expect. The pain was like having a very bad period. As it got worse, I lay there and wondered how bad this pain could get. After a cervix check, I was rushed to the delivery room. Dr Judy was nowhere to be seen. I'd wanted her to be there for me. Much to my relief, she appeared, and my legs were placed into the stirrups. I felt so uncomfortable with them up there. The nurses were rushing around and I couldn't understand what was happening. I looked at

Dr Judy as she stood at my feet and the pain became more intense.

I heard them say, 'Push, push, come on, Christine, push.'

'I can't,' I said.

'Don't you feel a bearing down feeling?'

'No. I feel nothing.' I had no feelings, only an intense pressure pain like a period. I pushed as they commanded, however I just urinated and pooed myself.

'Quick, she's dirtied herself. Clean her up now,' said Dr Judy. I couldn't feel anything. Dr Judy told the sister to prepare an injection. She leant in and said, 'Christine, we are going to give you an injection. We have to help you bring the baby out because you can't bear down.'

I was so naïve and nodded in acceptance. The injection was inserted down below. I felt nothing but heard them say get the forceps. With no pain on my part, only a period pain, the baby came out and the period pain left. He cried, accepting his life.

I was told I'd had a boy, a perfect, beautiful baby boy. He wasn't given to me for a while. I had to wait. I was told he was being cleaned up. The sister announced, 'You had to have two stitches.' I still couldn't feel a thing. I just wanted to see my baby. I had Julian at 4.30pm on the afternoon of September the 1st, 1970. The nurse informed me Julian weighed seven pounds seven ounces. Later on I was asked his name for his name card.

'Julian Juan,' I proudly said.

'Juan?'

'Yes, it's spelt J U A N.'

She went off. Juan was after Javier's older brother, Juan, who they called John. I hadn't wanted Julian to have any family name, but I'd given in. After all, he was Javier's child too.

Wrapped in a bunny rug, he was finally given to me. Looking at him, I smiled and kissed his little forehead. He was so beautiful and seemed so at peace. He wasn't fighting against his life; he was coming in gladly.

Dr Judy interrupted me. 'Christine, his head is a little pointed. Don't worry, that will go down in a few days. It's because we had to use the forceps to bring him through.'

I smiled, not even noticing anything imperfect about him. To me, he was perfect. I heard her and I didn't hear her. Looking at her for a moment, I said, 'He's so beautiful.'

Dr Judy smiled and left the theatre, after giving instructions to the staff. He was taken from me and I was taken back to the ward.

The other mothers, who were still waiting to deliver their babies, asked me eagerly, 'What did you have?'

'A boy; he's beautiful.' Slowly I was put into my bed. After a while, sleepy feelings came over me and I relaxed.

The waiting mothers-to-be were not so calm, and I sensed their anxiety. I wanted to tell them there was no need to worry; all the pain would be quickly forgotten. Unable to move and totally relaxed, I closed my eyes and lay there in peace. Later that evening, Javier and Mum came to the hospital to see me. He was happy to have a son and she was pleased. Julian was her first grandchild. Mum was a young grandma, only thirty five. I felt so different, a changed person, after giving birth to Julian. I was peaceful and content.

Javier went with Mum to see Julian; they were away for a while, and on their return, Javier said, 'He's down there smiling and he's got his eyes open.'

I laughed and thought, yes, he's ready to live.

Javier never held my hand or cuddled me. He sat on a chair as if visiting a friend. For that matter, which I'd never expected, my mum never showed much excitement either. She sat there smiling, and through her smiling, I could see she was pleased. None of us knew how to show any joy or love to each other. We each sat in our own space. There was never any real show of affection between Mum and me as a child. It was only a peck on the cheek goodnight until I was in my teens and demanded a kiss. Since marrying Javier, he'd gradually got me to stop kissing my parents, even though it was only on the cheek with no great emotion.

He'd said as I kissed them goodnight, 'Do you have to do that?'

I didn't answer, but knew what he meant, and slowly stopped kissing them.

Sister Phillips said, 'That Spanish baby of yours is jumping out of the cot.'

I smiled at her shyly.

She adjusted my bed covers and said, 'Your baby doesn't want to stay in his cot and he has the most beautiful, big, black eyes.'

I looked at Javier. I could see he was pleased. So was I. They had to go because the visiting hour was up. Javier gave me a quick kiss goodbye. Mum said goodbye, and looked around at the other mothers-to-be and their visitors. I guess she was leaving space for me and Javier if we needed to say anything to each other. I didn't mind them going because now I had my baby. I was told again that my baby was jumping out of the cot. For me, there was no reason why Julian was so active other than he was ready to enter and experience the world. This baby of mine was acting so differently to me on my day of my birth. I slept and wouldn't cry or eat; I was so reluctant to live.

The next day, Javier's family came to the hospital. On seeing Julian, my father-in-law was brought to tears. Normally, he was always acting tough and bossy. I knew they'd lost many babies, one around the age of two, and after twenty-five years, they were still crying over that child.

During my pregnancy, Mum had told me I should have a boy circumcised. She told me it was cleaner and better for the child. Not knowing what it was, I requested it to be done and Dr Judy told me she'd do it before I took Julian home. This meant I had to stay in hospital a little longer for them to keep an eye on Julian. We were sheltered as children in our family and no one taught us about our body.

The idea of further confinement didn't agree with me. The longer I stayed there, the harder it became for me emotionally. It caused me a lot of grief. I hated being confined at any time and my guilt around not being a proper mother producing milk for my baby didn't help.

The guilt that raged in me made me upset and annoyed with the women in my ward, who had milk overflowing from their breasts. I couldn't understand why they didn't want to breastfeed their babies. Their answer shocked me. I was told because they didn't want to lose the shape of their breasts. I couldn't comprehend such thoughts. I'd never even thought about my body at all during my pregnancy and I only put olive oil on my skin to prevent stretch marks because my mother told me to. If she'd never told me that, I'd never have known about stretch marks. I still insisted on trying to feed my child, regardless of what my breasts turned out like. One time I was feeding Julian and my breathing was slowly closing down on me. I had no control over it. I was turning blue. One of the mothers, Polly, in the bed opposite me, noticed me turning blue.

I heard her sing out to the nurse to come quickly. 'Nurse, quick - look at her,' Polly shouted.

The nurse rushed over to my bed and took my baby. Another nurse came in. I could hardly hear what was going on. I was given oxygen.

I came around and Sister asked, 'What happened?'

Dazed, I said, 'I don't know. I was trying to feed Julian, and I lost my breath and my throat felt like it was being strangled.'

'We'll get the doctor to look at you this afternoon.' Sister informed me. With care she said, 'Christine,' and she placed her hand on my hand. 'I feel you shouldn't feed your baby, not for the moment, anyway.'

I quietly pleaded, 'No, I want to feed him.'

She could see I was distressed and she comforted me. 'Okay,' She didn't want to upset me more than I was, so she reassured me, saying to wait until the doctor saw me, suggesting in the meantime I fed him with a bottle. Her face showed concern and I had to agree with her. So a bottle was prepared and brought to me with Julian, and I fed him with a bottle. He gulped the milk down and he was hungry; I could see he wasn't getting enough from me.

Dr Judy came in later that day and gave me the bad news. 'Christine. You can't feed your child by the breast.' My face changed and she stated, 'Because it's affecting your thyroid.'

I sadly said, 'No, I want to breastfeed my child, Doctor Judy, please.'

She looked at Sister Phillips and said, 'Alright, you can try; it's your decision. But remember, he's not getting enough from you, and it's not safe for you.'

I was so sad and wanted so much to breastfeed him. 'I will try to feed him,' I persisted.

Dr Judy and the sister stared at me. Sister patted my hand and they left. Sister Phillips came back after the doctor left.

'Christine, you can try to feed your baby and we will leave the oxygen tank near your bed. If you need it, you use it.'

I nodded and she showed me what to do.

When Javier came in that night, he saw the cylinder and asked, 'What's this for?'

Casually I answered, 'Oh, I had a small problem breathing today. It's nothing. It's okay now.' There was no need to go into any details or explanation; the choice was mine and mine alone. My confinement ended up being for ten days. With little to do, I spent most of my time sitting and waiting, and walking to the maternity section to look at Julian. I wasn't a person who read at that time.

Eventually, the day came for us to go home and all those feelings of being restricted left me. Javier came to pick us up. It was Javier's first chance to hold his son. I found Sister Phillips and told her my husband was here for me. She called the maternity section and Julian was brought to us. Sister Phillips asked Javier if he wanted to hold his son. He held out his arms, took Julian, pulled the rug from his face, stared down at him and kissed his cheek. I smiled. Javier was really happy with Julian; I could see that. I was so proud of my baby. After thanking the staff and receiving last minute advice from the sister, we went home.

I saw Mum out the front of the house, because the dogs had started barking the minute the car pulled into the gate. The farm was so quiet, and all the different sounds became distinguishable. We could always tell who was coming from the way the dogs barked, or the sounds that broke the silence. Mum was standing there patiently, as well as my dog, Lucky, and Blue. Lucky was the most excited. Even before Mum could get near me, Lucky was at the car door trying to get in as I was trying to get out. Mum dragged him away and I got out, and then he jumped up on me.

I pushed him away, saying, 'Get! Get away.'

The dog still jumped up on me and I turned my baby from him and pushed the dog away with my foot, telling it to get, Mum also shooing Lucky. Javier jumped in and the dog stopped jumping and stood motionless, not understanding. Then and there, I had forgotten how I had treated the dog like a baby. I guess he wasn't that lucky after all.

In the shade, still outside, Mum said, 'Let me look at the baby.'

I opened the rug to show her his face. 'He's beautiful, isn't he, Mum?' I bent down to her level to show her.

She was in awe. 'He's so beautiful.'

I could see her eyes welling up as she stared at Julian. We smiled at each other and walked into the house. As we did, I silently vowed that my child was mine and no one would take care of him, only me.

In the kitchen, I let Mum hold her grandchild while Javier took my things to our room. Mum was so thrilled; her face was teary with joy. As she nursed Julian, he made little grunts as if he was so contented, happy, and at peace. We both became very gaga over him. We had to introduce him to Grandma.

At the door, I said, 'Grandma.'

She looked up. 'Christine.'

'I have Julian to show you.' I walked over to her bed and even though I knew about her not being so clean, I let her nurse my baby, making sure she didn't put her fingers near his mouth.

Her old, wrinkled face was so happy and she said he was so beautiful.

'Julian is your first great-grandchild, Grandma.' The old woman nodded, and an old hand at it, she nursed the baby. The baby was content with Grandma, and he didn't seem to be disturbed by either of the women. Glancing from Grandma to Mum, both looked like coy old women. After a while, I said I'd better put him down to sleep.

Mum followed me, and she said it was good that I let Grandma hold Julian. I thought, of course she had to; he's her great-grandchild. I said, 'Mum, I feel so different now, and I will care for my baby all by myself. I'm a changed person.'

Puzzled, she asked me, 'How?'

'I don't know, but I feel changed, and not the same person I was.'

We put him in his bassinet and let him sleep. My Dad and Maxine loved Julian, and I was generous in letting everyone nurse him.

However, strange feelings came over me during my time at home. I was experiencing unnatural jealousies around my mother and Javier; I couldn't leave Mum and Javier alone together. I asked myself why? Why am I feeling this around my own mother? The whole thought was ridiculous, and I told myself no, I don't want to go there. I'd been feeding my child in the kitchen around them when Dad wasn't home. I had to stop these silly thoughts. Eventually I did, and breast-fed Julian in my room. The fourth day at home was difficult for Julian, and I had to surrender the breastfeeding and put him permanently on the bottle. He flourished.

In the mornings, after bathing him, I'd wrap him tightly in his bunny rug like a little papoose, and place him in his bassinet. Julian was admired wherever I took him. He had the biggest black eyes and an endearing face. The perfect child; after getting Javier off to work in the early hours of the morning, I could go back to bed and sleep, because Julian was also happy to sleep until he was hungry or needed a change.

I was so close and protective and wouldn't allow anyone else to care for him. He received all the love I didn't get. Somehow I knew it was very important that the mother cared for her child completely, and not to hand her child over to any other caretakers. This was essential in the bonding process between the mother and child, and for me that bonding was imperative for my child's growth and security. I determined my child would feel a mother's love and not be affected by other role models in his formative years. I knew zero to age seven was crucial in his development.

Being out on the farm wasn't the answer. I started to see the true state and deterioration of our old farm house. Mum was not a good housekeeper and she'd got it to a state of no return. The house was never the same as when Grandma cared for it. Not having been happy there, I was becoming very lazy. I reasoned the house wasn't mine, and I had no desire to clean it. I tried to keep Julian's things as clean as possible, however I became lazier, even with Julian's things. I was living a lie; nothing was true. I didn't understand that then. We had to get our own place. I was more determined than ever to knuckle down this time and get serious.

After my pregnancy, I needed new street clothes, due to only having miniskirts and minidresses before our marriage. Javier now forbade me to wear those clothes. When I put them on, he told me I had to lower my dresses. Clothes were expensive. I liked to buy good quality clothes, rather than quantity. Now I had to change. Mum and I went shopping into Wentworth and found some good, strong, cotton summer dresses for one dollar ninety-nine. I was so happy to wear them for summer, that I would wear them into the winter, if need be.

Julian was a good baby, but sometimes he'd play up, and it was hard for Maxine to accept Julian's crying. A couple of times, she jumped on me, telling me to stop him crying. I had no problem with him crying; my patience with Julian was great. Maxine's tolerance was limited. I thought, when she had her own baby, it would be different. When she was home, we confided in each other. She was very worried about her future with Collin, because his wage was so low. I didn't know what to say to her, but listened, and while listening to her, I thought how lucky I was, because at least Javier was making good money in the construction industry. Wages were starting to increase quickly, and Javier was doing some extra work as well. His work enabled us to look at buying a house. Regardless of his good wages, Javier didn't see my point of view about buying our own home. I had to work hard, pushing him, motivating him and encouraging him to see beyond his parents' lifestyle. He had no ambitions to have a nice house. His parents rented all their married lives, but no way was I renting. I wanted us to own our home.

# Chapter 15

# Now Maxine Was Gone, Mum And I Fought More

Maxine and Collin got married in October, 1970. I was her matron of honor, and it was a beautiful wedding in the small, quaint, stone church in Spencer Shire. The church was so quaint, even the resident mouse attended the wedding, deciding to make its appearance during the middle of their ceremony, much to everybody's shock or delight. Their wedding reception was a very beautiful party, and there were no Coca-Cola bottles filled with cheap wine for them. This time it was done right.

Maxine left home to live with Collin at Lachlan Vale, renting a house there. For the first time, I missed my sister. We'd just started to develop a special closeness we'd never had as children and I could speak to her, and she to me. We didn't lose her completely, and we would go out for lunch and shopping together. This seemed to bond us more. I was realising how important my sister had been in my life. Even when we were children, she had been very important in my life. Regardless of our squabbles, she'd made my life in that farmhouse more bearable and relaxed. Many times she was an unaware protector of me in the family unit.

Sooner or later, tensions had to build between Mum and I, and they were building up fast. I began to realise I had no idea of what my mother was doing to me emotionally. I didn't realise how much she'd brainwashed me all my life and now I hated her for it.

She had me totally to herself and she was dumping all her problems on me. I wished I could tell her I didn't care about her shit life; it was her problem, not mine. I wanted to tell her to stop telling me her crap, but I couldn't do it; I was too afraid of her. I listened begrudgingly and bottled it all up.

My demands on Javier, due to my mother's crap, were worsening; we needed to hurry the process up of getting our own home. My determination to get out of that farmhouse and into my own home grew and grew. Dad was playing up and Mum was becoming more and more obsessed with this. She knew something was wrong, because Dad was starting to stay out until late at night: attending meetings, he told her. She had to contend with the added worry of Barton. I was being emotionally dragged into their issues.

Mum's anger, frustrations and worry over Dad and Barton were being released onto me, causing me to be angry with my mum, because I couldn't tell her how I really felt about her throwing her shit on me. So my anger was aimed at Javier, and in my frustration at having to endure her crap, he suffered. It was a vicious cycle. Javier knew what was going on. When I'd start getting cranky with him, he'd say, 'You've been fighting with your mother again.' I'd jump at him, saying no, and I'd blame him for our predicament.

I was unforgiving towards Javier when I married him. He had nothing but debt because of his recklessness, drink driving, and the accident he caused not being covered by insurance. They'd wiped him. To make matters worse, we were paying off a car he'd never had. The pressure was great, too great with these added debts restricting us from renting our own home, and there was that maintenance for his brother's child. On top of my mum's burdens with Dad, my brother and Grandma, I was suffering. Things were weighing heavily on Mum and her isolation and lack of freedom were tipping her over the edge. Nonetheless, I was a changed person, and I was not prepared to suffer these family issues anymore. I had my own issues to deal with, bringing up my child differently to how I'd been brought up. I wanted to offer my child a chance in life, and the only way to do that was to move out of the farmhouse. Living in my childhood home, I could see I'd married back into a familiar family pattern of adults who were non-achievers and had no ambition to further themselves. Javier did not have the same aspirations I did for our family. His family was very similar to my own. No one was progressing past the familiar.

Fighting was our biggest problem. It always centred around other people and I felt it always would. Dad had decided it was time for him and Javier to make regular outings to the pub. This was causing a big rift between Javier and I. No way was I going to take this and the day came when all hell blew open. On Javier's arrival home after a drinking binge, I stood at the gate. Dad was in a drunken stupor, a grin from ear to ear. He got out of the car and started to be stupid with his grin and many excuses, but there was no excuse for what was happening. We had to save money.

Javier sheepishly got out of the car and I nagged him with a hundred and one questions why. 'How could you?' I said. 'What do you think this is? You're inconsiderate and selfish.' Then came the accusations. By then, Dad had high-tailed it into the house. I accused Javier of doing the wrong thing by going to the pub and drinking. 'How could you do this now we're married?' I remonstrated. 'You should be with me and Julian, not Dad,' I screamed at him.

He started to walk down the hill towards the bottom gate and the road leading to Dawson Hill.

'Where are you going?' I questioned him. As I followed, I hounded him, pestering him about not being fair, that he's away from the house for hours, and that I'm stuck there and have to listen to all my mother's shit.

Suddenly and unexpectedly, he stopped. I halted in my tracks, losing my voice. He stared at me, as if searching me, and quietly told me that he was leaving and not coming back. Then he walked off.

A million things went through my mind, but the thought of being left there with my parents was too much for me to bear. I had to change my tactics and soothe him. I had Julian to provide for, and I wanted better things for my children. I'd never achieve that trapped out there. It took time to win him over, but I did, reminding him of his responsibilities to his son. Javier never said a word. He just turned around and headed back to the house. I stood there watching him walk back and I looked at that house I was born in. There was a choice of two hells: with him or with them.

I couldn't stay there with my parents and put up with their self-created hells of hatred, hurt and guilt. I took my chance with Javier. I realised he was the wrong man for me, but I now knew how far I could push Javier, and with my strong determination to rise above my present life for the sake of my child, and our future children, I surrendered to the fact that Javier was a good worker and he'd be a good provider. That day, getting out of that house was all I wanted.

Every now and then, he'd go out with Dad to the pub, and I think the reason why Javier went was to avoid the conflicts and tensions between my mother and me.

# Chapter 16

# Pia's Pregnant Too

Not long after Javier and I had moved in with Mum and Dad, Javier's family became regular visitors to the farm: almost every day. Javier's family were noisy, and like tornadoes. On hearing them screaming in general conversation, my grandma screamed from her bed, 'Who are those people in my house?' On their first visit, I'd taken them all into her bedroom to show her my new family. 'Grandma, this is Javier's family.'

They weren't the quietest people and I was always asking them to speak quietly. Our house had been so quiet you could hear a pin drop. His people were so overbearing and they didn't realise that these Australians weren't that way inclined. Sometimes my patience ran thin with them, because they never listened and had no boundaries. You could never offend them, and they just did as they liked. But luckily, with their warm hearts and kindness towards my grandma, they soon won her over. Grandma actually liked them and they liked her. My mother-in-law cuddled her and Grandma would cuddle her back. Not that Grandma was big on cuddling; however she was won over, and that was a good hurdle to leap.

Grandma's health wasn't good, and she was in and out of hospital often, so this also eased a lot of the tension on my mum and on the visitors. As a rule, Grandma was very private in her life, and she'd even stopped Mum and Dad from having friends.

On one of their visits in November, Julian was still in bed when they arrived and they wanted to see him, but I didn't want to wake him, so I made them coffee and they waited for a while. I chatted to them about an hour, then I decided to go and get Julian because I could see Javier's dad was getting impatient. Gema, Javier's sister, came with me.

She seemed a bit edgy and I asked, 'What's up, Gema?'

She looked back to see that we were alone. I thought her behaviour was strange, because no other family member ever came to my bedroom. I placed my left palm flat on the door, turned the handle with my other hand, and quietly opened the door. We sneaked in and went over to the bassinet. Julian was still asleep.

Looking at Gema, I smiled and whispered, 'I don't want to wake him yet.'

'Don't then, Chris; leave him for a bit,' she suggested. 'Let's sit, Chris. I have something to tell you.' There was an urgency in her tone.

'Okay.' I indicated for her to sit up on the bed with me.

The bed was very high, almost as tall as Gema; she was four foot nine and had to face the bed and virtually climb up onto it by grabbing the back of the bed posters. I gave her a small boost up to help her. Then I placed the palms of my hands on the edge of the bed and hoisted myself up backwards. Settled, she became anxious again and said, 'Pia's pregnant.'

I looked at Gema, surprised.

'And she's not going to tell the old man yet.'

'Oh, Gema, why not?' I asked innocently.

'She's afraid to. The old man will kill her,' she stated, concerned.

'But Gema, she has to tell him soon. Does your mum know?'

'Yes.'

'Well, she'll help her and go to your father with Pia,' I said encouragingly. For a moment, Gema drifted off somewhere else in her mind. She knew her family and I could see her reason for being worried. Their father would kill her. I guessed Nick was the father and asked, 'Is Nick the father?' My face was taut, as if to say, ouch.

'Yes,' she replied and hung her head.

I knew Pia was seeing Nick; he was one of Paco's school friends. I also knew he was sneaking into her bedroom through the window at night. I really felt for Pia, because she wasn't allowed to have a boyfriend. She was the oldest of Javier's three sisters. Pia was never allowed out of the family's sight. If she did go out, she had to be chaperoned by a brother. Paco only had younger friends, and so Pia met Nick, who was very young. He was fourteen when she first met him. I'd met him a few times, but never took much notice of him.

'Your mum should help Pia, Gema.'

'She won't, Chris; she's afraid of the old man too.'

I sighed. 'Gema, what can I say.'

'Nothing, Chris, and there's nothing anyone can say.' She was resigned to the fact that this wasn't an easy situation, and it was too late to turn the clock back to prevent it.

Sliding off the bed, I said, 'I'd better get Julian up.'

I gently wrapped my hands around my sleeping baby. He looked so cute, all bundled up in his bunny rug. He pursed his little lips in objection to the rude awakening. 'Come on, little man. I'm so sorry, but your grandparents want to see you,' I placed him in the middle of my bed. Gema was still sitting on it. I said, 'I'll just get a clean nappy.'

'Okay. Hello, Julian, this is your Aunty Gema,' she cooed at him.

I came over with a clean nappy, and unwrapped him out of his bunny rug and commenced to remove his wet nappy. He started to wake up. Gema crouched over him making goo-goo sounds. He stared in her direction. I re-wrapped him and we both headed for the kitchen.

As we walked, Gema grabbed my arm and said fearfully, 'Chris, not a word, and not to Javier either.' I totally understood and I reassured her. 'Gema, you know me by now. I'd never do such a thing.'

We stepped into the kitchen. A lot of pensive people were sitting there waiting for us. On seeing Julian, they soon changed their looks: love and joy replaced upset. There was a touch of sadness for Javier's dad, because all babies reminded him of his lost baby. I immediately handed Julian to my mother-in-law. Jules, the baby of Javier's family, hung over his mum's shoulder to watch her. My father-in-law stood near her and they talked to Julian, touching his cheeks and puckering his lips. While they goo-gooed with Julian, I prepared his bottle.

They truly loved him and all their grandchildren, and they were so excited to see him.

It would be a couple of months before Pia could gather up the courage to tell her father she was pregnant. It was because she'd reached the point where she had to tell him of her pregnancy, because it was becoming obvious. Nick and Pia had told Nick's parents, and they were shocked, I'd heard. His parents accepted Pia. To break the news to Pia's parents, Nick's mother and father advised them to do it in their house. So it was done at Nick's home, and it was a good idea, because seeing Nick's parents supporting them emotionally allowed Javier's family to accept the situation. So they were married when he turned sixteen. Their baby was due a month later in May. Fortunately, they could get married and Nick's parents were very supportive and really lovely people who understood people and their situations.

# Chapter 17

# My Brother

When Julian was three months old, we went to Cloverbrook to see my brother, Barton, who hadn't seen Julian yet. He was at Cloverbrook Boys' Home for stealing a car with his mate, Patty. He'd been in this home for the past nine months. Mum was devastated over it. She already had lots of nervous problems, suffering tension in her head and the back of her neck, and this problem just made her life even more stressful. She was caring for Grandma, worrying over Barton, and stressing over Dad's behaviour with the other woman, who Mum said was Hilary. Barton was her biggest worry, and her own personal isolation concerned her, having no way to get away from the farm except through Dad or me. She couldn't drive, so she was trapped. Mum did try to learn to drive, but she was too nervous.

The Boys' Home was set in a lovely garden area, and we had a picnic and tried to enjoy ourselves, but Mum's anguish was too obvious, and we all felt it. Barton genuinely seemed well-adjusted; nonetheless, Mum worried if he was safe or not. Barton reassured her he was and told her he got on well with one of the officers looking after him. He said he liked it there, the people were nice, and he'd met some good blokes in there. I believed that, because Barton was like that; he could befriend strangers so easily, and they always seemed to like him. Time changes things, or maybe it was his way of reassuring her.

Unfortunately, the punishments Barton had received from Dad were way out of line, in my opinion. It was all because Mum loved Barton too much. He was her favourite child, which never bothered me, or Maxine, for that matter. Dad couldn't cope with it, and he abused Barton verbally, using horrific name-calling tactics, constantly telling him he was stupid or an idiot. I guess if you're told that often enough, you'll believe it and become it. I don't know how Barton felt about what happened to him, but I know I felt his pain. Not only was it verbal abuse, but physical abuse as well. It was incomprehensible how someone could do that to their own flesh and blood.

My brother was difficult to understand because he was so closed and acted as though nothing fazed him. I couldn't relate to my siblings; they were like strangers living in a house I shared with them. This was because there were too many years of separation between us during our childhood. When Mum had taken Barton away with her for two years, we didn't re-connect with him. Again, Barton was taken out of my life, and again, it was hard to connect with him; it was hard to connect with everybody in my family. Barton seemed to be my biggest puzzle. Not understanding life then, I didn't realise the puzzle was within me and that I was trying to seek myself. Not connecting with my siblings was my inability to know myself. Not understanding how life worked, there was no chance of understanding anyone else.

I don't ever remember cuddling or kissing my brother or sister; we only fought. There was no expression of love.

My brother's sufferings haunted me for many years until I found out why I was so affected by what he'd endured.

Barton turned fourteen in January, 1969 and he got his first pair of long pants. To get a black suit was traditional for boys in those days when they turned fourteen. Prior to that, they wore shorts. Barton was so short at fourteen and he never seemed to grow much. At our wedding in February, 1970, he got to wear his black suit. Not long after our wedding, Barton went to the Boys' Home. He turned fifteen there. I remember the day he returned to the farm house in 1971. He seemed to have shot up very quickly.

# Chapter 18

# Barton Returns

I remember the day he came home. I was home on my own with Julian. Mum and Dad had just gone into town. I was in the living room watching some TV while Julian was sleeping. I heard the dogs barking and went outside to see why. I saw this person coming through the top gate. Straining my eyes to recognise who it was from such a distance, I watched intently. As the person came to the middle gate, I realised it was my brother. I sung out, 'Barton!' I was so excited to see him and I ran to greet him. When I reached him, I wanted to embrace him, but there was no penetrating the shield he had up. He looked like a driven machine and he marched on, so I walked with him. He was as stiff as a board, rigid, unable to be malleable, but then he always was like that. He said, with a deep and expressionless voice, 'Hello, Christine,' as if he should at least greet me, and he pressed forward. I noticed his changed voice, and he was so much taller: not a boy anymore. Ploughing on, I tried to talk to him again, asking how he was and getting one-word answers. He seemed as if he was on a mission and not hearing me. I felt he was walking through me. I couldn't connect, so I stopped trying and eased off my pace. I allowed him to press forward, and I walked in silence behind him. I didn't understand the mentality of a person who'd been locked up. Not only had Barton been a prisoner in a boys' home, but he was a prisoner in his body as a baby - strapped in his cot for long periods of time, a whole year with eczema - and now he'd ended up a prisoner in adolescence. What is the meaning of what we do?

Six months later, Barton would bring sorrow once again to Mum, and again she'd be devastated and suffer badly through worry and stress. Her life was already miserable and Barton was just adding to it. Next time he'd go in for stealing pit property. September this same year I would once again be separated from my brother and he'd be put into a boys' home for another six months. Confinement was something he was so used to. I couldn't work it out, because no one else in our family was ever in an institution that I knew of.

As he got older, if he got into trouble again, he'd have to go into prison. Mum would die, for sure; I didn't think she'd cope if that happened. Barton's mind was impenetrable, like a solid brick wall, showing emptiness and disconnection. What was behind that wall, and what did he think about, I wondered. When I was around my brother, I personally felt he was a person to be feared.

Even so, in a way, I did understand why he was like this. It was because of his childhood and Dad's attitude towards him. How my father must have hated Barton, because Mum loved him more than anyone else.

Somehow, even though Mum loved Barton, and it was obvious to us all because she'd shower him with kisses and pet him and not us, I never felt any jealousy or dislike towards my brother. All I ever wanted was to know him.

I felt my brother and I were brought into this life to endure suffering, regardless of me not knowing enough about life to tap into why things are as they are. I was nineteen going on twenty, too young and inexperienced about life and the reasons why things happen as they do. I wanted to understand why we were with the people we were with, but my life had been so sheltered and protected from reality.

What intrigued me was Barton's reactions to his suffering, telling my sister and I, who stood watching him being belted, he never felt it. He must have, though, because I was feeling it when Dad belted him.

Barton told us that during the floggings, and after it, it didn't hurt, and he went off with a smile that I couldn't fathom. How could he endure those whippings - because when I got belted, which wasn't as severe, it hurt me. It would take me many, many years to understand it. Unbeknown to us, he'd learnt how to escape his body in times of unbearable pain, be it physical, mental, or emotional. In doing that, he ended up blocking his feelings. Instead of living and feeling our pain, we choose to ignore the pain; and so, the pain keeps presenting itself in various forms to be experienced, felt and dealt with, for the lessons needed around it.

As children, we learned to internalise our feelings, and none of us shared or expressed how we really felt. None of us knew what the other was thinking or feeling. When we got angry, it was stopped, suppressed by our peers. Throughout my childhood, I didn't realise I'd stopped feeling and learnt to detach to survive. In detachment, one can't feel, so when we try to understand love through the mind, love becomes a thought, not felt from the heart. I thought I loved Javier, but I was simply infatuated with an image, so my mind said I loved what I saw, but my heart was closed to feelings. I felt my sister, brother, and I were all the same. I would remain that way until my early forties, and then I would find my voice.

# Chapter 19

# My Sister Has Her Baby

In April 1971, my sister was rushed to hospital to have her baby. After Collin had taken her to the hospital, he came out to the farm to let us know she was in labor. As soon as he told us, I felt instantly for my sister. It was so strange. Now we were closer, I was feeling for her. Collin didn't stay after he gave us the news. He wanted to go back to the hospital and be with Maxine. Later on that day, they had a son and named him Alex. I was so happy for her, and now Julian had a little cousin to grow up with, just like my sister and I. We grew up with our cousins, Gerry and Hope, and we became very close. The following day, Mum and I went to the hospital. We had to take turns to go and see Maxine, because babies weren't allowed in the ward. I waited with Julian and Mum went in first. Then it was my turn. On seeing my sister, pride filled me. She looked so lovely and I kissed her, congratulating her.

We talked about her birthing and her new baby. Later I went up to see Alex. He was beautiful. Instantly I knew he and I would be close. I went back to Maxine and told her how beautiful he was. She was beaming. We both had our first sons and our journeys were to begin.

This same month, Nick's parents signed the consent form for their son to marry Pia. Javier, Julian and I attended the registry office wedding, and it was good to see them eventually married. There was no reception, only a small gathering at Nick's mother's house where they would be living. In May 1971, their first child, Sonny, was born.

Gema and I were always close, even though there was seven years difference between us. She seemed to trust me and liked being with me. I guess I never criticised her and I accepted her the way she was. Pia never changed, even though she was a mother. She still had her unkind attitude towards me. She seemed to delight in hurting me with her cutting words. I don't know if I was afraid of her, or in shock, but I couldn't defend myself. Most of the time, I never reacted and just wondered why. Again, I had to face humiliation by a family member, like I did as a child from Dad and Mum. Now it was Javier's family's turn. Despite the torments, it was good at Javier's mother's house, because we were away from Mum and Dad for a while. As time went on, I realised how much I was kept out of Javier's family circle, in regards to the older members. I was put with the kids for a reason, so that's where I spent my time while in that family. Gema and I enjoyed our time together and became very close; she seemed to stick to me like glue. I don't know which was the hardest to suffer, the torments of Javier's family, or the emotional traumas of my mother. At least I could escape the farm by being there. It was like being in heaven to be away from Mum and Dad.

Even though we constantly went to Javier's mother's house on the weekends, they still insisted on visiting us on the farm. They were on our doorstep nearly every day through the week. They had no boundaries and they didn't care that it wasn't our home. They'd stay for hours and hours. I couldn't understand this, and found it hard to find out why, or a reason why they'd come all that way from Dawson Hill to see us every day. Dawson Hill was twenty miles away. Later on in our married life, I questioned it and complained.

Pia and Nick would have their second child in May the next year. I felt for her and having two babies so close was hard on her. Pia's life was already hard, and I could see her life was going to be a struggle. Her husband, Nick, was so lazy; even though he had turned seventeen he was still a boy. Also Nick had started drinking, and he didn't drink small bottles of beer; he often carried around a large bottle in his hand.

# Chapter 20

# Strange Happenings

Dad convinced Javier to buy some cows. It was a good idea, as we could make some extra money, especially if they calved. Both Dad and Javier bought two cows for us. One was very young, the other a bit older. We intended keeping them for a season. The money could go into the block of land we'd purchased. Not long after we got the cows, the older cow was in calf. It was moving into August, and September or October was the best time to sell. During these months, I became unsettled. I felt some hesitation in leaving this older cow until the following month to sell her. I suggested to Javier that he sell her now, while she was in calf. He wouldn't entertain it and told me I was being silly, and that we'd wait until the spring time. A few days later, I pestered him more and more to sell the pregnant cow. The weather was changing, my feelings got stronger, and an inner voice was telling me we should sell this pregnant cow that was nearing her birthing time.

Javier eventually got sick of me pestering him, so we went and asked my dad.

Javier threw it on me. 'Max, Chris said we should sell the pregnant cow now. What do you think?'

Dad looked at me and snapped back, with a smirk and a snigger, 'Don't take any notice to her: wait until the spring.'

I couldn't, at that point, overrule my father, so Javier listened to him. My feelings intensified. I knew the prices for cows at the market weren't too bad at that moment, and a pregnant cow would, of course, bring in more money at the sale yards.

Telling Javier the prices were good at the market, I cautioned him to sell. 'Sell the cow before the spring, Javier,' I pleaded.

'No, your father said no - and no.'

'Okay. I won't say any more about it.'

A few days passed by. There was a raging storm and there was nothing I could do. On waking the next morning, I got up and moved the curtain aside to see outside. It was blustery and the sky was still heavy with rain. I felt there was a problem, because the storm was so bad all night, and the wind was still blowing a gale outside. Julian was sleeping; it was early.

I quickly dressed and shook Javier out of his sleep, whispering, 'Javier, we have to go and look for the cow. There's a problem.'

He moaned and groaned a bit, but he went along with me. 'Alright, let's go.' He got up out of bed, pulled on his pants, and threw on a jumper.

As we walked through the living room, I said, 'The weather was so bad all night. Did you hear it?'

Wiping the sleep out of his eyes, he mumbled, 'No.'

When I opened the kitchen door, the enormity of the night's storm was evident. There was rubbish strewn around the yard and left-out washing blown off the clothesline. Not sure where to head to search for the cow, I started to walk towards the pump house. Javier was following me.

In the howling wind, I screamed out to him, 'Where is she? I can't see her.'

He said nothing but kept walking and looking in the paddock. I was frantic for the cow's safety, and I turned this way and that, searching the paddock for her. Javier must have thought I was mad.

Nearing the edge of the lagoon, my feelings were getting stronger and stronger. Then I saw her and I screamed out above the wind, 'Javier, there she is. She's dead.'

He hurried over and peered over my shoulder at our poor cow. We both remained silent. She'd rolled down the embankment into the lagoon while giving birth to her calf, and both mother and calf were drowned in the lagoon. My intuition was starting to become stronger, and many times it would tell me things and it would be right. I would advise Javier to do things to our benefit but he never listened to me. As a consequence, we lost out on many good opportunities.

We still had the younger cow. She would have her calf soon. My feelings rose up inside me again. I told Javier to sell this cow and her newborn calf. 'Sell them now, Javier, while the market is reasonable,' I told him.

Javier told me no. He said my father had said no.

I complained, 'But Javier, remember what happened last time.'

'It was just a freak accident. The cow rolled into the lagoon and nothing more, and your stupid thoughts had nothing to do with it,' he snapped.

I stared at him. I knew my thoughts weren't stupid. It was just this man would never listen to me, but he'd listen to my father and take on his bad advice. The market for cows was better in August, just when I wanted to sell the older cow. In September, the market was reasonable, but Javier was waiting until early October. Then the market plummeted. Once again, we lost lots of money, and I realised my husband was weak around my father.

I knew without knowing things, and it was to become stronger as time went on. I was becoming more aware on a level I didn't understand, and I was having some flashbacks, remembering the vision I'd had in my teens in the dead of night when I was around sixteen.

We were driving home from an outing. It was a strange evening, and on the crest of the hill, on the lagoon side of the road, I was looking over at the farm. As we were descending the hill, I turned and looked at Javier. I looked back again to the landscape as he drove us along the dirt road.

'Javier, I want to ask you a question.'

'Yes, what is it?' he moaned.

'Javier, I've never, ever confided in anyone about a night when I was sixteen.' He was my husband, and I felt he should understand me, and help me to understand what I was going through.

'Well? What?'

'When I was sixteen, I saw a vision in my bedroom of a ghost. I was wondering what you think it was.'

He said straight out, 'It was probably the Devil.'

I jumped back in shock at the thought of the Devil. Such thoughts had never entered my world. No one in my family ever mentioned the Devil. I'd never given any thought to God or the Devil. I looked at him and said, 'No, it wasn't. It was a transparent-looking woman and she had on a veil.'

He changed the subject and I knew we'd never relate to each other on any topic or in any area of conversation. I needed to talk to someone for answers about what was opening up in me, and there was no one.

# Chapter 21

# More Strange Happenings

November and springtime was with us. We were still living on the farm, and my awareness was getting stronger. I could tell if something was going to happen. I was usually an early riser, even on weekend days, because I got up early on work days to get Javier off to work and it was habit. This Saturday morning, I stretched and moved around. Javier and Julian were fast asleep.

Julian was one year and two months, walking everywhere. He was so cute and loved his dummy, which he called his Ber. He called his bottle his Bor, and water Aqua. We didn't know where he got these words from, because no one else used such words. He was also cutting his teeth, and constantly chewing on his dummy; it was a good pacifier.

Lying there, I straightened. I was on my back, and anticipation came over me. I felt I'd see my cousin Kelvin today. He was going to pay us a visit. I said, frowning, 'Hmm, Kelvin. That's unusual. He's in the army and preparing to go to Vietnam any day now.' Letting the thought go and getting out of bed, I went over to the window, pulled the curtains back and held them to inspect the day. Smiling as I peered out and saw nature at its best in the early hours of a morning, I dropped the curtain again.

I'd had enough of lying in, so I removed my nightie and placed it over the back of the bed poster, went over to the couch where my house clothes were, and put on my short cotton dress for the day. This room was so spacious. As children, we'd been truly lucky to have been brought up in such an enormous house. I went over to Julian and watched him for a bit with his little pursed lips, and he looked so sweet. He was still in a deep sleep. I quietly left the room and made my way to the kitchen. I went over to Grandma's door, because she was always awake early. 'Hi, Grandma, how are you?'

She glanced around from her book and smiled. 'Fine, Christine, and how are you?'

'Good, Grandma.' I turned away, saying, 'See you,' and continued on to the kitchen. Mum was already in the kitchen sitting over a cup of tea. I could see she was in anguish.

She told me, 'I couldn't sleep.'

I reassured her. 'Me either, and I can never sleep in on the weekends, and I wish I could.'

'Do you want a cup of tea?'

'No, Mum, not yet. I'll eat first.' I went to the cupboard and pulled a box of cereal off the top shelf. Mum placed the milk in front of me. Thanking her, I took a bowl from the centre of the table, placed cereal in the bowl, and said, 'We're going to see our cousin, Kelvin, today.' I looked at her for her reaction.

She looked at me as if I had some inside information she didn't have. Her look was asking me if I was in contact with Kelvin, and why didn't he tell her. Annoyed, she finally asked, 'How do you know that?'

'I feel he's coming.'

She looked at me strangely. 'No, he's not coming; he has to go overseas soon.'

'I know that, but I feel he's coming, and it's okay if you don't agree with me.' Taking the milk carton and opening the spout of it, I commenced to pour the milk onto my cereal and watched the cereal disappear under the flow of the milk. I closed the spout of the carton and returned it to the refrigerator. As I did that, I thought how repetitious our lives were. I was not aware in those days of the changes that were happening to me, and I never realised we changed constantly. I was truly a princess in a deep sleep, held captive in a castle by witches and huntsmen. I didn't know I was awakening into my spiritual world.

Around 10am, Dad, Javier, and Julian came to the kitchen for breakfast. By 10.30, breakfast was over and Mum and I washed up and put the dishes away. Not long afterwards, around 11, a car turned into the top gate. Dad came into the house announcing, 'Carol, someone's coming.'

Mum asked, 'Who, Max?'

'I don't know; I don't recognise the car.'

I said, 'Maybe it's Kelvin.'

My mum looked at me weirdly. We all moved out to the front gate. This is something we did when people came to our house. We were all out at the front gate waiting, because there was a fair distance between the gates, and the car was coming through the second gate, opened by a young girl. We all wondered and stood watching as this old station wagon pulled in closer.

'It's Kelvin,' Mum shouted in excitement. She ran to him in raptures, because he was her favourite nephew. She was beside herself.

Kelvin jumped out of the car, all smiles, and he grabbed my mum and gave her a big bear hug. 'Aunty Carol,' he bleated, and Mum laughed and cried tears of joy at seeing him.

It was too much for her. She was overwhelmed, and they cuddled tightly; you could see they really loved each other equally. As I watched them, I felt she loved him more than her own two daughters; but not more than her son.

When they broke their hold, Dad shook hands with Kelvin saying, 'God bugger me, we didn't expect to see you here.'

Kelvin grinned from ear to ear. 'No, Uncle Max, but…' He grabbed Dad and gave him a big hug, which shocked my dad, because he never would hug a man. Dad was a bit flabbergasted.

I walked over. 'Hi, Kelvin, so good to see you. I felt you were coming today.' He gave me a hug and I hugged him back.

He smiled and said hello to Javier, who was holding Julian. Then he said, looking over the roof of the car to where the pretty, young girl was standing, 'I want to introduce you to my girlfriend.' He put his hand out and nodded, and this pretty, young girl came around to him and took his hand. Kelvin, who was a real Aussie, said with an almost Texan accent, 'This is Brooke, and Brooke, this is my favorite aunt, Aunty Carol.'

She said, 'Hello, Carol, I've heard so much about you, and I'm glad to finally meet you.'

'And this is Uncle Max; Christine; Javier, her husband; and their babyyyy.'

I said, 'This is Julian. Hi, Brooke, lovely to meet you.'

Kelvin hadn't met Julian yet, so he didn't know Julian's name. We were all so excited to see him.

We all liked Brooke, who was a shy and reclusive kind of girl.

Kelvin announced, 'I am leaving next weekend to go to Vietnam.'

Mum couldn't contain her fears, and she cried. Kelvin put his arm around her and reassured her. 'Now, Aunty Carol, I'll be alright.' She made a promise to see him off in Rosemount. As she promised Kelvin, she turned to my dad for confirmation of that promise and asked, 'That's right, Max. We'll go down to Rosemount and say goodbye to Kelvin.'

Dad, in his yeah-non-committal voice, said, 'Yeah, we'll be there.'

We all moved into the house, and it was one of the best days ever on the farm. Through the day, looking lovingly at Brooke shyly lowering her eyes and head, Kelvin also announced, 'Aunty and Uncle, we have some good news to share with you.' We all looked at him in suspense, waiting eagerly for his news. Brooke blushed coyly. 'On my return from Vietman, Brooke and I plan to marry.'

We clapped and gave our congratulations to them both, and we were extra happy for them. Mum's eyes welled up with pride, love and joy for her favourite nephew.

When Kelvin and Brooke left that day, everyone spoke of how surprised they were to see Kelvin visit us.

But not me; I knew he was coming somehow. Mum never remembered or acknowledged I'd told her earlier that morning. My intuition was never understood by others, and for that matter, by me either.

Many times I knew things prior to them happening: like I knew who incoming mail was coming from, or if a particular person was going to contact us or visit us. I was tapping into impending losses as well; I seemed to know if/that someone was going to die.

The following weekend came, and Mum wanted to go to Rosemount to see Kelvin off. Dad refused to take her there, and she was devastated. But the most tragic thing was that she never recovered from the guilt of not keeping her promise to Kelvin to go and see him off. In this guilt she created another hell for herself to live with. During Kelvin's tour of duty in Vietnam, Mum and him constantly wrote letters to each other. I was so glad she did this; at least this enabled her to explain to Kelvin why she couldn't go to Rosemount to see him off. Mum apologised numerous times to Kelvin and he lovingly accepted her apology, but she could never forgive herself.

# Chapter 22

# Boredom

It was around December, 1971, and things got rough for Dante and Nita in Cloverbrook; he lost his job with the contractors. So they moved back to Dawson Hill to live with Javier's mum and dad. They had no money, so they had no chance of buying a house. Dante was a very handsome man, and his good looks intrigued me. He had a serious face and his dark looks were appealing; the more I saw him, the more I liked him. Not that I would've ever done anything in my marriage; however, I started to notice Dante, and I watched him from a distance, not allowing my eyes to give me away. I was starting to feel real unhappiness with Javier.

Dante was married to Nita, who was of European descent. It was a strong marriage, but Javier's family actually disliked her so much, that they all talked badly about her behind Dante's back. Simply because Nita hadn't been a virgin; she'd had a few lovers before Dante and had even lived with a man for a period of time before Dante married her. She was considered a bad woman. Dante loved his wife, regardless of her past, and he trusted Nita. For me, it wasn't an issue that Nita had loved others. I couldn't see what the problem was, because it was prior to them meeting. What surprised me the most were the younger brothers and sisters, who had been influenced by the Australian culture, were up in arms about Nita and her past. These younger family members were under the age of eleven when they'd arrived in Australia in the 1960s. They were still influenced by old beliefs and thinking. The older brothers I could understand, because they were in their teens and were influenced by their culture. Dante, sixteen when he left Spain, had let his old cultural beliefs go, and took a woman he loved for his wife. They'd married the day after they met. When Dante brought Nita home and announced they'd just married and that was it, shit hit the fan, so to speak.

John, on the other hand, could get away with murder; I saw that the day I met him at the boxing match. I had picked up he was a volcano; an impulsive, temperamental and violent man who could change at the click of your fingers. He'd hit you and ask questions later. I later learnt he had a background involving mafia, but I seemed to have won John over. He seemed to like me a lot. These two older brothers would come and go, living in different towns throughout my marriage.

The three older sons, John, Javier and Dante, didn't mix with the younger siblings from Pia down. John, Dante and Javier weren't reachable. The other eight siblings were kept as children and looked on as such by the three older siblings; when you looked at the eleven siblings as a group, you too could see the younger eight were child-like. They were from a different generation or time frame.

Javier was the youngest out of the three oldest, and then came Pia, then Bernat, who was my age. The gap between these younger ones was great; there was a child that had died between Javier and Pia. This child was still being mourned by the parents. Pia, Bernat, Paco, Vince, Alexandre, Bianca, Gema and Jules didn't have a hope in heaven of being understood by the three eldest.

The younger ones had the old parents' belief system pushed onto them. I could see clashes with the younger ones and their parents. The older ones had a clearer memory of life in Spain and its traditions, and what was expected from the family and the culture. I felt it must have been hard for the younger ones to synthesise their culture, when they had been influenced by an Australian culture at a young age. This led to having to take on the beliefs and hearsay of the older brothers and their parents, who hadn't been back to their own country for years, which I was sure was changing. A country and a culture will never remain the same as you leave it.

A virgin bride was very important in the marriage for this culture, and Javier boasted I was a virgin. Now I wonder, did Javier just marry me because I was a virgin? In Australia, women were becoming freer and making choices in what they wanted. I personally wasn't ready for sex, so he was lucky to scoop me up. Javier dated both myself and Charlene at the Bolt Steel Fabricators Plant, but she wasn't a virgin. I knew he liked her, but she just didn't fit the criteria.

Dante had committed a sin to marry Nita, a free-minded woman. John had married Sarah, a virgin. He'd got her pregnant, but she walked out on him after the birth of their third child, Mitchell. They'd had two girls before Mitchell arrived, Marisa and Zara. Sarah disappeared, not to be found by any of the family. I was told John was very cruel to her, and they fought all the time, so she went back to her parents and later found a place of her own, and never told John where she was living. John had constantly accused his ex-wife of being lazy. He told the family all she did was read books and wouldn't have his dinner cooked when he arrived home, or his clothes washed and ironed, ready for him to go out and live the high life while she stayed home to mind their kids.

Personally, I felt John was a non-committal person, and one wife may not have been quite enough for his male ego. No way was I going to allow that with Javier. Sure enough, he would have his dinner on the table and his clothes washed; but as far as him coming home and dressing up and going out, living another life outside of our marriage - no way.

I don't think John was really worried about losing his family, because he was too busy enjoying his life with different women. I would get to know a few of those women as time went by, and I'd see for myself his other side. John tried to present an image of Mr Nice Guy, but even with my naivety, I worked him out. He was a person to be watched, and not upset, or you could be the victim of a surprise, explosive attack.

# Chapter 23

# Family Conflicts

When Julian was older, and Nita and Dante were living at Javier's parents' house, Javier and I were still spending our weekends at his parents' home, and the four of us started to go out occasionally for dinner. This was also a very festive time; as Julian was older, I was able to take him out with us, so we attended some of the family's friends' parties. There were many parties and we seemed to be attending one each weekend. At one party, I was holding Julian and standing, watching the crowd with Gema. Javier was getting so drunk, he started to embarrass me; not in a humiliating way, but because he was stupid.

He was dancing very stupidly with another woman. This didn't worry me because I wasn't jealous of Javier. I trusted him completely and never suspected him of cheating on me, but he looked so ridiculous. I asked Dante to tell him to behave.

Dante was grumpy and growled at me, 'Tell him yourself; he's your husband.' He walked off snarling, and I realised what all the family were saying about Dante and his jealousies. He'd just shown me how jealous he was of Javier, because Javier was popular, even though he looked stupid. I saw Dante's other side: a cold, unhappy, envious man. Dante was a very serious, grumpy type, and full of pomp, the type of person who couldn't see the fun in life. My infatuation with Dante left me as quickly as it had come. His good looks had blinded me to his character. Sometimes that's what happens: we see an image we like, and we get so caught up by its beauty, we don't look beyond the beautiful image to see the true, hidden nature of that beauty. Sometimes the image of a beautiful man or woman isn't transparent. Dante stormed off, cursing Javier; he wasn't happy.

Javier and I had decided to start trying for our second baby. Nita and Dante found this out, and because of his jealousies, they announced they were trying for their third child. When I heard this, I couldn't believe that someone who was struggling financially would bring another child into their lives, just because someone else was going to try and have a child. It didn't stop there either; Nita's mother got wind of Nita trying for a baby, and so she jumped on the bandwagon and announced they were going to try for a baby. Nita's mother wasn't psychologically stable, due to some traumatic experience; I'm not sure what. That made three of us aiming for another baby. I was confused by their behaviour, and I didn't pay too much attention to it all; because I wanted a baby, not because others were trying to have a baby to compete with other family members.

In March, on Barton's return, Dad bought him a car. It was time for Barton to get his licence. There were no problems teaching Barton to drive because he already knew how. He was driving Dad's tractor when he was young. He just had to have his Learners for three months, and then he could go for his test to get his Provisional licence. We all thought if he had his own car, he wouldn't have to steal someone else's car to drive.

All hell broke loose in the house of Javier's father. There was a big blow-up with my father-in-law; he was telling stories about Dante's wife, Nita, and how she was entertaining men in their bedroom at the house, also spreading rumours that she was going out and not staying at home. Dante believed Nita when she said it wasn't true. He fought with his father, and in April, they'd left Dawson Hill and moved to Chester Hills for good. They got away from the family and their hatred of Nita. Dante's jealousy was too much for him to cope with, so it was probably best they left.

I did miss them, because sometimes we went out to dinner together, and it had been nice to have that release from the daily routines of life. I thought Nita was a nice person, even though she was very naïve and played the innocent, which upset the family. When I think about it, she was only trying to be nice, and fit in and be accepted, but she never was.

In May, Pia had her second son, Daniel. Regardless of all the jealousy and competition, at the end of May I became pregnant with our second child, before Nita. During the first stages of my pregnancy, I had to have blood tests to make sure there were no problems. It was found I'd either had or come in contact with German measles. I remembered having rose pink spots on my stomach, but I wasn't sick. The doctor thought I'd probably had German measles. I had to have a second blood test which showed I had more antibodies than other people. Dr Ling told me this would protect my child. I never worried about having measles or thought there'd be any consequences for my child. In my second month of pregnancy, Julian got the measles, and straight after the measles, he got chickenpox. On visiting my doctor, he informed me this can cause blindness, deafness and muteness in a baby. There was protection from my extra antibodies, but I had to have an injection. I was told I'd have no troubles. There were no worries on my part, because I always felt safe.

My cousin, Gerry, was carrying her first child at the same time as me, and she was going through the same issues; she'd come into contact with German measles, or had had them, and she had the blood test and it showed she too had more antibodies than other people. She'd also come in contact with chickenpox and had the injection. We were so lucky. I don't know where the extra antibodies came from in our family, but it was a blessing.

# Chapter 24

# Reminiscing

I was dreaming and woke around 2am. I felt wide awake, so I turned off the alarm; it would have gone off at 3:30am and woke the baby. Awake, I stretched my body and looked over towards Julian. There was no movement. My thoughts of him made me smile and I realised having Julian had been the best thing that'd ever happened to me - and to think I didn't want to have children. I looked at Javier. He was still in a deep sleep, so deep his mouth was agape, showing his teeth. Those teeth, my goodness me; when I first met him, they were terrible. Thank goodness I'd got him to clean them. They did look much better. When we first got married, it was obvious he'd never been instructed in basic bodily care. Now he was taking more pride in himself, and regularly went for dental checks with my dentist, Mr Pounder.

That brought to mind my own experiences around going to the dentist. Stretching, and snuggling back down between the sheets, I recalled the time I'd had a bad toothache. It was so bad, and I whinged so much that Dad and Mum took me into town to see Mr Pounder. My father was complaining to Mum about how he didn't want to listen to me whine for another minute. Mr Pounder was booked out, so Dad asked if there was another dentist close by. The receptionist explained that there was another dentist across the street. Terror seized me. I couldn't run and somehow the pain left my tooth, not that I could tell Dad that. He would be ropeable. Without any say in the matter on my part, Dad decided to take me across the street to the other dentist. I didn't want to go. Fear was gaining a firm grip over me and I was so terrified. Now I can laugh about it.

Javier stirred, and he turned around to face the wall. I went back to my reminiscing on the day I had to face a strange dentist. I could see Dad dragging me across the street, telling me how he's not putting up with me screaming in pain for another night. By now, the tears were flowing, and the fear was getting higher. In my mind, I envisaged an ogre who would yank out my tooth.

We entered the building of the other dentist. I felt my dad didn't care about my feelings. There was a long staircase. Looking up those stairs, I started screaming at the top of my lungs and gripped the banister. No way was I going up to that monster. Dad couldn't unlock my grip; my fingers had become part of the railing and my screaming wouldn't stop. Dad became very angry with me, and people in the building came out to investigate. Poor Dad; he hated any public embarrassment made by his family.

Finally Dad gave in. I could feel his defeat and I released my grip. He grabbed me, saying, 'Come on, we're going home.'

Sobbing, I followed behind my parents. When we walked out of that building, I was relieved. A child's fear is so great. I don't think I could ever trust another dentist, even today.

Dad was always going off at me for being lazy with my oral hygiene. I hated to clean my teeth, but later, I taught Javier to clean his. Fortunately, habits do become routine.

Routine. That is how I felt my married life was: a routine. Everyday, I would get Javier off to work; every day of my married life, I had to keep to routines to suit others. I sighed, whispering to myself and feeling the heavy burden of responsibility. 'Marriage, truly; I don't know.'

There had been some hard times in our marriage, and some incidents that I couldn't really understand why I'd responded in the way I did. I couldn't understand my behaviour.

Like the time we first got together, and went to Javier's friend Pepe's marriage to Camilla. At the wedding, I felt such jealousy over a girl that was talking to Javier. After I had Julian, I was so jealous of my mum around Javier. It was ridiculous behaviour, because I'd never felt those kinds of feelings of jealousy before with anyone, not with my sister, brother, mum or dad. Thank goodness it came and went, and there had been no more jealousy around Javier.

Things were better, and I was more tolerant of Javier. Despite this, there was still some tension between us, because of my clashes with my mother. I slid my hand gently over Javier's head and wondered where all this would lead us. I often wondered about our future, especially my children's. Soon we would have two children to be responsible for. Moving away from him, I pulled the cover over me again. Another day and we were still on the farm, but not long to go. I asked myself: how long will it take to build our house? How long do I have to stay here? I sighed, thinking: as long as it takes.

I felt like I was being cheated of a married life that should be free of parents. I was still here with them, and I couldn't break free from them. Stress engulfed me, and I sighed deeply and quietly, running my hands over my body as I stretched again. I fell into the foetal position, wrapped my arms around myself, and cuddled myself and rocked my body. One more quick sleep and then I must get up, I thought.

# Chapter 25

# Daydreaming

3.30am. Slowly I sat up, lifted the sheets and struggled out of bed so as not to disturb him. The old bed was very high, a long, three-foot drop to the floor. The beds in that house were well over eighty years old, and still had their original mosquito netting on them. As children, we never used the netting, so they smelt of dust from eons ago, which made me think of how old this house was, and if only walls could talk; what a story they could tell. I wondered about the memories this room held. Glancing up at the wedding photo of my grandfather and grandmother that sat perched over the large door into the bedroom, they both looked so regal. What a beautiful couple they were. Nonetheless, my grandfather's eyes; I swear he was watching me, and he followed me around the room. I never knew him. Nor did my father know his own father. All of us only knew things about him from what Grandma told us. Out of the family members in my immediate family, and besides my grandma, I'm the one who felt a deep love for my grandfather. So much so that I wanted to know him.

The bareness of the floor was cool under my bare feet. I liked going bare-footed on the floor, and I hardly ever wore shoes around the house. I loved to feel the ground under my feet, especially when I walked on the grass. When I did that, I felt connected to the earth and nature, more than I felt connected to my own body. Honestly, I never worried about my body. Even before I met Javier, and after meeting him, I'd dress up in my mini-skirts, put on my make-up in five minutes, and out the door. I rarely stood gazing in the mirror at myself.

Leaning against the bed, I pushed myself off of it, and picked up my brunch coat that was lying on the chair near the French doors. Sliding my arms through the sleeves and pulling it over and around me, I buttoned it up. I needed to peek at the day ahead, so I went to the French doors and gently pulled back the curtain. It was still dark out there. I didn't fear the darkness outside, but I feared the darkness of the rooms in that house. Out there, it was safe and free, with no walls to bind you, or for things to hide behind. The openness was all upfront and real. In that house, there was no realness; everyone was lost in their own worries and sorrows. I turned to look at my child in his cot and I smiled; I knew what was real. Closing the curtain, I felt wonderful feelings of motherhood engulf my whole being.

Looking down on him in his cot, I could see how gorgeous he was. His lips pouted and I felt like kissing them. His face was so serene, and he had his little arms out of the covers. He stirred. He must have sensed my presence. I moved back, because I didn't want to wake him yet.

Carefully, I opened the big, heavy, wooden door, so as not to make that creaking sound. I gritted my teeth and hunched my shoulders as I did this. The quieter you try to be, the noisier you are, I thought. Julian wriggled in his cot. I smiled and slipped out the doorway, leaving the door ajar.

The hallway had to be at least twelve feet wide and still had the beautiful, old, oriental carpet runner up its centre. Grandma said she had bought that when she first got married and came out here to live. Being in this end of the house, I actually felt like a house guest. In its heyday, it had been used as a guest house for Grandma and Grandfather's special guests. They'd stay in this very bedroom. The formal lounge room was also only used by guests.

The formal lounge room was the eeriest; I would fly past that room and pretend it didn't exist. If something was to come walking out of there, I'd die on the spot. I wondered if Grandma knew there was something down there. If she did, she never said anything to me about it.

To the right of the archway was my parents' room. As I passed their door, I dreaded them waking up. I closed my eyes as if to pretend they didn't exist.

# Chapter 26

# Grandma Locked In Her Past

Grandma was awake; I figured she'd been awake most of the early morning, reading her magazines. Her small lamp threw a shadow over the room and I could see her propped on her pillows. There was a terrible smell of urine that wafted from her room. Mum had tried to remove it as best she could, and she kept it all clean, but it just lingered. I guess it was because of the old floor boards. There was lino on the floor, old and cracked. If anything was dropped, it went straight through to the boards beneath, and they'd soak it up, absorbing the mess.

It was about 1968 when Grandma really decided to go to bed. Before that, she used to get up and sit in the family living room, and then go back to bed. With time, she became so tired, she decided to go to bed permanently, refusing to leave her bed. Sometimes Dad forced her to get out of bed, and she'd scream and cry. Witnessing her pain, I felt her whole body must be aching. Sometimes, Dad acted very cruelly towards Grandma. This left her sobbing as she sat in her chair. It used to upset me sometimes, his powerful hands dragging her to the sitting room. Fortunately, it got to the point where she couldn't be moved. Her whole body must have seized up: moving her was too cruel. Then Mum took care of Grandma. Mum had to learn how to change the sheets with Grandma in the bed. Sometimes Dad would help; however he was too cranky, and instead of being loving to his mother, he seemed to be hurting her. During the process, all you could hear was Grandma saying, 'Max, you're hurting me.'

Grandma had given my mum a hard time all her married life. She'd never accepted Mum as her daughter-in-law, and now Mum was the one, and the only one, caring for her. None of her children wanted anything to do with her, not even Dad. As Grandma deteriorated more and more, he didn't want to touch her. Mum cared for Grandma, but she was paranoid about germs too. She'd always had a thing about germs, and now her fears were enhanced, and she included us in her paranoia. The biggest shock for Mum was when she caught Grandma masturbating. Mum was in disbelief. Every time she washed Grandma's sheets, she'd scrub out the washing machine and used loads of disinfectant on everything. Her paranoia stopped all of us touching Grandma for fear of getting her germs.

Uncle Oliver was so disgusted with us and our attitudes towards Grandma. One day, I had freaked out when Julian stepped into her room without me knowing. I grabbed him and refused to let him go near Grandma. Uncle Oliver was very angry with me for not letting Grandma nurse Julian. He shouted at me that day, telling me how dirty money was, and that I never washed my hands after touching money. I just stared at him in shock, but Mum had trained me well, and I couldn't break the training.

I'd make a little noise to let her know when I was approaching her door. She turned as she heard me.

'Hello, Grandma. How are you?'

With her toothless smile, she answered, 'Good, Christine. How are you?'

From the doorway, I replied, 'Good, Grandma. What are you reading?'

She turned her opened magazine towards me to look at the page she was on.

In response I said, 'Oh, you're on the latest fashion pages. They're beautiful, Grandma.'

Grandma had told me she didn't wear clothes from a shop; she and her sisters handmade their clothes, and she was a seamstress in her younger days.

She flipped through her magazine, and as I watched her, I felt she was completely happy where she was. I never saw her as a lonely person, or maybe I didn't notice her being lonely. I knew she missed Grandfather, who had died at 42, and Uncle Donny, who had died young. There were no feelings of pity for her. She had on her favourite pink bed-jacket. Up until the mid-60s, she'd never worn coloured clothes, only black. After the death of her husband and son, she went into black. Somehow, Aunty Connie had managed to get her into grey, blue-grey or dark blue dresses. Just before her major bowel operation, she was into pinks and pale blues: how we can all change eventually.

'I'd better go, Grandma. It's late. See you later on.'

'Hmm,' she said, not even noticing I was still there.

I never saw her get bored or upset in that room. She truly was in her own world.

As I walked off, I could still smell her room; the smell seemed to linger in my nose for a while. There was not only the smell of urine, but also an old, musky smell, because the windows were never opened in that room. To think, as a child, I shared that room with her; but back then, she was a different woman, strong and demanding. She let herself go, surrendered to others, and lost her will to control them. Once we all feared her, then we shunned her in her unhygienic, old age.

At the kitchen door, I switched on the light. Nothing had changed in here either. It was like we were all trapped in an era gone by. A feeling of annoyance came over me. I had to cook Javier breakfast and prepare his lunch for work. In an hour's time Mum would be up.

'Oh, I wonder what today will bring me,' I muttered. I dreaded the thought.

# Chapter 27

# Nature Resolves The Days Of Dread

Before I did anything, I had to go to the toilet. I'd been daydreaming. I couldn't help it, and stuff them, I loved to daydream. I was always in trouble for daydreaming, but now I could. That was the only thing they couldn't intrude on, or take from me: my mind.

I rushed to the kitchen door and took out the old poker that barred the door. Every night, it was thrust into a big gap between the door and the kitchen floor. The key for the front door was lost years ago. The poker did the job. Opening the door and stepping out onto the old wooden verandah, I spotted the cat. It saw me and came running over. The animals, as well as my child, made my day.

'Hello, Ginger, gorgeous pussy cat,' I cooed, as if talking to my child. It responded by meowing, and purred and rubbed its body through my legs. I gave it a pat and picked it up, tightly cuddling it. It meowed and pulled away. 'Sorry, pussky, pussky.' It pushed away and jumped down. I laughed, knowing I was too hard with it, but I couldn't resist cuddling it as tight as I could, feeling the love that welled up in me. It shook itself. I felt gentle towards it and patted it softly this time.

Blue, the dog, lifted its head and stretched, just looking at me, as if to say, oh, it's only you, and it's that time of the day again. I know if I called him, he'd bounce up and run to me, but it was getting late, so I walked up the front path and through the old, wooden gateway. There were hardly any palings left on the fence, and only the frame of the old gateway. Everything was falling around our ears. There had to be a closing to this house's life. Nothing had been repaired or renewed.

Dad and the pit management said no to repairs, and Mum and Dad held onto Grandma so they wouldn't have to go into town and pay for their own home, and start to pay bills. I told myself to run to the tiolet. I was really in a hurry to go. The toilet was about 20 feet from the house. I dodged my way around the cows, and one of the cows threw its head back and stepped out of my way. I switched on the light and sat on the wooden seat of the dunny. Dad had to rebuild the toilet when we were kids. Being a sanitary pan, Dad and Barton had to bury the dead, as they called it every fortnight. Then Javier had to help with that job. I was glad to be a girl. Sitting there, I could hear various noises outside. That was one good thing about being a country girl; you got used to noises. I heard a cow brushing up near the toilet. The cows didn't worry me. I was just hoping the spiders were still asleep. The toilet was very clean; Dad was a stickler for that. He was always pouring phenol disinfectant into the pan, and on emptying days, he washed out the pan and the inside of the loo. I guess there was a method to his madness, because he seemed to be the one using it the most. It was like a safe haven for him. I couldn't understand why anyone would want to sit on a toilet for long periods of time. He also had a variety of reading material to entertain himself, but there was nothing educational, only magazines on fishing and boating.

Opening the door, I saw the two dogs waiting outside. 'Hello, Bluey, hello, Lucky,' I said invitingly. Funny how animals sense when it's okay, and not okay, to come near you. Blue wagged his tail and nudged into my leg. I went to pat him, and Lucky bit Blue on his snout. I tried to pat them both and keep it equal. The older dog could only tolerate Lucky's antics for a while. He snapped, and when Blue snapped, you stopped mucking up. Blue must have been at least ten years older than Lucky. Blue had been a good, faithful dog and he did love us. Unfortunately, Blue didn't like Julian, and we had to watch him around Julian because he'd started to bare his teeth at him. It was hard for Julian too. He was never frightened or cried when Blue did this; however, we had to protect Julian from Blue. Mum and I would tell Julian to not go near bitey Blue. Lucky was a good dog, and accepted Julian. It was good that Julian could learn from both their personalities, but it soon came to an end. One day, Blue didn't see my dad come onto the verandah. If he had, he'd never have showed his teeth to Julian until it was safe to do so. Good thing he did slip up, because Dad seemed to come from nowhere, and as quick as a flash, Blue had Dad's foot in his ribs, giving him an almighty swift kick. The dog ran away down the paddock. That was the end of his growling at Julian.

Dad was like that; he didn't say much, he just acted, and before you knew it, it had happened, but also you knew what it was for. Blue got the message. To nip things in the bud is always the best policy. Sometimes, in regard to his family, Dad didn't always leave room for explanation in his retaliation towards you. I was still finding it hard to get past Dad's stern looks, and to find the courage to tell him where to go. Well, maybe one day I would when he pushed me too far. But for now, I was glad he'd sorted out Blue with Julian.

Looking at Blue, I said, 'I want you to live with Julian, and we still love you, you silly old dog.' As if he understood, he turned into a pup and jumped up on me as we ran back up the paddock to the house. I went into the laundry to wash my hands and Blue waited on the verandah. The water was freezing cold. We had a chip heater in the bathroom on the opposite side of the verandah, but not in the laundry. While washing, I thought of Blue, and how he'd been number one for so long. Julian was Dad's pride and joy, and he took a lot of Dad's time. It was hard for Blue, being replaced.

Returning to the verandah, and in sympathy with Blue, I said, 'Poor old Blue. I know what it feels like to lose your position in the family.'

# Chapter 28

# A New Life Awaits

I slowly moved into the kitchen, and my whole temperament changed. I was free in the fresh, crisp air with myself and nature. I wondered at times, did this house really exist for me in such spendour as I'd seen it as a child? Had I created the splendour, or was it from nature I saw the splendour?

I had started making Javier's sandwiches for work; he liked salami and sardines. We didn't eat such foods. The salami was smelly and slimy on my hands, and my fingers smelt after touching it. I couldn't come to eating it myself. With the sandwiches made and wrapped, the clock showed me it was 4.30am. I rushed down to our room to get Javier out of bed.

Creeping into the room and glancing over at Julian. I said, 'Javier, Javier,' in a quiet voice, 'it's time to get up.'

In his sleepiness, he let out a groan. Once again, I told him it was time to get up.

'Okay,' he answered, moving away from my insistent voice and drawing the covers over his head.

'Come on. You've got to get up.' I didn't tell him it was me who was running late.

'Okay, okay,' he announced.

I laid out his clothes for him. I did this because his mother told me to, which was a bad move. I shouldn't have listened to her. Now it'd become a habit of mine and Javier made no attempt to find his own clothes. Things could be under his nose and he'd call me, asking me where such and such was. There's an Australian saying that suited this scenario: why have a dog and bark too. I guess I was just taking over where his mother left off. Although Javier'd been away from his parents' house, on and off, over his working life, I guess when you're back in the family way, old habits resurface and you want what was familiar to you in your first family.

'Javier.' I pulled out his socks and checked to make sure there were no holes in them. He got cranky if there was. He didn't answer me. 'There's a fog today; not a heavy one, but it's there.' Still he didn't answer so I left him, thinking, he'd need to take it easy going to work. We were in a small valley at the base of the mountain slopes, and the fog came in and settled for a period of time, and then lifted. Actually, it kind of crept in.

He answered, 'There's a fog?'

'Yes.'

He sat up, reached for his glasses, and wiped them on the sheet corner, then pulled his frame from under the sheet and sat on the side of the bed. 'What are you doing today?' he asked me in a quiet voice.

'I will play with Julian, and maybe take him for a walk around the paddocks,' I said. We didn't have time for conversation. 'I'll see you in the kitchen.'

The sooner he went, the better it was. Then I could come back here to the bedroom and be with Julian. I wanted Javier to go to work so we could have money to get out of here. Ten minutes later, he was up in the kitchen. I made him his coffee and he drank it. Javier amazed me, because he didn't have to go to the toilet straight away on rising in the morning.

I was busying myself packing his lunch into his bag and I heard, 'I've got a big job on today.'

'Really,' I said in a disinterested voice, forgetting myself. I thought I'd better be more interested. 'Will you be late coming home, then.'

He downed his last sip of coffee and breathed out a loud ah, as if to compliment the satisfying taste of the coffee. 'Could be.' He stared into his cup, contemplating what he just tasted. Next he was describing to me the procedures of the job.

Oh, shit, I think, here we go. I smiled and nodded, answering, 'Oh yes,' to look as if I was interested and understanding what he was saying.

I'd found out the hard way that I had to pay attention to what he had to say. If I didn't, he could get unreasonable to live with. I found his conversation boring; he had a voice with one tone and it became monotonous. In spite of that, I guess he had to get it off his chest if it was an awful job.

When Javier and I first got married, he never ate breakfast, but now he was starting to want it. I made him some eggs and placed them in front of him. While he was eating, I made him another cup of coffee, and one for me. As I sat there, I felt some love towards him - or was it pity? Putting my coffee down, I went around and gave him a kiss on his cheek and wrapped my arms around his neck.

He asked, 'What's that for?'

'Oh, nothing.' I broke the embrace, wondering why he had to question everything I did. Sometimes I just did things without there necessarily being a reason for them. If my feelings welled up, I was spontaneous and I played them out. The more he questioned me, the more distant I became.

He got up and went to the toilet. Not long after, I heard him in the laundry, washing, so I waited for him to come back into the kitchen. As I waited, I wondered how our lives would be in the future.

He entered the kitchen, smiling, and said, 'I've got to go.' He still carried a heavily-accented voice.

I thought he would never lose that accent, but he had improved with his word pronunciation.

'I'll be late tonight. There's a big job on,' he reminds me.

'Yes, you told me,' I reminded him back, getting his bag for him.

To Javier, work was everything. He'd always worked since he was ten years old in Spain, and I didn't think he could ever understand relaxation. Sometimes his job took him out of town. He'd be gone for a week or so. I didn't mind because I was with my parents, and I didn't question Javier in regard to this. He had explained to me ages before that in the construction industry this can happen. I knew they worked long hours. We moved out of the house and into the fresh morning air. I walked to the car with him. The car was parked near the front gate. It was going to be another warm day when the fog lifted, I thought. Springtime is lovely in Australia, and especially in October when everything is in the process of new growth.

Javier was still travelling all the way to Bryson Power Station and working with contractors, which was good because there'd been a lot of new construction work going on in the past five months. He often worked seven days a week, and well into the night, since May. It'd been really good, money-wise. The travelling was the problem, being a two-hour trip. There was a car pool in town, but he had to travel eight miles into town to get to the car pool. I was grateful for that, because it saved us some wear and tear on our old car, and I could have the car to go shopping on days Javier didn't drive. At the car, I went to cuddle him, but Javier was not like that. Cuddles, for him, were strictly for the bedroom. He didn't respond, but I still swung on his shoulder. The dogs had joined us, wagging their tails, and Lucky was wobbling between our legs. That dog was craving affection as much as I was. I laughed at its antics; to me, it was cute. Javier couldn't see anything cute or funny in the dogs; he acted so seriously. At times, I thought Javier and I were worlds apart.

I let go of Javier's shoulder, and turned to look at the old, rambling house. It really had fallen into pieces, and I felt a heaviness around it. If I didn't live there, it could've felt like an eerie old house.

My thoughts were broken with, 'Chris.'

'Sorry, I was just thinking.' I could never tell Javier how I felt about things, and we didn't ever get into an in-depth conversation. I quickly forgot my thoughts, and planted a kiss on his lips. He opened the front door of the car, and I wrapped my arms around him, saying, 'Have a good day, and I'll see you when you get home.'

He held my waist then dropped his hands, and climbed into the car. As he sat there warming up the car's motor, I went over to the side window, reached in and gave him one more kiss on his lips. He kissed me back quickly, and took out a cigarette to smoke as he waited for the engine to warm up.

I thought how I hungered for love. I wasn't sure what love was or meant. Sometimes he found my needs were too much for him to handle, and he wasn't a loving man. We never, held hands, and he never, ever cuddled me in public. He didn't show any form of affection towards me near his family. For that matter, neither of our families showed any affection to each other.

He checked the dashboard, and put on the wipers to wipe off the dew. The fog was not that bad now. He looked at the passenger's seat, so as not to draw my attention.

I patiently waited until he was ready to move. The silence in the air was so refreshing and I heard the birds. Nature was once again stirring as the sun rose. The cat appeared and jumped up onto the old, closed-off well. I smiled as I watched it preen, its tongue moving up and down its legs, and side-to-side in a quick motion. It sensed it was being watched, stopped, looked my way, and blinked its eyes. The car moved, and I was reminded of where I was. As he pulled out, I said, 'See you tonight.'

His head was turned away from me and he had his arm over the steering wheel as he drove the heavy, old car out of the passageway between the clothes line and the house fence. He did a tight swing and drove the car into the open yard, making a right turn.

He pulled at the wheel to straighten the wheels, drove off to his right and went straight up the open paddock.

He never looked back or waved. At the middle gate, he got out of the car and opened it. My attention was drawn to the cows, as they moved around the yard just near the toilet. The morning light was coming in fast as I stood there. Javier was going through the top gate onto the main road. Glancing around, I thought I wouldn't miss this place when I finally left here. It was just as much a shambles as the lives of the people inside it.

# Chapter 29

# The Pains Of My Mother

I dreaded my mother getting up. I heard her approaching her bedroom door, so I rushed into my room. I wondered which I feared the most, her or these rooms. There was too much memorabillia in that formal lounge room, people I'd never got to meet. They seemed to be living in that room like they'd never died.

Funny there's no photos of my dad in there, I thought. Actually there was only one photo of him as a child in the whole house, and that was kept in our bedroom on the mantelpiece. I looked up at it, a small, white, oval photo frame of a small, fair, curly-haired, boy of five. Now I had my pride and joy, my little boy; he was so precious. I bent over his cot, kissed him, and he moved. I smiled at him, thinking I could stand here forever and just watch him.

I didn't fear the future. I liked the idea of knowing what was ahead of us. For me, change was important; I didn't want things to stay as they were forever. This was my mother's problem; she didn't like change. Mum was always telling me if she had her life over again, she would never change a thing. My goodness me,

I thought, I would. I'd change my life in a flash, and if I had her life, I'd change everything. No way would I take the crap she'd been taking.

I moved away from Julian's cot, and went and put on my cheap dress I'd found in Wentworth just after having Julian. I vowed to wear just two dresses through rain, hail or shine, summer or winter, until we'd paid off our land and started to build our house. After I had Julian, I'd had no practical street clothes. All my clothes I'd bought before meeting Javier were mini-skirts, and very short. I wore some of these after having Julian, and Javier went right off and told me to lower my dresses. I got upset when he said that, because I'd just started to find myself when I was working and had bought lots of nice mini-skirts and dresses. I was only eighteen, and I wanted to dress young; but I was stripped of my youth just as I found it. I missed not being able to wear my mini-dresses, but to keep the peace, I complied and lowered my dresses. Owning our land and a house was more important and what I wanted, not expensive clothes, or to waste money. As I looked at my reflection in the mirror and admired my cheap A-line, flower-printed, cotton dress, I thought I was lucky to find these practical dresses for one dollar ninety-nine each. A real bargain, I must say, and during the winter just gone, it wasn't too bad wearing them with a cardigan. I was warm enough. I did splurge and bought myself a couple of cheaper, nice dresses to go to dinner in with Dante and Nita when they came to live at Dawson Hill, because Javier wouldn't allow me to wear my mini-dresses.

The first four months of my pregnancy with my second child was so bad. I was always sick. I don't know how women can say they enjoy being pregnant. Feeling better, I made the bed. The old netting over it released its dust. I'd asked Dad if I could wash the netting. He told me if I did, it would all fall to pieces. He was nice about it and I understood, so we had to bear the smell of dust. I pulled up the old, pink chenille bedspread that had had its day. I didn't want to use any of my new things here. I thought how good I was with money, and how lucky I was to have picked up some good bargains. At a store called Ben's Manchester, they had a big promotional sale on. For one hundred dollars, you could layby manchester and kitchen appliances, which I did, and now all those things were stored in the formal lounge room. I'd also found a furniture store that had a full house of furniture - a lounge, bedrooms, and dining table - at a bargain price. This store allowed us to layby the items and they would be paid for by the time our house was built.

Javier was right in saying to hang on and wait. Now the waiting was nearly over. I had enough basic household equipment and furniture to start off our new life. We'd just paid our land off, thanks to Javier and the sudden boom of work in the past five months. He'd been working seven days a week.

Next week, we planned to take in our deposit to the bank to get our housing loan, and we had enough money for a solicitor's fees as well. Then the builders could start to build our house. All was progressing, and we could tighten our belts a little more, if we had too. I sighed, thinking I would have to be patient with my mother and just let her groan. It wasn't as bad as when Maxine first left. We couldn't see eye-to-eye, and many times Mum ran screaming to Javier, telling him to take me from their house. I guess it must have been hard for him, having Mum telling him to get me out of the house, and me telling him I wanted to move because I hated it there, and I couldn't stand my mum's behaviour. He'd almost plead with me to be patient and to just let my mum rave on, because we couldn't manage to pay rent for a flat and save for a house. He was right, we couldn't, and he gave me an option, asking me what do I want, a house or a flat. Putting my head down and diverting my eyes from him like a sulky child, I surrendered and agreed with him. I wanted my own house.

I also felt bad, because I wasn't working and he had to do it all. Maybe there was some guilt on my part, not working and contributing to the house costs, that was making me angry. If I hadn't got pregnant, I could have worked. Yet Javier didn't believe in women working, so there went working anyway. For me, work wasn't rewarding, because I didn't get to do the job I wanted to do.

I sat up on the big bed and went through some financial papers. I heard a noise. Julian was standing in his cot, rocking backwards and forwards, smiling a big, cheesy smile. I'd say he'd been standing there waiting to get my attention. I pushed the papers aside, went over to him and lifted him out of the cot. He was wet from last night. I cuddled him and showered him with kisses, taking him to my bed. I lay him down and took off his pyjamas, talking to him. 'Who's the most beautiful baby in the world?'

He smiled and giggled. As soon as I removed his nappy, he wiggled away from me so I couldn't put on a fresh nappy straight away. He crawled quickly to the other side of the bed.

I laughed. 'Come on, Julian, let Mummy put your nappy on.'

He laughed in defiance and snuggled into the bedspread with his face. 'No,' he said.

'Yes.' I ran around to the other side of the bed.

He was in full laughter as he tried to crawl to the other side, but I grabbed him and tickled him and he laughed.

I picked him up and cuddled his half-naked little body and he smelt so fresh. That baby smell brought in a deep feeling of love. We played 'what's this?'. I pointed to his nose. 'Nose.'

He giggled.

'And what's this?' I pointed to his eyes.

He said, 'Eyeee.'

Putting him back on the bed, his attention was drawn to the toy I'd put on the bed earlier. As he played with it, I lay on the bed and snuggled into him. What glorious peace this child brought me. The changes I had gone through having Julian had been wonderful for me. I put on his fresh nappy, and dressed him in his play clothes for the day.

As I did this, I thought of how lucky I was having such a wonderful, intelligent child. Julian was two years old and I remembered how, when he was eighteen months old, I'd caught him playing in the lounge room with no blocks, nothing around him, but he was building something out of nothing using his imagination. He was always pretending to be something, either a mechanic or a fisherman. His imagination was excellent, and I encouraged it to grow. While watching him at play, I often wondered if he'd lived those lives before his birth to me, and he was recalling some past memories, because not only did he perform these acts as a fisherman or mechanic, he'd tell stories about them and what he was doing. Sometimes I couldn't understand what he was saying, as if he'd gone off into some other language. As mentioned, he was using some strange words to descibe his bottle, dummy, and water. I didn't discourage him or insist on him speaking properly. I believed in letting my children experience whatever came in for them. Julian liked to rearrange everything in the lower kitchen cupboards. He removed everything and placed everything back in order. He seemed to have a lot of order in his life. I felt he was way ahead of other children in his intelligence and bodily development. Even one of our family doctors, Doctor Hobbleton, asked me what I was feeding him and said he's a fine specimen of a boy. I just smiled proudly.

When Julian was around six months old, I started to read stories from the Golden Books to him. I'd bought quite a few of these books, and he looked at the pages; gradually, as he got a little older, he'd listen and point to the items as I named them. Around eighteen months, he was so eager to learn, we'd sit for hours and read his Golden Books together. I taught him to pronounce his words by using syllables, breaking the words down as I pointed to the words, and as I sounded them, he could easily say really big words. I guess he was lucky having been surrounded by adults.

My parents really loved him, especially Dad. He often took him over to the shed with him. I did worry about Julian being with my dad. On the other hand, I knew Dad wouldn't hurt my child. Julian loved and trusted his grandfather.

Dad had caught a baby wild pig when he was out shooting. He'd brought it home to rear it and he'd called it Grumpy. It was a morning and afternoon ritual for Dad and Julian to go to the shed where it was penned, and feed the pig. All Dad had to do was ask Julian if he was coming to see the pig, and Julian would go out onto the verandah and sit and wait for Dad to put on his piggy boots, as we called them. He loved the pig, and Dad was careful with Julian around the pig. It was still a wild animal. The pig grew very quickly and became too hard to handle, so Dad organised for it to be butchered. When Grumpy came back home as pork chops, no one could eat him. We had to give the meat to someone else. We'd all become too close to him.

The farm experiences brought my child into contact with some lovely animals. At the time, we'd also had a lamb. Often Julian and I would go and pat it. Julian was such a loving, gentle child and he'd kiss it. There was a magpie that hung around the house, and Dad had caught the bird following Julian. It would be picking up Julian's biscuit crumbs or just following him. Dad told me he'd seen a snake following Julian for his milk, as he walked with his bottle tilted, spilling his milk. Animals sense no harm from children.

My cousin Kelvin returned from Vietnam and he came to visit us again. Kelvin, Dad, Javier, and Julian, on Javier's shoulders, all went to the water's edge of the big lagoon with their rifles. Of course Julian's pet magpie flew over them, following Julian. Sadly, before my dad could see what had caught Kelvin's eye, he was aiming his gun in the air and shot the magpie. I think Dad was more distressed than the others, because it was Julian's pet. Dad went off at Kelvin, which he shouldn't have, and Kelvin apologised. However, it was too late; the bird was dead.

'Okay, Julian, let's go for breakfast. Are you hungry, my little man?'

He looked up and squeezed his face, causing his little nose to go up. 'Yes, Mummy.'

I kissed his face, and he kissed me back and snuggled in to me. We headed up the hallway. 'Poppy and Nanny will be up now.'

'Poppy,' he said excitedly. He really loved my parents and they loved him.

'Hello, Grandma. How are you?' We'd called in to say hello to Grandma.

On seeing Julian, her eyes lit up. 'Hello, Julian,' she said.

'Say, 'hello, Grandma,' Julian,' I said, looking into his puzzled face.

'Hello, Grandma,' he said.

Grandma spoke to Julian, asking him how he was. I held him to me as they interacted, because I wouldn't have him go near my grandma, due to the ignorance of my mother and her fear around uncleanliness. Mum imparted these fears onto us. As I looked at my grandma, I wondered why she ended up as she did. She had been such a strong woman, now totally dependent, and I wondered how she could bear to be in her bedroom, day in and day out, never leaving or wanting to leave the confinement of her room. The room smelt of disinfectant; it was in her pan that was always near her bed. I guess she was comfortable, and she had an array of bits and pieces on a tray stand, but the whole room looked unhealthy.

'We'll go now,' I said. 'We'll call in to see you later on, Grandma.'

Julian waved his little hand and she waved back. On leaving her room, I glanced back. She'd picked up a magazine and started to read it. She buried herself in those magazines and in that bed.

At the dining room table, I stopped. Before entering the kitchen, I needed to take a deep breath; facing my parents and their long, unhappy faces, I felt the life force about to leave my body.

I breathed in and put on a mask, never sure what to expect. Smiling, I edged to the door, as though we'd just been doing that all morning. Entering the kitchen, I gently swung Julian in my arms. He was laughing. I said, in a chirpy voice, 'Good morning, Mum and Dad.'

They both looked up, and of course, I was right; there was a no-speakies going on between them.

'Hello, Julian,' Poppy said.

Julian's face beamed, and he pushed down from me and ran to Poppy.

'Hello, my little man,' Poppy said, as he lifted Julian up and cuddled him.

The child was an ice-breaker in the family, and Mum forced herself to say, 'Hello, Julian.' She smiled for an instant, and then went about her work. The tension in the air was thick. Mum would have something to whinge about later on when Dad went to work. Dad put Julian down.

I was thinking that Julian was a blessing for all of us, and he broke the hatred in that house. I said, 'Goodbye, Dad. Say goodbye to Poppy, Julian.'

Julian showed a cheesy, toothy smile. 'Bye, Poppy.'

Dad said, 'Bye, Carol,' moving in closer to her, hoping she'd return his offer of a kiss. She pulled away, and he became angry, and stormed off out of the house, growling to himself.

Oh, God, it's on, I thought, and tried to dismiss it all.

Julian stood there waiting for Nanny to talk to him, but she was too cranky.

'Come on, Julian, let's go and wash for breakfast.' I picked him up and took him to the laundry. I didn't want to be in their disharmony.

# Chapter 30

# Mother's Moods

At the breakfast table, Mum didn't say anything. Her head was down, and her face was flushed. I gave Julian his cereal. He wasn't doing too badly at feeding himself. I played with him as we ate our breakfast. Looking over at Mum drinking her tea, she was sad and depressed. I heard the cup hit the saucer; she was now supporting her head in her hands.

Julian noticed my attention was on Nanny. 'Nanny.'

She didn't respond to his call.

He looked at me with wide, wondering eyes. 'Nanny,' he said again.

Mum looked up. He smiled at her.

'Nanny's not well, Julian,' I said,

His face changed. He pushed away from the table and went over to Nanny.

'Julian,' she said, as she picked him up and cuddled him. He was happy, because finally she'd noticed him. In Mum's preoccupation with her own problems, she'd forgotten to given Julian a cuddle. She played with Julian and he snuggled into her, telling her a story.

I watched them as I ate my breakfast.

'I'd better feed your grandma.' She put Julian down on the floor, and he looked at her. She looked back at him. 'Nanny has to give Grandma her breakfast.'

He stood near the stool, and watched her put together the breakfast on a tray. When she'd left the room, I sat Julian back up at the table to finish off his cereal, then placed him on the floor. Julian was one of those children you didn't have to entertain; he could always find something to amuse himself. He found the cat, who was sitting on the sofa, all curled up in the corner. The cat seemed to trust Julian, and it let him stroke it.

I stacked the plates from breakfast.

Now and then, Julian would look up at me and say, 'Pussy cat, Mummy.'

'Yes, Julian, pussy cat.'

The old cat seemed to wink.

While putting the cereal away, I thought, I will be twenty-one in a couple of weeks. Mum broke my thoughts. Suddenly, she flew through the kitchen door in a huff and went straight out the door that faced the verandah, cursing to herself, carrying Grandma's bedpan. That's why she was so long in there with Grandma, I thought. Grandma must have had to go to the toilet when Mum brought in her breakfast. I knew when she came back in, she'd whinge about it, and I'd have to let it go and say nothing. It wouldn't be long, I told myself, and we'd have the deposit for our own house.

Javier and I had already found the house we wanted the builders to build for us. All we needed was the loan from the Dawson Hill credit union, and next week we'd make our appointment to see the manager.

Julian was playing on the lino with one of his toys. The lino seemed to be a million years old. How old everything was here; even the people seemed old in their grief.

'Come on, Julian.' I picked him up in my arms.

He turned his head from side to side. 'No.' He was occupied with his toy. I needed to walk outside to gather my senses. He wanted to stay, so I put him back down and walked out onto the verandah. I saw Mum coming back up the paddock from where she'd washed the bedpan by the old trough that sat near the clothes line. There was a garden hose there just for that reason. I was glad she was a fussy woman and feared germs, because there was no fear of her lapsing in her hygiene. In a flurry, she ran back through the front gate and onto the verandah. I noticed her face was red, probably due to her anger this morning with Dad and Grandma. She never said a word as she flashed past me, but I felt her tension and I had to let it go. She went back into the house and I breathed.

I felt for my grandma; she wasn't well. Grandma was never a kind person to my mum, so I could also understand Mum's dilemma. Our family had left all the caring and responsiblity to her. I'd suggested to Mum, on her better days, to refuse to do it and to tell the others to take turns. Her remarks shocked me. She stated she couldn't do that, because Grandma relied on her. It was all contradictory at the time. She whinged about cleaning Grandma up, and then asked me what would they do if she left. When I heard her in these moods, I'd think well, leave and let them find out how hard it is, and get them to take responsiblity for their parent. But I couldn't say that. She'd take it the wrong way, and think I wanted to take her place in the house, because she'd implied that to me in one of our arguments. That was never my intention, to take over this household, and I had no idea how she could even perceive such a thought. This was the last place I wanted to be. Her words were, 'if you want it, you can take it over.' She must've been crazy to even think that. I stared at her on that day, and told her, 'No way do I want your life.' How could she think I'd want her life and this house and its misery? She was so wrong. Living here was showing me what I didn't want, and that was misery.

Back in the kitchen, Julian was still playing. Mum reappeared, and went out to the laundry to wash her hands. Her dilemma was a struggle, but then her whole life had been a struggle. Mum was very disorganised, untidy and slack in the house. Nothing was ever put away, be it her clothes or things in the kitchen. Everything just mounted up in piles around her, either on the table, the old fuel stove, or the old sofa. I looked around at the shambled life here, the oldness and the accumulation of rubbish.

She came in from the laundry and said, 'Do you want another cup of tea?'

'Yes, please, Mum.'

She made a fresh pot. I knew her life was hell. With Grandma's bowels done for the day, she could relax. She seemed to be in a better mood. Also, Mum knew she had to keep on my better side, because I was her only link with the outside world to get out of the house. Little did she know, she didn't have to be like that with me, because I wouldn't ever be nasty to her and not help her or Dad. I'd always complied with them. However, time would solve that too.

Julian had climbed up onto my knee and was swinging side to side as I moved my leg. He was talking to me and his toy. I watched his little, intense face as he played and I stroked his head and face. He looked up, and when our eyes met, I felt a welling of mother-child love. I looked up from my child to my mother, and saw her sadness as she removed the cover from the teapot and poured our tea. It was like hell was on her back, and she couldn't shake it off. Every move she'd made in her life, there was a repercussion.

I looked at my baby, and wondered if my mother was ever happy. I couldn't ever recall her being happy. I don't think she was. Lately, Mum had been constantly telling me about her life here with Dad, but she wouldn't leave him.

'Christine.'

'Yes, Mum,' I answered, almost standing to attention. She still had that power over me.

'Tomorrow, when we go shopping, I want to go to the doctors. Is it alright?'

'Yes, of course, Mum,' I said in a nervous, child-like voice. Underneath it all, I thought I was in for another long day. Her indecisiveness and fastidiousness while shopping drove me to madness, and being with her was a nightmare. She examined every label, reading all the information on it. I felt she did it deliberately. Even with Julian, I could go around the supermarket in half an hour and get all I wanted, but Mum, no. She'd take her time at our expense. My next mistake as we drank our tea was asking her what was wrong. As if I didn't know.

'I feel unwell and I need a check-up. I think I have a bladder infection, and I'm feeling sick. It's probably cystitis,' she droned.

'Okay, Mum, we can do that.' I laid Julian across my knee, and swung him from side to side on my legs to break my real feelings.

# Chapter 31

# Nature Protects Me Again

Julian got tired, and he snuggled into me. He liked to sleep in the morning. I finished my tea and stood up, telling Mum I was going to put Julian to sleep. I took him to our room, and placed him on my bed and changed his nappy. He started to act like a little terror, wanting to play and hold my attention longer. I got him to lie down, stroked his eyebrows, and he became really tired. Eventually, he fell asleep. As I placed him into the cot, I could smell his baby smell, a smell that gave me a sensation of new life and freshness.

I edged my way back to the kitchen. Mum was preparing another cup of tea. This was the sign she was ready to dish out her shit on me. I sensed her fears and anxieties, but I really couldn't help her; she had to do it herself, put her foot down and tell Dad what she thought. Then she started. 'Your father...' and he did this and did that. The same old stories. It went on and on. I thought, it's never Max, or my husband. Goodness me Mum, he's not just my father. You married him, not me. She acted as if it was my fault she was with him. I didn't ask her to get pregnant. I knew what she wanted, so I said the dreaded words, 'What's wrong this time, Mum?', hiding my own pain. If I did have pain, she'd never know. I felt she was oblivious to any other human having pain.

As I listened to her rant and rave about Dad, I realised she did feel for others, it was only me she couldn't feel for. I must've seemed like a solid rock to her. I had never gone to her for help.

'He's not coming home until late. He says there's a meeting on.'

'What type of meeting, Mum?' I asked.

'Union business. I know he's going to see Hilary.' She cried.

I tried to soothe her worries, gently saying, 'Mum, you don't know this.'

'Yes, I do,' she screamed hysterically.

I shuddered because I couldn't handle her stress. I had my own stress with Javier, and meeting my baby's needs, and I was still dealing with hers as well. I guess I was so fortunate Julian was a good baby. I had to listen to her, and I couldn't tell her off. If I had, there would be holy hell. I thought of hell raining down on me from my mother's mouth. I didn't like going through these issues with her now I was carrying another child. I didn't want this child to hear this crap because to me; all is heard by the unborn baby. She'd affected me as a child and I hoped her behaviour wasn't affecting Julian - but anything for peace.

I listened to her fears and we finished our tea. We took all the stacked breakfast dishes to the laundry. After listening to her, I felt like throwing them on the floor and just walking off. I felt like my whole self was caving in on me with this negative energy of hers.

Mum threw the plates down on the counter and got out the plastic dish to do the dishes in. There was an old copper at the rear of the laundry which didn't get used anymore; our hot water came from a chip heater in the bathroom across from the laundry. Those memories of those days; how I loved wash days when Grandma was doing the washing. I had loved to watch Grandma, Mum helping her, as they fed the sheets and towels with a big stick into the boiling water in the copper. Grandma would add a blue bag to give the white sheets that extra whiteness. The old stone sinks, used for washing clothes you didn't put into boiling water, or to pre-wash heavily stained clothes, were near the copper. I could still see Grandma scrubbing our clothes on the scrubbing board made of glass with a wooden frame. There it was, still sitting stately in the corner, retired from its numerous hours of service, gathering dust with the old copper. These had all been replaced by a modern washing machine. Despite its convenience, the machine would never hold my attention like the old copper routine. I was so glad I experienced the old world, as well as the modern world. Those women seemed to have more time to pore over their housework.

Just at the entrance to the laundry was the sink we did the dishes in. As Mum performed her ritual of preparing to do the dishes, I watched her in another space in my mind, and I lost myself in the movement of her body, and in her process of doing. I watched her as she poured the dishwashing liquid into the dish. It sprayed across the dish, and in a flurry, the hot water was poured in and the suds scrambled up the dish, as if it hurt them; and the cleanliness in the disarray seemed to bring in hope of better times. She rhythmically put on her little cotton gloves, and then the rubber gloves over them. She seemed almost like a surgeon about to perform a major operation. She began to wash up the plates, placing them on the dish rack for me to wipe up.

She started in again with her insidious worries about Dad and his affair with Hilary, and how she was worried, because Glen wasn't a stable man, and if he ever found out, he'd kill my father. I sighed. I knew Glen had been in and out of mental hospitals for threatening to kill someone, and I'd actually sensed there was something amiss with him years ago. All I could do was listen to her, and that's what I'd done ever since I was a child. I diverted my attention to the cleanliness of the air that I smelt, in between the 'Yes, Mum,' as I acknowledged her. The spring air wafted in with the smell of the cows that had come close to the fence. I wanted to go and look at them. Then the cat stretched, as if to say, don't forget me. I smiled at him and he winked at me. I winked back, my head turned away from my mum, and I threw the cat a kiss. It sat up and had a longer body stretch. I said, in a childlike way, 'Mum, look at the cat; it's so cute.' She didn't really hear me, but managed, 'Yes, yes.' She continued on in her droning voice, and I looked at the windows in front of me, and wondered when those windows had been painted to filter out the severe summer heat. Summer was around the corner. Oh, how I love to go swimming, I thought; and we can go down to the lake house for the weekend – oh, yes! This brightened me up.

Spring brought in wonderful smells of the earth, and newness of life. In the peach tree just outside this door,

I heard the birds chirping, enlivening the silence of our existence. I heard the rustling of the branches in the gentle breeze. This brought in more smells to tantalise my senses. I walked to the door to look at the peach blossoms, and to see the bees at their work, buzzing from blossom to blossom. Mum didn't even notice this beauty around her. I looked at my mother, with her strained face. If only I could have pulled her into my world, to see the beauty that surrounded us. She'd quietened down; I guess she got it all off her chest.

The cat had decided to go back to sleep, and its paws were hanging over the side of the table in a relaxed way. I felt like picking it up and cuddling it. The cat felt me looking at it, and half-opened its eye, yawned and closed it. I turned back to Mum. She was overweight, her hair was a mess, and she didn't seem to be able to control her physical body anymore. She was looking ugly at that moment. This stress was not helping her. I knew she could look great. I thought of the photo of Mum and Dad, taken with her sister, Betty, where Mum looked like a girl, so slim, and so beautiful. I frowned, thinking, Mum, what happened to you; where did that beautiful, young woman go? You're looking like an old crone.

This was too much to bear, and I thought of myself. I'm not so pretty in my cheap dresses, and I never looked good during my pregnancy. But this will only be for a while. I must always look good, for my own sake. These days, I was noticing how vacant I felt, and how bored I got. Out of the blue, Mum startled me. 'Christine.'

'Yes, Mum.' I jumped in my own skin.

'What are you doing?' she squealed.

'Nothing. I was just admiring the cat.'

'The cat.' She looked at me as if I was crazy.

'Yes,' I smiled at the cat. 'It's so cute.'

She shook her head, not understanding me at all.

'I love the cat, Mum,' I said in my own defense.

'It's just a cat,' she informed me.

'I know that, but it does cute things.' I felt like I was going crazy, and wondered if I was listening to her comments about me.

'Christine, I need to go to the doctor tomorrow. Do you think you can get the car?'

'No problems, Mum. I told you I can have the car, and I'll take you to the doctor,' I reminded her.

Mum repeated herself often, as if she'd just thought of it, and had to tell me. So I got the same story again. 'I need more valium. I think I have a bladder infection,' she complained.

'Yes, you told me that.'

'And it's probably from your father, this infection. He's playing up with that Hilary,' she reminded me hatefully.

I couldn't answer her. I found it too hard to talk to her about sex. I never could. I went back to my childhood again, and thought of when I heard about periods, and she couldn't even talk to me about that.

'It's okay, Mum. I'll take you to the doctor. Don't worry.' I had to reassure her. She was always going to the doctor for answers that no one could give her, and that she would not find in a bottle of pills. The doctor must've been sick of her problems, and her need for attention. It's like I owed her, for just being her child.

Maxine had long gone from the house, and Barton had gone away to Robertson, out west, to visit his girlfriend, Lorna. He was doing that every weekend. Everyone had left, except me, so Mum was more reliant on me. I saw her with Dad, and she was constantly bitching to him about something. Mum was never happy, and she was demanding. People get tired of little girls in women's bodies, I thought. She needed to grow up. All that had been going on was of her own doing. I better be careful, I thought, as this is the type of woman I'm capable of becoming, because I know I am nagging Javier. I thought of Javier and my life with him, and how it could be hell, especially with his points of view on marriage, and the wife's role in the house. He'd never let me work, and I'd have to be resigned to staying at home with the children. Our conversations were very limited, and he was not affectionate, or loving, to me. Before we were married, he had seemed different. Marriage had brought out a personality I hadn't met before. I sighed. Truly, I really didn't understand a lot that went on around me.

The house crackled as the day warmed up. The sounds knocked me back into the here and now. Mum had been talking on and off, but I had skipped off in my mind, and she had stopped her job and was staring at me. She swished her hair back off her small face, throwing me reminders by telling me I hadn't done the last lot of dishes that were sitting in the rack.

Looking at her frail face and thin hair that was falling into unmanageable parts due to her stress, I felt for her.

'Sorry. I was daydreaming.'

She didn't comment. I wiped up the stacked dishes. If only I could give her a cuddle, I thought, but we didn't even cuddle each other. We were too afraid. I looked up at the wall above me, as I wiped the last pot, and I saw a thousand spider webs. I watched one large, black spider edge its way along its web to a trapped fly. The fly knews its fate, and it struggled against the misty, illusional web that lured it in there by its softness. It was a disguise, a deception, and its ultimate end was death. I felt like the fly trapped in a web, a web of tangles, disarray and delusions. As the spider moved in on the fly, the fly buzzed in its final endeavour to free itself. It seemed like it was trying to ask the spider to have mercy on it, but this spider was a merciless creature, and it edged in. The fly ceased to move, and laid down its life. I felt for the fly. It would be dead in a moment, just as I was dead inside. I wasn't living. I looked at my mum, and she was red in the face; her anger had soared. I looked back to the fly, and the spider was at the back of it, ready to make its final pounce. I had to look away. I couldn't bear to see it killed - and devoured.

# Chapter 32

# Putting Our Deposit On The House

Javier decided to take two weeks off work, to finalise all the arrangements for our house loan. The time had come: our land was paid off, and we made an appointment to see the bank manager. With Javier's good wages for the past five months, and the few extra cows we'd bought that spring, to sell next spring, it would help us with the collateral we needed to secure the loan. The loan was approved and granted. In a few days, we had everything signed, sealed, and ready to go, all within the week. With the loan in hand, we went back to Fenton Brothers, the builders, and let them know our housing loan was approved, and we wanted them to start building the house we'd picked. It was a deluxe HardiePlank home. The weekend after everything was approved, Javier arranged with his brothers to come and help him clear our land. There had been a lot of rubbish dumped on that land over the years, so my Dad and his brothers helped us out.

Later on, Nick and Pia's car appeared at our front gate. Nick was carrying a large bottle of beer. He seemed to be always doing that. They'd come without their sons, Sonny and Daniel, leaving them with Nick's mum, and they'd brought Gema along. They were late; the other men were already well into the work. I'd given Nick the address to go and join them.

It was a big job, clearing that land, and the men needed to be fed, so we girls and my mum prepared lunches to take in to them. I'd bought lots of cold meat, cheeses and salad foods, and while making the sandwiches, Pia started to put aside the best sandwiches for Nick. I never said anything, just let it pass. With the sandwiches done, Pia, Gema and I went into town to deliver the sandwiches, and I had a few big containers of mix-up cordial as well. The land was looking great. What they'd done was a vast improvement on what it was, and it all seemed to be coming on fine.

A week later, the house was started. Javier's two weeks were up, and he had to go back to work, so I was left to pick the interior and exterior paint, the tiles, kitchen cupboards, the kitchen appliances, and all the bathroom accessories. Even though I had to do all this work to get our house built and completed, I was happy to do it. I carried Julian around on my hip to do the selections with my Mum. It got a bit hard carrying Julian around, because he was so big, and I was getting bigger in my pregnancy; I was actually carrying two babies around. Some days, I was so exhausted, and the running around continued right up until the house was completed. I was lucky, because Javier was such a good worker, and his attitude towards working impressed me, and made our lives comfortable.

After we'd got everything on the way, Javier decided he wanted to ease off working the whole weekend. I agreed, and he worked weekdays and Saturdays, and had Sundays off. It was good for all of us, because when he came home Saturday, we'd sometimes go down to his mum's house in Dawson Hill and stay there, and come back to the farmhouse Sunday night. Even though I found his family intrusive, I really did have some good times with them, and I'd visit my mum-in-law's friend, Clea, who was a very fastidious lady, and who liked me and Julian. Julian would just stand near me, and he wouldn't move or touch anything. It was like he knew at home it was okay to touch or move some things, but things belonging to other people weren't to be touched, even in Javier's mother's house. Julian never touched their possessions.

If Pia's children visited Clea's house, Sonny would be so unruly, running around this poor woman's perfectly-kept house. I believe you must teach your children at a very young age to respect other people's things: good disciplining, with explanations of why it's so important, so the child understands. If you scream at a child, they're not learning. I loved to teach Julian; he was a great student. He learnt values and ethics, and the discipline was taught with lots of love. Love and discipline go hand in hand for a child to understand the right and appropriate ways of living. A child needs guidance, mixed with love.

I loved my mother-in-law, and I knew she loved me, even though we couldn't understand each other. We had developed a way of communicating through body language. I never felt she was intrusive; it was Javier's father I felt intrusion from. Mum-in-law was also a great cook, and it was truly like going to a restaurant. Javier's family was the opposite of my own family; they weren't very clean people, and I had to overcome issues around cleanliness - and I did. Sometimes I'd find food still on the cutlery that hadn't been properly washed up, and I'd discreetly go and get another piece of cutlery.

It was strange when we were at his mother's house. Javier was always away somewhere else, and I was not sure where he went. I didn't question it; I was preoccupied with Julian and Javier's younger siblings.

In my boredom, I became intrigued with another family member, Paco. He was younger than me, seventeen years old, and he had been away from the family for a short period of time. On his return, he seemed different. He'd grown up, and was very handsome, and he'd grown his hair long, much to the disapproval of his father. I liked his rebellious nature, and how he stood his ground. I'd watch him from a distance and admired him.

If Javier was working on the weekend, or he had to go out of town to work, Julian and I would stay on the farm. Javier's parents always visited us. Julian and I never set off to his parents' home without Javier. Summertime was a good time, and from when Julian was three months old, we'd sometimes go to Spring Lakes, and stay there all day. Javier's brothers would play cricket, and us girls would talk. It was a bit of a strain for me, because Javier was so possessive, and he was even jealous of his own sister, Gema. Sometimes, he'd ask me what we had been talking about. I'd look at him strangely and wonder why he was so concerned. After all, it was just girl talk, and what could I do with her, a girl?

# Chapter 33

# On The Farm

My mum was having more problems with Dad and his running around. To her, his unfaithfulness seemed to be getting worse. It seemed more real and obvious for her, but I had to close off to it. Mum was taking lots of sedatives, and I didn't like her behaviour, and could see the effect those drugs were having on her. She said, when I questioned her, that she needed them to cope with life.

Maxine and I had discussed this issue between ourselves, and we both were against it. We'd vowed we'd never take drugs under any circumstances. I'd reasoned that one could cope under any circumstance. I was closed to her pains, cut off; I'd lost all compassion. Sometimes I'd laugh inwardly at other people's troubles, but I'd pretend to be compassionate. Drug-taking in any form, be it doctor's prescription for sedatives or hard drugs, was unacceptable to me. Surely, one could cope in life, and deal with issues. I silently coped.

I knew it was hard for Mum, because she couldn't drive a car. She was totally stuck on the farm, and she had to rely on me or Dad to take her places. I knew

Mum had issues, but I didn't want to hear about them. I did not want to be involved in her hell, and at times I wanted to tell her, but I couldn't. This caused my whole internal being to scream inside me, and I wanted to tell her to shut up and leave me alone, you're eating me alive and driving me mad.

Unfortunately, there was no way to escape her misery, only through Julian. He was my salvation, and he showed me how to love another human being, and actually care for them.

My child and I spent lots of time together. He was the icebreaker for me and Mum. His stories delighted us and kept us sane, and away from the nightmare life we'd all created. I never discouraged his make-believe stories, and I believed he really did have his invisible friend, Goofy. I felt I understood him so much and could see myself in him from when I was little and had had a wonderful imagination, and probably invisible friends. My parents never understood such things, and it was probably ignored, and gradually wiped out of my mind.

As I gazed upon my child's innocence and watched him at play with his toys and his imagination, I marvelled at this giant of a two-year-old child, and I saw my own imagination had been harshly squashed by Dad, who caught me talking to my dolls, and the cat, and had called me a stupid idiot. It was his favourite word for all us kids. Now, I had my own precious child, and I made sure his imagination was nurtured and encouraged.

When she came to visit us with her son, Alex, Maxine was another form of relief. Her life was going better, now Collin had completed his apprenticeship, even though they struggled. Our times together were wonderful, and we were so close. Julian loved Alex so much, and he wanted to cuddle him all the time. Alex couldn't handle being cuddled, because of his breathing problems. He was a very sickly little boy, and developed eczema at about four months old, followed by asthma not long after. We both loved our children, and sometimes we'd go out for the day. It was worth the early morning drive into town at 5am to get Javier off to work, so I could have our car for the day.

I had to be back in Hastings Crossing by 8pm to pick him up. While I waited for him, the security guard at Bolt Steel Fabrications used to come over to my car and talk to me. We'd talk about world issues, and other topics of interest. On arrival from Bryson Power Station, Javier caught him talking to me once. He'd never told me not to talk to the security man. Following that event, I noticed the security man didn't come to my car as often to talk to me, or if he did, he made sure he'd moved well away before Javier arrived on site. After that, I just sat and waited alone. When Javier did come to our car, I wanted to talk to him about my day, or other topics. To start the conversation, I'd ask him how his day was, and he'd say it was alright, and then gradually I told him about my day, but he wasn't interested; our worlds were too far apart.

# Chapter 34

# Small Town

I could see lots of changes in our small town of Hastings Crossing in the early seventies. Money was starting to become evident in our society. Wages of everyday people had increased with the new Labor government, industries were popping up, and shopfronts were modernised to attract the more well-off people. Larger, new supermarkets were springing up and taking over from the smaller corner shops. Over time, these shops closed down. This was progress. I liked progress, because it meant change. With change and more money came a darker side of life, and an unsavoury element was starting to overshadow it. It was becoming a fairly active town, and there seemed to be corruption in all areas.

At this time, there were some girls offering their services in the streets, using vans as their workplace. I actually knew some of these girls who had decided to take up prostitution. Wendy was an unmarried mother, and as a young girl, she'd attended our high school. She wasn't a local; she'd come to our high school in my last year. She was well-liked by many of us. She had told me this work paid well, and she could make a pile of money and get out of the business quickly.

Wendy was an exceptionally pretty girl, and we'd even thought she'd make a great photographic model. As I look back, I can't reason why or how she could have done that work. The thought of having to make money that way baffled me, and it made me realise I needed to keep my husband to guarantee us a better life. I couldn't think of anything worse than having to be a prostitute for a living. The girls involved were a year or two younger than me.

Some weekends, we'd go and stay in Dawson Hill with his family, which was becoming more of a blessing in disguise. If we stayed at home, Dad became a problem, and sometimes on the weekend, or even occasionally through the week, Dad would drag Javier off to the pub, causing Mum and I to complain. Our complaints fell on deaf ears with Dad. He didn't care, as long as he had company to go to the pub.

Dad had a saying as he left the house: we won't be long; we're just going in for a couple of beers. We never knew how long they'd be away; it wasn't a couple of hours. My father was very selfish when it came to getting what he wanted, regardless, of others' feelings. Javier was always sick after heavy drinking, which caused him to vomit. My father could drink lots of beers, and drink them fast, and it would never affect him. I could imagine he'd be making Javier keep up with him. The next day, after a drinking binge and vomiting, Javier would vow he'd never drink again. I'd tell him, don't go with my father, but he couldn't say no to him. I saw my father's gleeful look as he took Javier off to the pub.

Many things were going on in that town. I had heard drugs were available and many of the people Javier knew, well connected people, were dealers in drugs and prostitution rackets. I think many small towns probably went through what I felt was a teething stage, then out of the chaos came the calm, and all the bad elements gradually weeded out. Lots of these businesses went underground, and only those involved knew where to look for them.

During this time, my husband brought home the crabs. He blamed my brother for the problem. In my naivety, I didn't understand what these were. I'd never heard of such things in my life, and I never questioned him in regard to it. It never entered my mind my husband could have been cheating on me. I trusted him completely. He did say something strange to me one night in bed. He said, 'Chris, you're as good as any sixteen-year old.' It was during lovemaking, and I was puzzled, but let it go. Maybe I was so detached from life, nothing was ever understood.

# Chapter 35

# Dad And His Personality

The karma Dad and I had, helped me to find myself through the secrets I held between us, secrets that would lead to the hidden, deeper ones that were not part of Dad and me. There were many secrets in my mind, and I would have a big journey in my forties that would open me up.

My dad and I were regarded as close in the family, and I was told that I looked like him and my grandma. Dad was a boy, and he never grew up until later in life. He had a short temper, which he could turn onto you in a flash. As a child, I looked up to him in awe. He was my dad, and my hero. At the age of seven, I was going to marry my dad. How that statement rang true and would play out in my life, and cause me to create turmoil in my life. Be careful what you wish for; it may just come knocking on your door. My dad was a tall, slim man, with black, receding hair and violet-blue eyes, deeper blue than mine. He carried no fat on his body; he was all muscle until he reached his fifties, then he changed. Dad was not an educated man, and he lacked the social graces. As a child, he had a vivid imagination that was never nurtured, and it became his enemy as he deluded himself. He tried to take others into his make-believe world. Unfortunately, people refused to go there, and this great gift of imagination turned him into a liar. Worst of all, he'd try to get Mum to back up his stories, his lies, and this was a great embarrassment to my mother. I never knew my Dad lied until I married. My husband took great pleasure in letting me know Dad was a liar. I could not believe my father lied. Apparently, he didn't lie to us children; he never had much to do with us, and I don't remember him telling us stories. I remember him always working or coming home from work late, or he was over in the shed when he was home. Unfortunately, his stories were told in the pub or the club, where he had an audience. As children, we were mostly outside playing, away from adult conversation. The old adage, children are to be seen and not heard, was a motto in our family.

My Dad was a pathological liar, and he couldn't control his lies. He was like Peter Pan, and had a highly imaginative mind. If he had been educated, he might have written many great books. His Uncle Max, who he was named after, apparently wrote books. It's ironic how we are named after a person and we can take on their energies or qualities, or the opposite aspects of their positive energies or qualities. It's all energy.

The problem was, my father was not cared for as a child. His father died four months before he was born, and in her grief, my grandma neglected my father, and he was virtually raised by others or passed around the family. Many times, he played hooky. It seemed like he wasn't loved or nurtured as a child. Nor was I.

What my parents did was bring in familiar patterns; my family was full of them. Dad married Mum, and she was like his mum; she isolated herself in her room. We children suffered the same fate. We had a mum who didn't have much to do with her children, and we weren't encouraged at school. I pushed myself to learn, and I loved school, and later on I would self-educate myself. My sister changed her life, yet my brother followed the family patterns.

One person's grief or losses can cause mayhem for others in a family. I was determined my children wouldn't experience those issues. They would be educated. I did learn familiar patterns; however, I was conscious enough to want changes for my children, and I made changes.

When Javier came into my life, I could join my parents on outings to the club. It was on one of those outings that I heard about my father's storytelling, which was very confusing, because I'd never heard him do this at home. From the beginning of our relationship, Javier was calling my father a liar. On further outings with my parents, it became more obvious that his stories were all lies. It got to the point where I was so shocked, I had to ask my mum about it.

When I was alone with her, and she was in a good mood, I asked her, 'Mum, are the stories Dad tells lies?'

She looked away in shame and said, 'Yes. They're lies. He can't help himself.'

I thought, can't help himself; that's an excuse she's making for him. At that moment, I was embarrassed by my father, and I realised I really didn't know these people who were my parents.

The constant reminder from Javier about my father caused us to argue, and this put a big dint in our relationship. I'd tell Javier not to go out with him, to stay away from him, but he wouldn't stay away from the pub. I don't know why, but I couldn't bear to hear my parents being called names, or ridiculed, by Javier. I'd end up protecting my dad against Javier's rubbishing. I hated Javier condemning both my parents. He was good at doing that. He'd accused my mother's sisters of terrible things, and delighted in telling me they were sluts, and he talked badly about my mother as well. The truth was out and I knew my father lied. This crushed my heart. I was caught between protecting and loving my parents, and not being able to accept the real truth that Dad lied.

# Chapter 36

# Standing My Ground

Our house was built, and all was going to plan. It was at the lock-up stage, and we were promised it'd be finished in a month. By then, our second child would be born. We hadn't decided on a name for this child. I loved the name Keith Alistair, but Javier didn't like those names. He liked the name Jerod, but I didn't. To me, Jerod was a sissy name.

Julian was always easy to teach, so the bottle and dummy had to go before our next child came. As we were driving home from Hastings Crossing towards the Darlington Bridge, I said to Julian, 'Dirty Ber and dirty Bor. Can Mummy throw them away?'

He looked at me and he laughed, the dummy poking halfway out of his mouth. As he was laughing and kicking his feet into his car seat, I put my hand out and said, 'Julian's a big boy now.'

He took the dummy out of his mouth, handed it to me and gave me his bottle. I wound down the window and threw them out over the bridge railing into the creek. Thank goodness we got rid of his Ber and Bor, as he called them, and he never once asked for them again.

I'd created a small problem with Julian by rocking him to sleep, and I'd ended up spoiling him. He insisted on being rocked, and having his eyebrows stroked, every time he went off to sleep. He was not requiring as much sleep, and sometimes he woke early from his afternoon nap. In the beginning of these new sleep patterns, I may not have always heard him straight away, because our bedroom was so far away from the other parts of the house, or I didn't expect him to wake that early. When I first heard him cry, they were cries of fear, causing me to rush down to him. He cried as if something or someone had scared him, or traumatised him. There was no one in the house; only Mum, Grandma and myself. I picked him up out of his cot that he was trying to climb out of in terror. He gripped me by the neck so tightly, saying, 'Mummy, Mummy,' and he was moving his head from side-to-side to avoid something or someone. His eyes were wide, and he was clinging so tightly to me, looking around the room, as if he was still looking at whatever terrorised him. As I comforted him, I could feel something watching us, but I pretended not to show it. I felt it. It worried me that Julian was exposed to this. After that, I made sure I checked him regularly. I knew how it felt to feel something down there in those rooms.

My dad decided to take Julian out by himself, without my mum. I was very uneasy about it. Both Mum and I were standing at the front gate watching them drive off, and without saying exactly what I wanted to say, I turned to my mother and asked her, 'Mum, will Julian be alright?'

She knew what I meant. 'Yes, your father will look after him, and he'll be safe.'

My sexual abuse by my father was never discussed in our house. From the day it was discovered, it was never re-opened or talked about. This was the first time there was a hint of me saying, I remember this happened to me. It was still in my mind, but Mum didn't ask me how I was coping. Even then, it was dropped. I had to resolve this in my own mind and in my own time, but I had to know Julian was safe.

My parents started to become more possessive of Julian. They were taking him out more often and it became too much for me to handle. For the first time ever in my life, I snapped at them, and told them that he was my child, and not theirs, and they couldn't just take him out all the time. My father reacted, quickly rushing at me with his hand raised to hit me, and I felt his powerful force.

I ducked, and I fell into the old, small cot that sat near the fuel stove, looked up at him sternly, and said, 'You can't do that now I am married.'

His face was snarling and his temper was seething, but he lowered his hand and walked off.

Gradually, I got myself up, and I felt right in my actions. He didn't have the right to treat me like a child. I was so glad I'd stared him down. He knew, there and then, we were separate, and I was not part of his control any more.

They could take Julian out, just not to take advantage of it, making it too regular. Fortunately, after that day, they didn't ask me if they could take Julian out until many years later, when Julian was around seven. They took him camping with them.

Julian had a very strong love for both my parents. I did feel a bit mean. Still, he was my child, and I wanted him back with me. He was the only person I had that actually loved me, and I loved him in return, and I wanted to protect my baby and keep him safe. A child can be ignorant of the consequences of the actions of older caretakers and suffer from the outcome of such experiences in the future.

# Chapter 37

# Separation

It was the 25th February 1973, a Sunday morning, and around 2am, I woke in pain, and I wanted to wake Javier. I didn't, because he had to go to work. So, I lay there in pain, and waited for the morning to come. 3.30am, I had to get up, and prepare his breakfast and lunch. 4.30am, I woke him for work.

'Javier - time to get up.'

He stirred; it took time for him to fully awaken.

'Javier, I think I am going to have the baby today,' I gasped, holding my tummy and waiting for his response.

He turned over and faced me. 'Do you think the baby's coming?'

I squirmed, and breathed in. 'Yes, will you stay home and come with me to hospital?'

Immediately, he said in a stern voice, 'No, Chris, I have to go to work.'

I was a bit upset, thinking work was more important to him. 'But Javier, I would like you to come with me to the hospital, and it's a Sunday. Please, and you've been having lots of Sundays off lately.'

'No, that's why I have to go to work today; you know Sundays pay well.' He moved out of bed, dressed, and I left him and headed back to the kitchen.

On my way there, the pain was so intense; it was like bad period pain. In the kitchen, I waited for him, and when he came in, I served him his breakfast. He didn't say anything about me going into labour. I didn't ask him again to stay home; he already knew what I wanted from him.

After he left the house, I went to Mum's bedroom door. I called out, 'Mum, I think I'm going to have the baby today. I feel a pain.'

I heard, 'Max, Christine's in pain; we'd better get up.'

I waited outside their door. I'd never entered their bedroom, unless it was with Mum, or only Mum was in there.

Dad stirred, and I heard his voice, 'What is it?'

Mum told him again, 'It's Christine, she's in pain.' Mum called out, 'Christine, we'll take you to the hospital. Go and get your things.'

'Okay, Mum, thanks,' I said, and walked off to my room. I was worried about leaving Julian with my parents, but there was nothing I could do.

I woke Julian, prepared him to go out, and got my bag, which had been packed for weeks. Julian was so sweet, and he walked with me, holding my hand. We got to the kitchen and Mum was there. I said, 'Mum,' pausing between the pains, 'I'm worried about Julian.'

'Don't worry; he'll be alright. I'll look after him,' she reassured me. This would be the first time Julian and I had been separated. I looked at my little boy. He was staring at me; I was in an awkward position. I couldn't sit straight.

He smiled at me, and I stroked his little head. 'Mummy sick?' he asked sweetly.

'No, precious, Mummy's not sick.' I giggled. 'Your brother or sister is coming today.'

Mum and Dad knew how to look after Julian, but I always bathed and fed him. There was nothing I could do. I had to hand him over. I questioned why Javier couldn't have stayed home. He'd been refusing to work on weekends lately, and spending more time at home, not that he spent it with us. Oh well, I can't make him stay, I thought.

Dad drove me to hospital, and on the way, I cuddled Julian as we sat on the back seat. I dreaded having to go through labour, and leaving Julian. I felt so alone, and there was no support from Mum. I thought, she could have turned around, and checked on me every now and then. I just wished it was all over. On arriving at the hospital, Mum carried Julian, and I took my bag, and we went to the receptionist's desk at the main foyer to book me into the maternity ward. I had to say goodbye to Julian there. That was the hardest thing I had to do. I cuddled him tightly and kissed him, telling him he had to stay with Nanny and Poppy for a while, and that Mummy would be home soon. As they left, Julian waved goodbye to me. Anxiety surged in me as we were separated, and his little, serious face was concerned for me, because he didn't understand what was going on. I felt he was being taken from me. I also wanted my mother to be with me - or Javier. Things had changed in the past two years; fathers, or a family member, were now allowed to go into the delivery room.

Sister took me to the ward, and she asked me to get changed into my nightie and get into bed; I did as she asked. The pain was getting worse. Later on, when the pain was more severe, I was wheeled up into a room. The nurse left me, and I thought she'd put on a light, but no, she left me in the dark room. I felt so alone, and feelings of being unloved and uncared for, welled up in me. I was overcome with sadness. I lay there in pain and wondered if they'd remember I was in here.

I called out, 'Mum! Julian!' I was shocked I'd called out to my mum. Why her? Julian, I understood; he was the closest person to me.

The nurse came back to check on me. Ready to give birth, I was taken to the delivery room. I knew what would be happening, but hysteria came over me, and I started to complain about the pain: how intense it was and how I couldn't bear it. Debra, who I went to school with, was the delivery Sister.

'Where's Dr Ling?' I asked.

Someone answered, 'He's on holidays.'

'Don't worry, Christine, I'll deliver your baby,' Debra said.

I became concerned and wondered if she could do it. My pain worsened and I became more hysterical. There was another older Sister with Debra, who was less tolerant of my suffering.

She shouted at me, 'Behave yourself; you're as bad as the Eyeties.'

Debra was more considerate, and she gently told me, 'Christine, try to breathe evenly, and slowly.'

I couldn't. I thought of what the older Sister had said. Eyeties; she meant Italians. How could she say such a thing as that?

Again I was told to behave myself, to stop being silly and carrying on - and to breathe.

'I can't help it; the pain's too much, and I can't bear it,' I screamed between clenched teeth, as I tried to push down.

Debra instructed the older Sister to give me some gas. Her compassion towards me was getting less and less. As she moved over me with the gas, I grabbed it out of her hand. Breathing the gas, I became nauseous, but relaxed as I breathed it in. The pain came back and I screamed. All of a sudden, the feeling to bear down hit me, and I had no control over it.

I heard, 'Stop it; you'll rip yourself open.'

It wasn't me. I had no control, and this bearing down was forcing the baby out. Then he was here, out of me, and had been thrown onto my stomach. I was relieved it was over. I saw this grey mess around this small, small baby.

'It's a boy,' Debra said.

My second son had come into the world earlier than expected; he was due on the 9th of March. He was left on my stomach for a short time, before he was taken from me. It was a wonderful connection with my child. With Julian, they never did that. He was taken from me and cleaned up before I got him, but things had changed, and babies were now given to their mothers straight away. Cleaned up, my baby was handed to me straight away. Dr Ling appeared. He was in his Hawaiian shirt. I thought, he must have just got back from holidays in time to sign the papers.

He asked me how I was, and I told him I was good, and very happy.

When he left, the older Sister, standing near me, snapped, 'You're lucky you didn't rip yourself open further than you did. You only require two stitches.'

'I couldn't stop it; it just happened,' I confessed to her.

'What are you calling your baby?' I was asked.

'We don't have a name for him; my husband and I can't agree on a name.'

He wasn't at the hospital, and we wouldn't have a name for another three weeks. I stayed in hospital for five days. This new baby would be circumcised when he was three weeks old. Again, I was unable to breastfeed this baby, even though I'd eaten all the right foods to help me produce milk. I couldn't do it.

Javier was happy with our new baby; Mum and Dad were too. Julian was able to come into the ward. It was so good to see him. I cuddled him heaps, and he got to see his little brother.

At home after three weeks, I gave in to Javier, and let him name our child, because I'd named Julian. I figured it was only fair he named one of our sons, because I wasn't having any more children. Our baby was called Jerod Alistair. Three weeks late, he had a name. He was put on the bottle, and he prospered.

# Chapter 38

# Leaving The Farm

Finally, our house was complete. We were given the keys to move in. I arranged for the furniture to be delivered through the week and had it all set up. We moved in on the weekend. Javier took time off work and arranged for his parents to help us take in our stuff, because they had a station wagon. There wasn't a real lot to move, just the linen and kitchenware and Julian's cot, which would be Jerod's cot. Julian would move into his own room.

28th March 1973, we moved into our own home, and Javier, the boys, and I ate our breakfast for the last time on the farm. It was a solemn morning, and hardly anything was said between my parents and I. Javier and Julian were the only ones doing all the talking. Javier's family arrived around 11am. Javier had disassembled the cot, and Gema, my father, and I carted all my belongings out of that dreaded, scary, formal lounge room, with all eyes upon us. My things were taken from our bedroom. I glanced up at my grandparents' wedding photo and said goodbye to them.

With everything cleared out, all that was left was to say goodbye to Mum and Dad, and to say thank you to them for having us. Javier shook Dad's hand, and kissed Mum goodbye. He went off with his parents and Gema in their station wagon.

Before I left the farm for good, there was something I had to do - go back to my childhood bedroom. Grandma was in hospital, which allowed me to go to my secret drawer, and not be disturbed. I had everything there in a box from when I was seventeen. I pulled out the shoe box, and opened its lid, and as I did, I smiled at the memories held in that box.

There they were, my love letters and other letters; some from Aunty Connie, and a pen friend I wrote to in America a few times. Picking up one of Ryan's near-perfect handwritten letters, I opened it and read it. My heart faltered, and I held my chest as I realised he did love me.

I took out his photo and scanned it to see if I could read his face, because I couldn't when he sent me the photo all those years ago. Still, it wasn't clear to me what he meant, or his love for me, or the meaning of his letters. The only ones who brought me any sense of love were my children.

I spied my autograph book. Dropping the letter, I picked it up, and smiled widely as I fingered through the pages, and saw the signatures of the radio announcers who were home-town celebrities in my high school days.

On closing the autograph book, I thought, there are some good memories in this box. Once again, I looked at my love letters. I ran my fingers over the envelopes, realising, there and then, I couldn't keep these letters. Javier would never understand. I would have to destroy them, but before I did that, I read Peter's letter.

*It's all due to the fickle finger of fate that we should be together.*

He'd signed it Peter. My heart stopped. How I had hurt Peter, and all of the boys who'd loved me. They'd felt things and saw things in me, or with me, that I couldn't see or feel. I had no love for anyone, no man or boy; my heart was too cold to love.

'Alas, Peter,' I said, 'we weren't meant to be together.' I couldn't look at Brook or Alex's letters. 'That's it; enough. I must stop this reminiscing.' I gathered everything up into the box, walked to the outside toilet, where we had an incinerator, and slowly fed everything into the fire. I watched my past burn before my eyes. It was time to let go of that life. A new life was about to begin. I turned my back on the burning memories and felt happy to be moving on. It was time to leave the farm. Jerod was one month old, and it was the end of March.

It had been unbearable in that house over the past two years. Now the day had come to leave it, and I thought it was going to be the happiest day of my life, because there were way too many issues between my mother and me. I was a mother of two children, and I needed to start my own family life, separate from my parents. I said goodbye to my parents, and for the first time, I noticed a look on my parent's faces that I'd never seen before. Their faces were saying, she's going, never to return to us. I felt for them for the first time ever, and I thought, they may have actually loved me; but I brushed off that look and moved on. There was only my brother left at home, but he was hardly there. He came in to say hello, stay a night, then left the next day to go back to his girlfriend's parents' house.

It was a quiet drive into town, and I watched the beautiful landscape of the farm areas on the Darlington Road, and the gentle, sloping land that nose-dived into the winding creek that trickled through this rich cattle-grazing area. Thoughts of Mum surfaced, and these thoughts interrupted my silence and calm, as I was losing myself in the landscape.

I sighed, diverting my eyes from nature, and I stared at the long, straight road ahead of me. Of course it was my mum's dilemmas that concerned me. I'd left her out there all alone, sharing a house with Grandma, totally dependent on Dad, who I knew would cause her more grief.

That house, and my grandma, had hated my mother from the day she arrived when she was seventeen, just married to my father. Mum was never good enough for Grandma, and she knew instantly how Grandma felt about her. All the same, she was the one who had endured the hatred, and ended up being the only one who would care for Grandma. Everyone else deserted her.

Then there was the incident between Dad and I, that was hard on all of us, I guess more so on Mum; after all, he was her husband. There were many limitations in our lives, due to others not taking responsibility. Lost talents, unseen and slipped away before our eyes; no general education; and no lessons on life and its workings. I had to self-educate myself by finding information to read. How I would've loved to have gone through school, studied at university, and learnt some trade or profession.

I entered the town of Hastings Crossing and sat up in my seat. All my life I'd wanted to be able to live in town, to do the things I wanted to do. Alas, that chance came and went, and no way would it return. Lost youth, lost knowledge, and it wasn't just me. Mum and Maxine married at seventeen. I was nineteen, and Grandma, she was twenty-one when she married. How young we all were, too young to marry. I hadn't wanted to marry until well into my late twenties.

Looking over the back seat at my two sons, I saw Julian in his car seat, strapped in securely, and Jerod asleep in the bassinet. Julian had dozed off, and his little plump hands clutched each other.

Turning into the driveway of our new home, I made my way up it to the back of the house. Javier and his father were there. I alighted from the car and stood there to survey our new location.

'How do you feel?' I asked Javier.

'Good, and you?'

'Good! And I'm glad we made it, and got our own home,' I admitted.

'I told you to wait,' he quipped 'and you see, it came.'

He was right. I had demanded on many occasions that we leave the farm, when I just couldn't take any more, and he'd just reminded me of my bad behaviour. 'Ok. You were right, and now we are finally alone as a family,' I shyly admitted.

He smiled. He was as happy as I was to be starting off on our own.

On the other hand, if I hadn't driven him, we'd never have got there, so my determination started the ball rolling. He would have been happy to live in a shack, and I wasn't. I knew what I wanted.

# Chapter 39

# Life In Town

It was so lovely to be in our own home. A three-bedroom, HardiePlank deluxe house with fairly big rooms, and living in Hastings Crossing was what I'd wanted for years. We had the basic essentials; I was not a very materialistic person. The most important thing was, it was ours. It was a modern home, so different to my childhood home: a modern kitchen, bathroom, finishings, carpet and venetians; we'd never had carpet in the house I grew up in. It was like I'd lived here always. I was realising I was an adaptable person. I could change my life easily, and I could let go of where I had been. Size-wise, this house was nothing compared to the house on the farm, but it was a beautiful house, and the big windows let in lots of natural light. This was one thing the old farmhouse never had, natural light filtering through it. It was always shrouded in darkness and closed up. Today, I could never finance the cost to build a house like that of my childhood.

My parents came to see us, and they were pleased with the house. Mum was still stressed, and of course

Dad convinced Javier to go for a drink, so Mum and I spent time with the boys.

Both Javier and I were happy living in town. I made everyone remove their shoes before they entered the house and walked on our new carpet. I don't know where that had come from, but it was a must. Javier was worse than me; he demanded I be cleaner, and never leave anything lying around. He expected the house to be perfect, and I was making sure all was put away. Something was changing within me, and from the rather complacent person I had been, I was becoming an angry person. My mum left things lying around in the farmhouse, but here I had to put our clothes away, and the boys' toys were always picked up and packed away after they'd finished playing with them. If I left the milk out of the fridge, or left a cupboard door or drawer open, or food on the table, Javier would scream at me to close the doors and put things away. I had lots of bad behaviour that upset Javier. He had become a perfectionist in the house and was forever telling me my shortcomings.

I questioned where that came from. He wasn't like that in the earlier part of our marriage. I realised he was showing me his true self behind his mask, demanding the house be spotless.

He ended up conditioning me into a perfectionist in the house without me knowing it. It's a true saying, it's best to train them young, and he did that; he trained me well. I soon learnt to put things away, and close cupboards to save arguments.

Javier left Bryson Power Station, because he was sick of the travelling to Cloverbrook. He went to work in a construction firm in Dawson Hill, called Hunter Steel.

Sometimes this job required him to travel to Chester Hills to work, which I didn't mind. While he was away, his youngest sister, Gema, came and stayed with us. I never questioned Javier going away to Chester Hills, and I always packed his clothes for the trip. I made sure he had a good set of clothes for going out at night to go to dinner, as well as his daily clothes and working clothes.

While he was away, the boys and I never heard from him, until he returned home. We didn't have a telephone then. The longest he stayed away from us was a week or two. I innocently wished him well when he went away and told him I'd see him when he got back.

Alone, I began to question myself. Here I was thrown into parenthood. Could I be a good and responsible parent? What lay ahead of me in my marriage? I had experienced lots of pain as a child, too much for me to bear.

I was changing, and I found my marriage was declining. I had feelings of being imprisoned in my own body. This echoed in my mind, and looking around the four walls of the house, I saw myself placed in a box in a house, to rot in my own private hell, to lie there sleeping until the hour came when the two princes, my sons, could move out of the castle.

I didn't know why I was so tired and felt lazy some mornings after Javier went to work. I'd go back to bed and sleep in, and when I got up, I'd wear my nightie around the house until late in the day. I was starting to sit and watch the boys, not wanting to do anything. A few times, Javier came home early, surprising me, and went right off at me. I had to change that habit. A lot of my own ways were disappearing. I can thank him for doing that. It got me out of some sort of doldrums I'd worked myself into.

I guess he was seeing I was lapsing into my mother's behaviour. There were two parts to me, one like Grandma who wanted everything clean. Grandma was an amazing cleaner; she'd be up at four in the morning, and she had all the floors washed before we got up. But there was another part of me which wanted to drop things and fix it later on. In due course, I was soon a trained and efficient housewife.

My days in the house were spent with the children. I loved having my children. We played together, and Julian loved his little brother, but Jerod wasn't as easy as Julian. Julian was an angel, and Jerod was testing me from the moment of birth. He'd wake at 5am, and I had to get him fed and back to sleep to get Javier up and off to work. When Javier left for work, I'd fall into bed. Julian was still a great child, and I had him toilet-trained by two and two months. He was always a willing learner.

Now Javier was working in Dawson Hill, he'd met an old friend of his that he used to work with years before. One afternoon, when Javier returned home from work, he brought this man with him, and I went out the back door to meet them in the driveway. I was introduced to Karel, a Yugoslavian, shorter than Javier, with fair, receding hair, and he had a stocky build. I was told Karel lived over in Southampton with an Australian lady. Javier was really happy about meeting up with this man after all these years. Now they could travel together to work. Because they were in their work clothes, I made them tea, and they sat on the back patio and drank it, speaking in Spanish. I started cooking dinner, and later on, Karel went, and Javier came in and showered, and sat with Julian while I finished cooking dinner.

This proved to be a bad blue for me and the boys. I'd got Javier away from Dad's influence, but now there was Karel, and they both ended up going out to the pub after work most days of the week. This time, Javier didn't allow me to dictate to him. Without my family around, I had to learn my place as a woman of the house.

# Chapter 40

# People Leave And People Come

As time moved on, Pia developed an illness. She was going through some very difficult times. Sometimes, Javier's parents looked after her children for her. So, Sonny and Daniel were often at Javier's mother's house when we went down to stay, which was good for my boys to see their cousins and get to know them. Pia had applied for a government house the previous year in November, when Nick left her. She still lived with her mother-in-law, which I thought was good of her mother-in-law to do that.

Eventually, she got a flat from the government in Newbridge South in a really nice suburb. She was quite ill, and she really needed help. This meant Gema was often called over to her flat. It was strange, because Bianca moved away around the same time as Nick, and I wasn't sure where she'd gone, or what had happened to her. If I asked about her whereabouts, all I got was that she'd gone to stay with some family friends. Witnessing Pia's life, without a father figure for their children, convinced me to stay and endure it with Javier. Even though I was not happy in my marriage, seeing her,

I knew I'd not be able to afford to give my children the care and education I wanted for them. I was determined to break the old patterns in our family. No one had attended university, but my boys were going to be educated and go to university.

Pia was so sick, and her sickness took a lot out of her. Her whole body puffed up like a balloon ready to burst. I felt for her. John, Javier's oldest brother, moved back in with his parents after he and Alexandria broke up, but like everything else in that house, no one told you the whole facts of why things were happening.

In August 1973, Barton decided to get married, and Mum had to let him go, even though he was her favourite, and the closest to her. Since he'd met Lorna, he'd been distancing himself from Mum. We'd all met Lorna and I liked her, but Mum wasn't that keen on her, and Javier hated her. So when Barton announced he was marrying her in Robertson, Javier refused to go. That meant I wasn't going to my brother's wedding either. He probably saw too much of himself in her, accusing her of everything imaginable. I didn't realise then, or know of the mirror, but what he was seeing in her was probably his own reflection.

Mum and Dad went, but Maxine was unable to go as well, due to financial reasons. Barton and Lorna decided to live with her mum in Robertson after they'd married. Some weekends, he and Lorna would come and stay with Mum and Dad at the farmhouse, which was good for Mum, because she missed him so much.

# Chapter 41

# Quality Time With The Boys

Julian turned three in the September. He was becoming more independent and wanted to dress himself. Gradually, over time, he accomplished it, and he could dress himself and do his own shoelaces up. I liked those qualities in him, and he was such a funny boy. He had some strange habits; he'd completely undress himself, stripping everything off to go to the toilet, then after going and cleaning himself up, he'd redress himself. I never stopped him, and he only did it at home, because at other people's places, I was with him. I guess he wanted to be comfortable on the toilet, and maybe he liked learning this task so much, he wanted to keep teaching himself to dress. I'd encourage Julian to learn while Jerod was sleeping, so we'd both watch *Sesame Street,* and I'd recite the alphabet games and words to him. He'd follow me and we'd cuddle. He liked to learn and loved this show. This show taught Julian some good basic concepts for school, we achieved a lot, and before long, he was reciting the alphabet. He was so independent and capable.

When Jerod was seven months old and becoming more demanding of my time, Julian started to change.

When I put Jerod to sleep, he'd wait until I was out of sight, and then he'd run past his brother's room and scream. He was becoming naughty. By the time Julian was three-and-a-half-years old, it had got so bad, I had to go and seek advice from my doctor. He told me not to worry; it was a stage he was going through, and Julian was testing me. I had to discipline that, and with time, and giving him some of my extra time, he started to behave. In due course, he started to lose that perfection he'd had before his brother came into the world.

Jerod was one year old, and my patience was being tried by these boys. I still joined in their games, and we'd watch the educational shows on television together. They were my responsibility, and I wanted the best for them - and me. Learning was as important for them as loving them. I liked to tickle and play with the boys. Their favourite game was Round and Round the Garden on their hands. They would roar in laughter. While Jerod slept, Julian and I started to read and write. I loved being able to teach him. As the time moved on and the boys got older, problems developed. When Jerod was one and a half, he soon learnt how to get his way. He learnt the more he screamed, the more I'd come running to find out what the problem was. He was angry with Julian. To keep the peace, I'd get Julian to give him the toy, or whatever it was he wanted. My stress was climbing with the noise. Of course, the older child would suffer due to the younger child.

Jerod was different. He would take longer in learning personal care, dressing, and learning to read and write. That was not for him. He preferred to be as close as he could to me. If he could have unzipped me and got inside my body, he would have.

I was also dealing with my own dilemmas in my marriage, which I kept separate from the boys as much as I could. Javier was coming home late most nights after work, and he and Karel were drinking at the pub straight after work. Javier knew not to come home and change into clean clothes to go out, because if he did, all of hell would blow open.

# Chapter 42

# Julian Nearly Bleeds To Death

When Julian was four, his eagerness to learn got stronger, which helped him so much when he started school. He was writing his name and reading, and when we had visitors - my parents or Javier's parents - he'd go and get his favourite book, *The Three Little Kittens*, and read it to any willing ear. He knew the whole alphabet and some of his numbers and could write his whole name before school. I thought this was amazing at the tender age of four years and two months.

Julian suffered a bad attack of tonsillitis, and it was suggested by our GP he have them operated on. Dr Ling was our GP and said he could perform the operation. We agreed to it, and Julian was put into the children's ward of the hospital. He had the operation very early the next morning. On calling the hospital around 10am to check on how he was, I was told not to come to the hospital until the afternoon, when he'd be fully recovered. Javier's parents had come up earlier from Dawson Hill to mind Jerod for me. Around 2pm, Javier's mum and I went to the hospital with some of his favourite toys. Julian was in bed, and he was so happy to see us. I cuddled him, and he tried to talk.

The nurse told him not to talk. She said, 'Julian, we told you, shh-shh.' She smiled at him, and I sat with him and held his little hand.

After a while, he started to cough up blood.

'Christina,' said my mum-in-law. We didn't like the look of that blood on his pillow case, and I immediately called the nurse, who rushed off and got the Sister. They told me they would have to call Dr Ling back in to examine Julian.

We waited and waited for the doctor, and he never came. I was going to the Sister, asking her why he wasn't there yet. She put it down to him doing rounds. We had to go back to the house, as Javier's father and Gema were there with Jerod.

The Sister said, 'Don't worry; I'll call you when the doctor comes.'

'But I don't have a phone on,' I said, concerned.

'What about your neighbours?'

So I left Mrs Innesvale's phone number.

At the house, Mum-in-law told Dad-in-law what had happened, and they said they'd stay until I had everything sorted out. I was so worried and told Gema how I didn't like the amount of blood Julian had coughed up. She tried to reassure me. At 5.30pm, Mr Innesvale came and gave me the message to go straight to the hospital.

When I arrived at the children's ward, I was told Julian would have to go back down to surgery to be operated on. Shocked, and not understanding why this had to happen, and why it took the doctor so long to come, from 2pm to then, I went to Julian's bed. He was blue. He was drained of his own blood. He'd been drinking it. The wound had not been properly sealed, and he was bleeding. I went into shock and couldn't speak. I picked him up and held him in my arms; his little body was so limp.

I cried, and asked the nurse, 'Why was he left for so long?'

She couldn't answer my question, and said, 'They had to wait for the doctor.'

Julian was taken to surgery, and an hour later, he was returned to the ward. I was told he had to have a blood transfusion. I was in two minds over this. I didn't know if I fully believed in this procedure of blood transfusions, but my son's life was at stake.

Meanwhile, Javier had arrived home from work late. He was greeted by his parents, who told him what had happened. He rushed to the hospital, straight to the children's ward. When I saw him, I was sitting holding Julian's almost lifeless hand. Javier edged over to us and when he saw Julian, he became very upset.

Our son looked so weak and lifeless on the blood transfusion. We both sat with Julian for a long time, not wanting to leave him. The Sister advised us to go home. There was nothing we could do for him. Leaving the hospital grounds, it was very dark, and I wasn't paying attention to who was around us.

Suddenly, Javier grabbed someone. It was Dr Ling. He had him by his shirt, and he told him, 'If anything happens to my son, you're dead.'

The doctor flinched, and fearing Javier, he assured him nothing would happen to Julian. Javier released his clothing, pushed him out of the way, and we both walked away from him.

The next day, I went up to the hospital as early as I possibly could, and Gema stayed to mind Jerod. On entering the children's ward, I could see Julian was playing with his favourite toy, his felt farm set. I went over and cuddled him. I could see he was on the road to recovery. I was so glad. Again, he was chatting away, but the nurse insisted on him being quiet.

She said, 'Julian, shh,' and put her finger to her mouth. He nodded. She went off, and as if he'd forgotten, he started to natter on again. I was so happy he was well; that's what mattered.

Julian played with his toy, and I joined in the game. He was completely different than me when I'd had my tonsils removed at seven. I'd screamed and cried the whole time. But I knew why. Julian was lucky he had me, a loving mum, who was always there for him.

# Chapter 43

# Dealing With My Husband

October '74, Maxine and Collin moved into town from their rented house at the pit. She was lucky to get a government house just up the road from us. I was so happy she was so close to me. Maxine had two children, Alex, and another son, Geoffrey, born in February that year. Javier's family had been dominating our lives, and now I thought my sister and I could get together as a family.

However, there'd be no freedom for me to spend time with my sister and her family. Javier's jealousy was too great, and he couldn't accept my sister's children. He kept me separated from them, because Javier couldn't stand me loving anyone outside of us four: him, me, and our two boys. Any sign of love to my nephews caused him rage.

Javier was always coming home late, and the boys and I were mostly at home alone. I'd just put the boys to bed, and I was waiting for him to come home to give him his dinner. Jerod started to cry, and I tried to put him back to sleep, but he refused to sleep, so we sat watching TV. As we sat there in the lounge room,

I had the feeling someone was outside around the house. The feeling was intense, and I had to check, so I stood up with Jerod in my arms and went to the kitchen window. Standing there with Jerod on my hip, I couldn't see outside. It looked black out there, but fear gripped me and I froze. Jerod whimpered, sensing my fear, and he turned his head back to look out the window, and then he looked at me. He murmured, grabbing hold of me tightly, and snuggled into me. He had connected with whatever was out there. There was a sound, like a stick being dropped on the patio, right near the kitchen door and window where we were standing.

I shuddered and froze again. Jerod grabbed me again, swinging to look, and he cried. I held his back and said, 'it's okay, Jerod, Mummy's here.' I cuddled him, easing his fear, and moved away from the window.

Ten minutes later, Javier's car pulled into the driveway. He came through the gate, and all the tension in my body was released. I reassured Jerod that Daddy was coming, and that it was alright now. When he parked the car at the garage, I opened the back door, and on the patio lay a stick. I told Javier what had happened. He was tired and said, 'It's probably nothing, and the stick was probably there, and you didn't notice it.'

He took off his shoes in the laundry and his work clothes. I peered down through the black of the night, and the back yard seemed silent and gloomy, but nothing stirred. We went into the house, closed and locked the door, and I gave him Jerod to hold, as I put his dinner on the table. It had been sitting over a hot dish of water to keep it warm.

The emotional abuse from Javier constantly running my family down was affecting me, especially if he'd met up with my father in the pub. He'd take it out on me if Dad had been telling his stories and lying. I still defended Dad. It was as if Javier wanted to brainwash me into seeing my parents as bad people. However, he was achieving the reverse. Instead of hating my parents, I hated him, and it was distancing us in our marriage.

Around this time, I got a surprise visit from Bianca. She'd been away for a year and a bit, and no one had told me why. When I had asked why, all I got was that she was staying with some family friends. She returned with a family of her own. I was so surprised, and happy to see her. She introduced me to her boyfriend, Henry, and their baby boy, Leonard, who was fifteen months old. I was just happy to see her again with her new family.

While talking to Henry, I said, 'You have a beautiful child, and he looks like you.'

Henry looked at Bianca strangely, and she stared at him and frowned.

Henry looked back at me and said, 'Do you think he looks like me?'

Puzzled and smiling, I said, 'Yes, to me, he looks like you.' The smirk on Henry's face baffled me. Then he said, 'Thank you.'

He looked again at Bianca. My mum-in-law came in from the bathroom, asking me for a hand-towel, and she broke my attention. In the diversion, I let it all go.

# Chapter 44

# Strange Family Incidents

A few days after this incident, Javier's oldest brother, John, came with Jules, the youngest brother, to visit us in Hastings Crossing. There seemed to be some urgency in John's voice as he spoke Spanish to Javier. After a while, John suggested Javier go with him to have some time with their mother. It was a strange request. John's gift of the gab convinced me that they'd not be long, and to save dragging the children down, they'd go themselves.

I agreed, and he said, 'We'll be back home around 5pm, and Jules can stay with you and keep you company.'

I continued doing my daily chores, and Jules played with the boys. When I'd completed what I had to do, the four of us chatted and played with the kids, and we had a good day together.

Close on 6pm, I checked the clock. Javier and John hadn't returned, and we didn't have a phone, but his parents had a phone. I had to go up the street to use the phone box to call them. I decided to wait a little longer. I cooked our dinner and we all ate.

While cleaning up, I told Jules my feelings. 'Jules, I'm worried about Javier.'

'Don't worry, Chris, he'll be here soon. You know they get talking and forget the time.' He winked, and twisted in his seat, trying to be cool.

'True, you're right,' I reasoned, but I was confused about the whole thing. I knew Jules hadn't been upfront, because he twisted and winked when he was lying.

Around 9pm, I put the boys to bed, and Jules and I watched TV. I was glad of his company. It was easing my distress about the whole ordeal. Javier was going out drinking a lot these days, but he always came home.

Midnight and I was really worried. Jules said, in his hoarse-like voice, as he stretched his shirt nervously, 'Chris, don't worry. Wait till morning. I'm sure he's just got caught up with John. You know what John's like.'

I really didn't know John that well, because he was living in Cloverbrook and he'd not long came back to live at his mum's. I felt John had a violent temper.

Jules kept easing my concerns, saying, 'He's at Mum's. What can he do there, and he's not dressed up.'

True, he went down in shorts, I thought. I let it go. Maybe they'd come home later on in the night. 'Jules, I'm going to bed.'

'Okay, I'll go in a little while.'

I must've dropped off into a deep sleep and woke the next morning. On waking, I looked over to Javier's side of the bed. Not there. I was very angry, and I got up, dressed, and got the children up.

'Jules, wake up.'

'Did they come back?' he asked.

'No, so as soon as we've eaten breakfast, we're off to your mum's. I've had enough,' I said, in a not-too-happy voice.

'Stop and wait a bit, Chris,' he begged.

'No. I've waited all night, and I'm going. If you want stay here, you can stay.'

'No, no, I'll come.'

He made himself a coffee. He was shrugging his shoulders, a worried look on his face; as if he knew something I wasn't supposed to know. I fed the boys and washed their faces. They were laughing between themselves, and Julian was doing funny antics to make Jerod laugh.

With the boys fed and washed, Jules and I put them in the car, and I drove out of the driveway, and swung the car sharply onto the quiet street.

'Aren't you shutting the gate, Chris?'

'No, not today.'

We travelled up to the main street of Hastings Crossing. I was speeding in my anger. I eased off the accelerator and listened to the car.

'Can you hear a rattling noise, Jules?' I asked him.

He listened, and it seemed to be coming from one of the wheels. It was really loud.

'Jules, do you hear it?' I repeated.

He sat up and pricked up his ears. 'Yes. What is it?'

'I don't know.'

'Chris, you'd better stop and check it,' he advised me.

My anger was so great, that I didn't care about the noise, or want to stop. I had the boys with me. If I was alone, I'd have ignored it. As we neared the tyre service shop, I slowed down and entered the premises, and eased the car over the cement speed bump Roy had to stop customers speeding on his premises. Roy, the owner, came out of his office and I drove to the garage section. Getting out of my car, I told him there was an unusual noise with one of the wheels. Roy grabbed the car jack, and I got the boys out of the car. Jules took Jerod, and I held on to Julian's hand. Then Roy cranked up the car and moved the four wheels.

'It's the nuts; they've been loosened. You're lucky you heard the noise, or you could have lost the tyre and had a bad accident,' he stated.

'It could have been that bad?' I asked him for further confirmation, stressing my request, due to me not fully taking in the consequences or seriousness of it. I was too angry with Javier, and all I wanted to do was get to his mother's house. Roy told me it was serious.

I informed him that we'd just got the new tyres on the car a couple of days ago.

'Well, whoever put them on didn't do a good job. I'll tighten them for you. You're lucky,' he said, as he went off to get his tools.

'Thank you,' I said, and all of a sudden, it hit me. My goodness me, that wheel, if it had come off, God only knows what would have happened to us. Now I was at boiling point.

Then there was a car pulling in behind us, and the noise diverted my attention from our car being repaired. As I looked up, I saw Javier and John.

Before he could ask me any questions, I screamed out, 'Where have you been?' Giving Julian's hand to Jules, I rushed up alongside John's car to where Javier was sheepishly getting out of it, and as quietly as I could in my enraged state, I stared hard at him, saying, 'You're not fair. We were nearly killed, me and the boys, by those wheels you had put on the car the other day.'

228

He put his head down and never answered me, then gave me a quick stare.

'I hate you, you bastard. You don't care about us,' I told him through gritted teeth.

He gradually moved from me to the side of John's car. He went over to talk to Roy.

John just stared at me from his side of the car, saying, 'Chris, calm down.'

'Don't tell me to calm down. Where were you all night?' I demanded.

'We were at my mum's, and time got away, so we decided to stay until morning, thinking you'd understand.'

'Well, I don't, and he'd better not do it again,' I warned.

The car was lowered off the jack, and I asked Roy if I could take the car. He told me I could and that it was safe to drive. I thanked him and ignored Javier. I called to Jules, who was still nursing Jerod and holding Julian's hand and talking to John, to come. Jules looked at John, and he nodded an approval to Jules to go with me. My eyes dug into John's eyes.

I got into the front of the car, and we went home. On the way home, I complained, and Jules was quiet. On reaching the house, I turned into the front gate and drove through, and parked the car in the driveway. I sighed and took a deep breath. The boys were trying to undo their belts, so I got out of the car and unbuckled them and bundled them out of the car. Jules had come up behind me, and he took Julian, and I carried Jerod. We made our way over to the back door of the house, and as we did, we stopped hearing the noise of a car. John's car pulled up behind ours. On seeing it was them, I continued to make my way over to the back door. While I unlocked the door, John hurried over to me.

'Chris,' he said.

'What?'

'Chris, we were at Mum's,' he promised.

'I don't care. You're a bastard like he is.' My tone of voice could have killed him. Forgetting they hated being called bastards - and really, it's just an Australian word most people use in anger - John jumped at me and raised his hand to hit me. I stood my ground and stared at him. He wanted to lash out at me, I could see it, and my eyes said, you dare.

Jerod flinched in my arms, and said, 'Mummy.'

John lowered his hand, shouting sternly at me, 'Don't you call me a bastard.'

I stood there and stared at him in defiance. 'Well, you are.'

Jules had backed away from the porch. When I looked at him, his eyes were showing some fear. Jerod lowered his lip and John took him from me. I knew what he did that for: to calm himself down.

'Come on, Jerod, to Uncle John,' he said, with a false grin spread on his face to put Jerod at ease. I let Jerod slip out of my arm to him and pushed on the back door to open it. Javier had been slow getting out of the car, when I saw him through the kitchen window as I forcibly pulled the curtains back. John was in the kitchen bouncing Jerod, and Javier came in with his head down and looking like a meek lamb.

I went to my bedroom and threw my bag on the bed. Returning to the lounge room where they'd all congregated, I took Jerod from John. Jerod was happier, but his little face was flushed. I didn't want the boys to be with them, so I took them to the bathroom and washed their little faces to cool them down, and myself. Immediately on leaving the men in the lounge room, they'd broken into Spanish. I spent quite a long time in the bathroom, playing in the water with the boys.

'Chris,' I heard. Jules was at the door of the bathroom. 'We're going,' he said.

'Okay. Thanks for staying with me. Good thing you did, because I would have gone to your mum's last night, and God knows what would have happened to us,' I proclaimed.

'Yeah, Chris, sorry. See you,' he said, glancing to the kitchen, where I could hear John and Javier speaking.

Sitting Jerod on the lounge room floor with his toys, Julian following behind, I settled them and they played. Javier just sat silently in his chair. He was acting very strangely.

I asked him pleasantly, 'Javier, what went on last night, and why were you away? You never do things like that.'

He didn't answer me straight away, then he said, 'I was at Mum's,' not looking at me and sitting with his elbows on the armchair, his hands up under his chin. There was no way I was getting a truthful answer.

I had to let it go.

He never, ever did it again. It didn't matter how late it was, eleven or two in the morning, he always came home. All secrets surface eventually, and the answer to this one would too.

# Chapter 45

# Laddie

We decided to get a pet when Jerod was twenty-two months old. The pet was for the boys. As children, we were always surrounded by dogs and cats, and I knew the benefits of having a pet. We found a stable, coloured collie dog, and it was love at first sight for us all. I named him Laddie, because he seemed like a Lassie dog, but he was male. Laddie loved Jerod so much, and Jerod loved him. They were inseparable when Jerod was in the yard. I had no worries leaving Jerod with Laddie, because he was always right behind him, and if he got too close to the gate, the dog would grab Jerod by his nappy and pull him back. Laddie was a good babysitter.

Jerod had been really naughty, testing my patience big time. He was going to the front gate and trying to get out onto the road. We lived on a busy, dangerous, main road. Having Laddie helped solved this problem, but the dog was getting stressed. I'd often hear him barking frantically, and I'd go out to see what the matter was. Sure enough, it was Jerod testing the dog. One day I'd had enough. Laddie was barking, so I grabbed Jerod by the arm really hard. He hadn't seen me come up behind him. My eyes made him cringe.

'Mummy, no.'

I pulled down his nappy and gave him the biggest smack I could on his bare bottom and legs, telling him it was dangerous to go out onto the road. I shook his arm, turned him to see the cars flying by, and told him if he went out on that road, he'd be dead. Tears streamed down his face. After that, the problem was solved.

Julian was still testing me, screaming when I put Jerod down to sleep. It was like the devil entered Julian. There were many little tests between the boys and me. Jerod was taking longer to toilet-train. He never had the same ambition as Julian. He wasn't willing to learn, and I couldn't read to him. He'd push the book away from us. The boys were chalk and cheese.

I'd become a fanatical cleaner, and I ended up mowing the lawns. I decided to mow the lawns to give Javier spare time on his days off, but I wanted an income from doing our lawns. I suggested to Javier he should pay me. I liked to do the lawns, because it helped me fill in my day. I was very precise with the lawns, so I earned five dollars, nothing for the amount of work I did, but it was something. All my money was mostly spent on Javier. I started to change him to the way I wanted him to dress. I bought him new clothes and made a new Javier from an image I had of him, but I didn't realise clothes don't change a man.

We can change our images through the physical, but to be a better person, we have to find out what is not appropriate within ourselves, be willing to accept what's not right, and change it. We can only do that if we choose to. We can only deal with ourselves, and not others. I had many fears around germs, and I couldn't get past those fears. If someone came into my house and used my toilet, I had to clean the toilet immediately. I was becoming very depressed and lonely, and cleaning took up so much of my time and filled in the day. Making my house clean was the centre of my life. I taught the boys never to sit on a public toilet seat. I couldn't touch things that were dirty, and if I did, I washed my hands straight away. This caused me to develop dermatitis. My hands were so bad, I had to peel potatoes with rubber gloves on. The hands healed, but not my phobias.

We still didn't have a home phone. I had to use the public phone box to make calls. Javier's parents and Gema were visiting, and I had to make a business call. I left the boys with them, while I went to the public phone box up the street. While on it, I noticed an old woman and a boy waiting to use the phone after me. After my call, I slipped out of the box, and stood there a moment to work out my messages I'd taken from the company I'd called. The old lady had gone into the box. She became quite distressed and beckoned me to help her. I freaked out. I physically froze when I saw she looked unclean. I sensed she had some mental disorder. I looked at the boy, and he looked away. The lady was so upset, I had to help her. I was so afraid of catching something, that I quickly dialled the number for her, threw the phone at her, and rushed out of the box. The boy looked at me strangely, and he went into the box and helped the old lady. I was so sorry, but my fear was so great, and I hurried home and washed.

I talked Javier into letting me get the phone on, and it saved me a lot of stress. I could talk to Gema more often. Gema and I had a good rapport, that became stronger as time went on. She was feeling more comfortable with me and started telling me family secrets. She told me about Pia.

'Chris, if I tell you something, you won't tell anyone?'

'No, Gema.'

'Chris, the old man was a bastard, and he slept with Pia.'

My body shut down.

I heard her saying, 'And he used her, because Mum was sick of him going near her, and when he did go near Mum, she'd get pregnant, and was having kid after kid.'

'But, Gema -'

'Mum made out she didn't know, but you knew, Chris. I think she allowed it, to keep him from her. She ignored what was happening to Pia.'

I was shocked, and just listened, as she told me more and more information about her father's behaviour. 'And his niece in Spain, he was using her. I heard that was one of the reasons why we left Spain.'

'Gema,' I said, flabbergasted.

'It's true, Chris.'

As she spoke, it was opening up my own wounds; I quietly put them back into my drawer in my mind and said nothing in regard to my own experiences of sexual abuse in my childhood.

'Chris, Pia's horrible to you, and you don't deserve it, and I wanted to tell you about her. Okay?' she compassionately said.

I could see why Gema was telling me, and all I could do was say, 'Thanks, Gema, and I'm sorry about Pia's trauma with her father.'

'Don't be, Chris; she's my sister, but she's a bitch.'

I felt Pia's experience was different to mine, because she must have suffered. Gema hung up, and I slowly put the receiver down, and dismissed what I had just heard.

# Chapter 46

# Many Changes Happen Around Us

I was a very ambitious person, and that ambition got us a lovely home. The first two-and-a-half years we lived there, we did lots around the house. We put up a garage, and Javier and his workmate poured concrete paths all around the house, which eliminated a lot of the grass area, and made it cleaner when people came into the house. Even though it was concreted, I still made people remove their shoes at the back door; plus, it made the whole place look better, and neater and easier for me. I took to hosing down the concrete with water, which I enjoyed.

Gradually, I learnt of Javier's weaknesses, and how to play on them to get my own way with him, even though he gave me a hard time emotionally. When the time came to play my games, I could, and I was very good at it.

Sex never interested me, and I can't remember ever being sexy with him. My pretend sexual prowess with him got me what I wanted. Javier was truly a basic, uncultured man, and for him, food, sex, and drink were what he needed. Not that he was an alcoholic, but he liked to have a drink. My main interest was for my children and my own comfort.

Barton and Lorna had been living in Robertson since they were married. In August 1975, they decided to move to Hastings Crossing, where their first son, Hank, was born. Barton never liked work. Actually, he hated it, and he seemed to always get out of having to work. He was happy to be on the dole. Occasionally, Javier got him a job in the construction industry, but he'd only work for about two months, and left the job without giving any notice, which annoyed Javier off big time, because Javier felt it affected him. I don't know how. Javier liked Barton, but when he stuffed up, he couldn't understand why. They were just two different people, with different aims in life. Barton loved his wife so much, that he couldn't bear to be away from her for too long. I think that was one of the reasons why he didn't work.

Dad and Mum had to leave the farmhouse around the same time, just before Dad's forty-third birthday in December 1975. After all those years they'd spent out on the farm with Grandma and staying on the farm due to Grandma's promise to Dad that she would die in two years, and to just stay with her on the farm for those two years - and they did. From the day they got married back in 1951, they stayed with her until 1975.

Grandma had begged them to stay, with offers of helping them. She was finally placed in a nursing home in Denver Shire. I was pleased for Mum's sake. She did so much for Grandma, and no one helped her. They'd been wisely preparing for this day, and fortunately, Dad saw the inevitable. All those years out on the farm, they had never saved a penny. They had no money and had to borrow money to buy their house in 1974. It was an old house, and he did it up himself, and then rented it to a family who had a store in Hastings Crossing.

Before Dad left the farm, he had to sell all the old furniture and items in the house. He never offered us kids any pieces of furniture or belongings. Apparently, when they cleared out Grandma's bottom bedroom wardrobe, there were lots of old letters from relatives, and from the two world wars, and many other valuable books and lots of family history. Dad had no idea of its value as family historical knowledge for the future; nor did I. He sold it all to an antique dealer for a song, I was told. My cousin Charlene, who was the bravest of us all, demanded the old brass bed I had slept in for the first two years of my marriage. All I could say was: thank goodness she won and got something. I wished I could have grabbed the letters and books, and all of my Uncle Donny's awards and scrolls.

Our horse, Star, was still alive. She was our last horse, and my parents couldn't bring her into town, so Alex took her out to his property for her to see out her last days. Dad wanted her to die of old age and not be sold, because she'd only end up in the glue factory, he said, and the thought of that pained him. Old Star was arthritic, and she had to be covered in the wintertime with a back blanket. She was already twenty-four years old. She had been a feisty horse, and Dad had ridden her a lot; so had Barton, now and then. Her trick was the same as her mother, Bonnie's. As soon as they'd turned around the top of the cow bales that stood before the shed, where all the horses' equipment was stored, they'd fly full speed to the shed, and there was no pulling them up. You just had to be prepared for it, and also be prepared for the sudden stop in front of the shed. If you weren't, you'd easily go over the horse's head. The two horses knew this was where their saddle and bridle came off, and they'd be released into the paddock. On the removal of the bridle, the last item to be taken off them, these horses would throw their heads back in the air and run off whinnying to the quiet of the middle paddock, their favourite spot, and graze, as if to say, thank goodness that's over and done with.

My mum had suffered badly when I left the farm, and she'd had no one to talk to about her concerns, Dad, and his alleged affairs; but it was like there was no solution to her woes. Talking to her, was like listening to a record caught in the one groove, and she was repeating the same lines over and over.

At this time, Glen was really in trouble, and he was placed in a psychiatric hospital for help, because he'd attacked a person. Maybe this would keep Dad away from Hilary, if he ever did go out with her.

Maxine and I didn't totally desert Mum. Sometimes, we'd go over to her house with our children, and take her out for the day. My house was a full-time job, and Javier's family were always on my doorstep. It was becoming too much for me; we never had any privacy and were never free of them. Javier didn't allow me to go to work, so I stayed home, but not always alone. I either had the company of Gema or Bernat. They'd take turns to come and stay with me. Through the week, all the family would visit me, and I found it more and more of an invasion. I learnt that if I created a fight with

Javier's father, I'd be spared for two months, because he wouldn't come to our house. The problem was, he'd retired from work just after I met Javier, and he had nothing better to do with his time.

What I needed was Javier to talk to me. I needed intellectual stimulation he couldn't give me, because he didn't possess an expansive mind. I wanted to talk to him about phenomena, or mysteries of life, and how did man evolve. If I did mention this, Javier would tell me I was stupid, and cut me off. Our conversations weren't interesting, and Javier hadn't had any formal education. He'd been working since he was ten years old, and that's all he knew. His conversation centred on his job. Many times, he'd tell me the ins and outs of a particular job, and I'd have to listen to his boring details. He even drew me pictures to make sure I was watching and listening. If I didn't, or I got bored, he'd go off in a huff, and then that would be it. No talkies, and he'd sulk. It would take me days to smooth him over. If someone came to the house, that was usually the best way to break the thick ice of non-communication between us.

'Don't rock the boat, woman,' I would say, and keep my thoughts to myself. 'Oh no, I've done it again,' was my other line.

Sometimes at Javier's mum's house, I had talked to his brother, Alexandre, who was still in high school. We talked about his school subjects, and one day, I noticed he had some interesting books I'd never seen before. I was never a reader, because books were never bought for us children, and I didn't think to buy books for myself. His books touched on topics I was starting to think about and question.

We were talking about life and its meaning in Alexandre's room, when Javier entered and asked me, 'What are you doing in here?'

Puzzled I said, 'I'm talking to Alexandre about science.'

He stared at me and said, 'Well don't, and I don't want you in here on your own.'

I looked at Alexandre, and he looked at me. He raised his eyebrows and said, 'For God's sake, Javier, we're just talking.'

Rather than start an argument, I said, 'Sorry, Alexandre.' I left his room, thinking, how stupid of Javier. He always had to have the last word on any decision.

If Pia was visiting her mum's house when we came down to see them, I'd suffer lots of abuse from her, and everyone backed her up, except Gema. She protected me. If Javier was around, she'd never torment me, and she acted like an angel. Due to this abuse from her and Javier, I started to become hypersensitive, and began to cry when I was being insulted. Pia was such an unkind person, even though she wasn't well herself. She delighted in hurting other people, especially when she had an eager audience to support her sly remarks. Her brothers, especially Vince and Bernat, were always her biggest supporters. The sadness I was feeling was enveloping my whole life. It was an obscene life of infinite sadness and hopelessness. All I had were my children, and they were being subjected to her taunts at me too. I didn't know how to handle it, and I wasn't an unkind person, and couldn't think mean thoughts. My children would just stare at these people dishing out offensive words and they'd look at me, questioning what was going on. I was too nice to be rude, and I took it.

# Chapter 47

# Women; I Can't Trust Them

I was so faithful to Javier; in all our married life, I was never unfaithful to him. I never talked about our home life to anyone, and everyone thought he and I had the perfect marriage. Bored, I started to notice a young man, who must have been about twenty years old. I questioned why I was so attracted to younger men, because I was finding Paco attractive as well. I would never tell these people about my feelings. The young man lived in the house on the corner of our street, near the swimming pool that was at the end of our street across the road. He often rode past our house on a bicycle. I liked his dark looks, which gave him an almost American-Indian look. I'd never caused a situation whereby I'd attracted his attention, but somehow, he helped me divert myself from my loneliness, and he gave me something to look forward to. Paco did the same thing for me. I felt an infatuation towards him, and when I saw him, he'd light up my life. I had to keep this all to myself, and not tell anyone. He didn't suspect; I was good at hiding my feelings, and I could keep things to myself, escaping from life through daydreaming. I could lose myself easily, and this was how I survived my marriage.

Pia was a snake in the grass, and one day, she tricked me before I realised what had happened, and I'd disclosed a secret. She'd caught me totally off guard. I knew she was dangerous, and it slipped out when we were talking about men, and how we found some men attractive. I mentioned to her that there was this very handsome boy in our street that rode past our house on his bicycle. We giggled at the time, and I told her he's just a boy that I'd noticed. I never told her anything else.

Not long after that, Javier's parents had come to see us. They were going back home, and Javier and I went out on the footpath to say goodbye to them.

A man went by on his bicycle and Javier asked, 'Is that your boyfriend?'

I looked at him as if he was mad, and said, with a screwed-up face, 'What?' I waved to his parents, smiling as if to say, what are you talking about? I knew straight away Pia had told him and had probably made it more than I'd disclosed. From then on, I never trusted her, and was very careful about what I said around her. Not long after that, I never saw that boy again. I guess he just came in as a temporary diversion. My life was so limited.

From then on, our fights diverted from my parents to me. He'd come home after drinking and accuse me of having boyfriends. This was the time that all hell entered my life. I had to defend myself, telling him I never had any boyfriends, and I wasn't interested in other men. He had started to raise his hand to me if I nagged him too much. I quickly learnt to back off, never upsetting him in his drunken state, and waited until next morning. Then he'd say I'd nagged him, when he wasn't feeling well after a night of bingeing. Fighting had caused another issue: silence. He was good at that. He could give me the silent treatment for days. I hated him so much.

I'd stare at him intensely, narrowing my eyes, and in a hateful voice I'd say, 'I hope you fall off a building today and die.'

Not speaking, he just stared back, opened the back door and left. When he'd left, I'd go into the lounge room and throw myself into the chair and cry. So much hate was building up inside me, and I didn't like this side of myself. My hatred for Javier just got worse over the years. He was the only person I hated. I couldn't bring myself to hate others, even Pia. I couldn't hate her.

Javier was still going away to Chester Hills now and then for work, and this gave me some space. One day, I was alone at home in the lounge room, and the boys were playing there too. Looking out the window, there were my in-laws pulling up. I just watched them. My father-in-law ran up the driveway around to the back door, and he rushed in saying, 'Christina.'

Mother-in-law, who was a lot slower, walked up the pathway with Bernat. It came to me that my father-in-law didn't trust me at all. What was he thinking? I knew Gema told me he never trusted anyone and suspected everyone of cheating.

I slowly walked into the kitchen and stared at him. He was holding onto the barrier that surrounded the stove, trying to get his breath. He'd sensed I'd seen him.

He said, 'We came to make sure you're alright.'

My antenna went up; didn't Javier trust me, or was it just him? Had they come to make sure I never had anyone in the house? It was too obvious and blatant for me not to question it, and there was nearly always one family member made to stay with me. Javier may never have trusted me, but I trusted him completely.

Around the same time, Barton became involved in a third theft incident. A lot of it was hushed up. He had gone to steal from a private home garage, and he must've known the people who owned it. He hadn't realised the people were home. Barton had gained entry through a window, and as he was entering their garage, the woman of the house had seen him. On seeing her, Barton had quickly jumped back out of the window. He'd landed on tin or glass and injured himself, cutting his Achilles' heel. He'd managed to get away but had to go to the hospital. Unfortunately for him, the people knew him.

Mum was hysterical, and I couldn't grasp that after all this time, he'd thieve again. Fortunately, quick thinking on my parents' part, going straight to their family lawyer, saved Barton from prison. He ended up with a limp and was cured for life of any other thieving. He was very lucky with this third incident. Being twenty meant jail; I think the reality of his actions kicked in. I must say, we were good at learning lessons that could cause us big problems.

# Chapter 48

# Fears Around Men

I wanted us to travel as a family. It took time, but I managed to coax Javier into taking holidays, so we bought ourselves a caravan. It wasn't clean - I think the previous owner may have kept birds in it - but it was cheap. I scrubbed it out, and it came up lovely. We found a great spot at Calm Lakes for our holidays. I wanted my boys to have a wide range of experiences, to travel and take holidays. On telling my parents about this great spot we'd found, they'd started to join us. I didn't mind them coming, but in a way, I wanted to escape the family. That seemed an impossible thing to do. I just wanted us to travel to other places in Australia. Unfortunately, Javier wasn't interested in travelling too far from home. I was grateful, for the time being, to go to the Lakes area. We'd go camping twice a year for two or three weeks, and often we'd go on short camping trips with Javier's parents for the weekend. That was the one thing I liked about my own parents; they'd always taken us on holidays a couple of times a year.

Javier was too protective of me during our camping holidays. I'd somehow gained the attention of another man, and my fears were so great. I freaked out when this man tried to talk to me when I was putting the washing out. I ran and hid from him. It was obvious he found me interesting, and I sensed it and feared it.

One day, this man cornered me and asked, 'What's wrong?'

I said, 'Nothing; I have to go into the van.' I was so scared.

As I moved away, he told me, 'Let's just talk?'

'No, I can't.' With that, I ran off. I was so fearful of strange men, and fearful of Javier's reaction if he caught me talking to a man. I was feeling the same fear I'd had if Mum caught me talking to Dad.

# Chapter 49

# Teaching The Boys

When it came time for Julian to start school, I insisted he attend the Catholic School. After giving Javier a list of all the advantages of a private education, it was settled. Julian and Jerod would attend the local Catholic School at Finch Town, so I went there and enrolled him for next year.

Julian seemed to know what he wanted in life. There was one thing he didn't want, and that was to be like his dad. He loved his father; however, when he saw his father's dirty work boots, he'd say, 'I will never wear dirty boots to work like my daddy.' He'd be swinging on the back of the stove barrier, where Javier took off his boots to go to the shower.

Later, I'd put them in the laundry, and I'd say proudly, 'Oh, won't you, Julian.'

'No, I won't,' he'd reply. Julian was also strong around Javier's father, and wouldn't let him boss him around.

The boys and I went shopping on Fridays to stock up the kitchen cupboards, and sometimes, we'd call in to the chemist to get my contraceptive prescription made up. Here, they actually got to experience their first instance in stealing.

We went into the chemist, and I handed in my script, busying myself talking to Connie, who was a good friend of Maxine's. My script was made up and ready for me. After paying for it and both of us saying goodbye, we left the chemist. Putting the boys in the back of the car, I closed their door, and went to the driver's side of the car and got in. I noticed they were remarkably quiet. Looking around at them, they both appeared sheepish, and they were hiding something.

I asked, 'What's up with you pair?'

'Nothing, Mummy,' said Julian, moving his head side to side.

My feelings were getting stronger that something was up: not much passed by me with them. 'Let me look at your hands,' I requested.

Julian's face was a dead giveaway; he was guilty, and his eyes were transfixed.

'Let me see,' I asked.

Julian opened his hands. He was clutching something.

I stretched over the seat. 'What's that in your hands?'

Julian opened his little fist wider and lifted it up to reveal a magnet.

Calmly and softly, I asked, 'Julian, where did you get that from?'

He replied, 'The chemist, Mummy, and Jerod has one too.'

Jerod said, 'Oh, no, I don't,' horrified his brother had put him in.

It was so cute, but I had to act quickly, turning away from them before I laughed. Turning back, I said,

'Okay, boys, we're going back into the chemist to give them back.'

There was no sound out of them; they knew it was wrong to take things.

We went into the chemist, and I went to Connie and said, 'Connie, I'm sorry, but the boys have something to give to you.'

They each handed back the magnets.

'Oh, Chris, it's alright; this happens all the time,' she said.

I looked at her, and waved my hand to say no, without them seeing, and said, 'No; they have to know right from wrong.'

'True. Thank you, boys,' she said.

I never made a big deal out of it, and on the way home, I explained to them, 'You don't steal things; you ask for them. If you get it, you do; if not, you have to learn to accept you're not to have it.' I asked, 'Do you understand?'

'Yes, Mummy,' said Julian. There were no more stealing incidents.

I know they were naughty, and they drove me mad at times, but I loved them, and loved having them. We'd play for hours, doing colouring-in or painting or playing games. Julian liked to get me to set up a tent scene with a sheet in the lounge room, and we'd all get into this tent and pretend we were camping. Sometimes, I'd sit and watch them at play. Julian's imagination was so great, and he'd be telling Jerod a big story about what they were doing in the game and where they were, and Jerod would go along with the game. I often heard him telling his brother what to do, and it was lovely how he gently and patiently got Jerod to follow his objectives. Julian was a good role model for Jerod. Some days, Julian got me to pack them lunches, and he'd take Jerod outside, where they'd pretend they were elephants, and they'd have these small wooden pegs in their mouths and act like elephants, and I'd watch them playing and take photos of them. After their big elephant scene, they'd sit and have their lunches. Jerod copied every move Julian made. He was skinny, and much littler than Julian at the same age. Sometimes, Julian called him Spaceman.

There were times when I was cranky with my sons, and they saw that other side of me more than anyone else did, and that side was not very nice. Most people considered me to be an angel, but deep within, lurked a demon I wasn't even aware of, and never saw through my own eyes. Often, my boys saw that demon, and cried out, 'Mummy, don't look at us like that. You're scaring us,' and they'd huddle together. When this beast rose up in me and glared out through my eyes, it brought terror to the boys. I had control over this aspect of myself, and I could soften my eyes, or push the demon back deep inside me. They weren't the only ones to witness this demon. Javier may have seen it as well, and he kept me well under his control.

I didn't know then, that as a spiritual person, one must enter all facets of the self, and view them and release them. I was suppressing my demon for another day, when it was time for it to show itself, for me to witness it, and accept it as part of me. So, I learnt to live with the demon and my angel self and let them both work through me. Javier knew how to suppress my potential and my power; but worst of all, I allowed it.

# Chapter 50

# Julian Starts School

Julian was five-and-a-half when he started school in February 1976. I missed him; it was no problem having the boys at home. I actually loved my boys being at home.

Finch Town Catholic School was run by nuns. Sister Carlotta really loved Julian, and each time I went to see her, she'd tell me, 'Your Julian is so gentle. He may be a giant of a child, but he's a gentle giant. And some of the boys think they can push him around because of that, but the other day I was watching them, and Julian turned and pushed the boy back, and because he's so big, it was a big push, and the other child stepped back. I was so pleased. And from then on, I've noticed they don't push him,' she told me, like a proud parent, as she lovingly watched Julian. I could see the love she had for Julian emanating from this lovely old nun. Six months later, the nuns had to leave, and the school brought in lay teachers.

Mrs Hopetown became the new Kindergarten teacher. She was amazed at Julian's height and shoe size, because he was in a size one shoe at five-and-a-half years old. After a week, she'd picked up on his special abilities, asking me, 'Chris, do you realise you have a very gifted child?' I did know this, because Julian displayed too many talents, and he was very gifted, because he could write his name and many numbers, and knew his alphabet. Plus, he could dress himself at three, and tie up his own laces. He could pronounce his words perfectly and proficiently. Unfortunately, I didn't fully understand how gifted he was. Julian always did well at school, until the time came where he had to make a choice to be accepted by his peers. It was either continue to excel, or fall back and be in the group, and he decided to let himself fall back, because he wanted to be accepted in the group, so he chose to not excel as much as he had been.

The school picked up many things I didn't notice, and Mrs Hopetown told me that Julian was colour blind. My brother was colour blind, and so were my mother's sister's sons, and my own sister's sons. This was acceptable. What threw me was that they'd found out Julian was totally deaf in his right ear. On hearing that, I freaked out, and all common sense and understanding was beyond me. This news changed my whole attitude towards this beautiful little boy, because of my own ignorance. I felt my child was imperfect, and this had an effect on my behaviour towards Julian. I questioned how I could produce an imperfect child. The perfection thing was an issue with my father; he hated anything imperfect.

I still loved Julian, but I distanced myself from him, and I knew I was not as loving towards him as I should have been. It was not his fault he was born that way, so I took him to a specialist in Dawson Hill. On the day of the specialist visit, it was very windy, and for some unknown reason, Julian was acting up and misbehaving.

When he misbehaved, so did Jerod. In the surgery, Julian was really naughty. The more I asked him to behave, the worse he was, and during his consultation, he was equally as bad. This really got to me, because normally the boys were always good in public. After Dr Thomas inspected Julian's ears, he told me Julian had an inner ear vacuum in the right ear, and there was nothing that could be done for him. He told me Julian had the hearing capabilities of both ears in his one good ear, and that's why we never noticed it. The specialist was right; it had never had any effect on his life. He did say it would affect him in later life in some jobs.

After our consultation, we left the surgery. I was really quietly angry with the boys for being so naughty. I couldn't believe they'd done this to me. It was so windy outside, and with their attitude and them still playing up, as we walked to the car, I let Jerod's hand slip out of mine and let him fly off almost with his light, little body in the strong wind. Julian rushed to him, and they both sang out in the howling wind. I could hear, 'Mummy, Mummy,' but I kept walking. I did stop and looked at them with piercing eyes, returning to them and taking Jerod's hand. From then on, they behaved, and I felt I'd shown them that if you don't behave, I can easily leave you to fend for yourself. After that day, it was a rare thing for them to play up while out, but Julian constantly tested me at home.

Jerod was an unusual child. I think he'd lived on this planet before this lifetime. One morning, I was cuddling into Javier's back, and I could see the boys coming in to our room. I was still tired, and didn't want to get up just yet, so I pretended I was asleep. Then I heard from Jerod,

'Come on, Julian, Mummy's happy Dad's stuck on.' I had to laugh, and peered over the sheets, watching this little boy take his older brother's hand and guide him out of the room. Julian was so innocent, even though he was six-and-a-half. I don't think he had a clue what Jerod meant. I thought, you've been here before, Jerod.

Jerod was always ahead of himself in understanding the body. I used to take them into the bathroom with me while I showered, and I had to stop it, because Jerod was telling Julian, 'Look at Mummy's bush.'

Gently responding to that information from Jerod, I said, 'Okay, boys, you can go and watch TV. And I won't be long.'

Jerod surprised me many times with what he came out with, and I knew he'd been here before. Julian had his recalls between the ages of two to four, but his recalls were on occupations, and these gradually left him.

Many years later, I found out the Scottish name for a woman's pubic hair was bush. I always wanted to call Jerod, Alistair, as his first name, but he got it for his second name. Alistair is a good Scottish name. I feel I knew something without being aware of it.

Julian was having swimming lessons with my neighbour's daughter, Donna, but Jerod didn't want to learn to swim; he still used his floater ring. Javier's work had a picnic day at the Collins Dam. We were on the side of the dam where people could go swimming, and I had both boys in their floater rings. I was in the water, with them playing next to me. They weren't allowed to go in the water on their own, and the water here was too deep for them; it came up to my waist. I was actually kneeling on the bottom next to Jerod, and I turned for a second to have a change of scenery. I heard Julian laughing, and turned back to see what was so funny. Jerod had disappeared out of his ring. I stood up immediately and screamed, 'Jerod! Where's Jerod?' Julian was still laughing, and I thrust my hands into the water and pulled Jerod up. He'd slipped out of his ring. His little face was silent; he was in shock. I threw him over my shoulder and expelled the water from him. He coughed and spluttered, but never cried or said anything. He just cuddled into me and coughed out the water. I cuddled him and soothed him as much as I could, and went mad on Julian for laughing at his brother. He should have told me. Julian looked sheepish, smirked and turned away as if he didn't care.

I went to the shore. No one had come to see what had happened. It was like in a movie when people see a tragedy, and no one responds. I was so shocked by these people's coldness and non-reaction to a child's almost drowning. I was mostly shocked by Javier's non-response. Javier and the other people were so strange. No one seemed to have cared, and no one came to help or enquire. Javier continued his conversation with his friend, Torres. I stood holding Jerod, who was so quiet, I wondered if I had dreamt this. Was I the only witness to this incident? After this incident, Jerod had many problems with water, and it was difficult to bath him. It took time and patience to coax him to overcome his fears. When I took Julian to the swimming pool, I'd slowly get Jerod into the baby pool. Gradually, he overcame his fears, and got his brother to teach him. He watched the other children as well, and both the boys became strong swimmers.

# Chapter 51

# The Neighbours

I liked our neighbours in Hastings Crossing. Mrs Delmore was my neighbour on our left side. She was a nice lady, but I found her a bit nosy. She was always gossiping to me about people I never knew or knew nothing about, and I did not want to get too heavily involved with her. She also had a son Jerod's age and she told me her son, Cody, was really her daughter's son, but she'd adopted him. Cody didn't know that yet. Mr Smallfellow lived on the other side. He worked in the Norton Coalmines, and he was always trying to tell me how to cook and the best products to buy for the house, and he was constantly philosophising about life. He was very friendly with the boys, which I was cautious about. The boys were outside playing in the backyard, and suddenly came into the house with a banana each.

Not thinking, I went to the neighbour and asked him nicely, 'Mr Smallfellow, I am sorry, but could you please not give the boys anything to eat, because I'm trying to teach them not to take anything from strangers, or go with strangers, or take anything from people.'

'Sure, Chris, it's alright. I understand your concern as a parent.'

I felt he did understand. He was always a good, kind neighbour.

After talking to Mr Smallfellow, I had a talk to the boys, explaining why I got them to give back the fruit. I sat on the lounge chair, stood the boys in front of me and said, 'Julian and Jerod, I know Mr Smallfellow is a nice man, but I don't want you to accept things from him, or from any other strangers, and please don't ever go with a stranger.'

Both boys looked at me with 'why' written on their faces. Jerod said, 'Mummy, if I go with a stranger, will he make me clean his toilet?'

I smiled and said, 'Well, he may do, Jerod.' That was enough to help Jerod not go off with a stranger. Jerod had a few more inquiries about being a slave. They both ran off and played happily, and knew why they weren't to talk to any strangers and become slaves. Jerod had really brought back some heavy past life.

My sister started working when Geoffrey was two years old, and I wasn't always allowed to go out with her or spend too much time with her. On occasion, I cared for Geoffrey while she was at work, but I could only do that without Javier knowing it.

Around this time, John re-entered our lives with his new girlfriend, Lois, and her son, Logan. They came and visited us on some weekends from time to time. I didn't mind Lois. She was a quiet person with a big frame, very tall with fair skin and short, brunette hair. She wasn't someone you'd picture John with, because she wasn't what you'd call pretty. This girl was madly in love with John and expressed her love openly by sitting on his knee and cuddling up to him. Her son didn't seem to mind, and he called John Dad. They all had a good rapport, and I was happy for John. He hadn't been able to have that family contact with his own children. Lois also had an older daughter, Jenny, fourteen years old, but she never came to our house or to Dawson Hill, or Javier's mum's house. We met her when we went to Lois's house to visit them. Jenny wasn't as keen on John, and I felt she could see straight through him, and that she didn't trust him at all.

Lois actually had a very nice house in a well-off suburb, and her mother was equally lovely. You could see they were good-hearted, trusting people, and John, with his gift of the gab, had won them all over, except for Jenny. Lois also arranged for me to get my ears pierced on one of our visits there, without Javier's permission. I had hesitated when she suggested it, but she insisted I should get them done, so I did, and they looked good. I don't think Javier approved, but it was too late, and John didn't want to say anything to Lois and unbalance his nest egg.

When Lois came with John to our house, she was too busy with John, and never once helped me to cook. Bianca and Henry decided to get married, so John and Lois came and stayed with us for the weekend of Bianca's wedding. At the wedding, I'd eaten pork, and got food poisoning. It was the most excruciating pain I'd ever experienced, and I felt like someone was putting a knife in my side and turning it. It was as if I was a slave, and I still had to cook, with no one offering to help me. I'd run to my bed, lie down and hold my stomach, rest, and then get back up and go to the kitchen to do some more cooking. It was as if my pain was invisible to others, and no one enquired or sympathized, or noticed I was sick. John, Lois and Javier, and even the children, were oblivious to my situation.

# Chapter 52

# Another Reminder

Javier's younger family members were becoming involved in the occult, and more strange happenings were occurring around us. The word occult terrified me; my fears were so great. I feared so much in life then. There was no one to talk to about these things, and to be honest, I couldn't talk about occult things. I'd scare myself thinking of it.

Bianca's husband's mother was big into séances, and she got Bianca involved in them, who got her sisters, Pia and Gema, interested, and then they got their younger brothers involved as well. I had no idea about séances, and I was so afraid of the unknown, and didn't want to even think about them. Again, I was being forced to face these fears of the other side, like I was as a child in our farmhouse. There was something living down in the two bottom rooms on that farm; on a deeper level, I knew without knowing that one should not interfere in the between-worlds.

I was home alone. Javier had gone to work, and Jerod was asleep. I got a surprise visit from the younger members of the family, which was unusual, because they'd come without their mother. I saw them coming down the pathway. It was too late to rush off and dress. I was still in my dressing gown.

Paco knocked on the back door. 'Chris, are you home?'

I came to the back door and said, 'Wow! Fancy seeing you here. Where's your mum?'

Gema piped up, 'We left her at home, and came to see you.'

Jules and Vince followed, and we all went into the dining room. I offered them coffee. We all joked, giggled and laughed at each other's funny sayings, and it was good to see them on their own. After the coffee and relaxing and joking, Paco suggested we try a séance.

Straight away, I protested, 'No. Don't do that. Not here. You shouldn't tamper with the other side; it's wrong.'

He insisted. 'Get a glass. Come on, Chris.'

My eyes widened. 'No, Paco, and don't joke with me on this matter.'

He got up and got a glass. The others were laughing, and I panicked. They thought it was a big joke, and Paco had a glass out of the cupboard and was laughing. I was pulling him away, and the others started to tease me more.

Jules was saying, 'Come on, Chris, it won't hurt.'

Paco was stronger than me, and I tried to push him away. He pushed me away, and one of them had put some words on the table. He put the glass on the table, upside-down, and he started to chant, asking, 'If anyone is there, please let me know?'

Jules and Gema were holding me back. The glass moved, and I freaked out.

'Stop it,' I sang out, almost crying. I was truly scared and wondered what they could have brought into my house. I had no idea of these things, but on another level, I knew you shouldn't interfere with the other side; it was not safe. They all laughed, but they'd freaked me out.

Paco admitted, 'It's a joke. I moved the glass.'

He hadn't moved the glass, and I think he realised he had made an error doing this, and if Javier knew what they'd done here, there'd be holy hell on. Paco tried to convince me that he moved the glass. We all went quiet, and all the joking ceased. I worried that something had come through, and it could possess us. I knew there was something controlling our house on the farm.

Many things were going wrong for the younger members of the family, who were dabbling in séances, and I started to experience strange events. I was having odd dreams that told me of events that were going to happen. I was spending lots of time on my own, and in this isolation, I was free to think. My mind was the only thing I truly owned and possessed. That was something Javier couldn't take from me, or own or control. He'd often ask me what I was thinking, and I'd tell him I was thinking of nothing. As if doubting me, and seeing something in my eyes, he'd say, 'Tell me, what's going on in that mind of yours?'

Casually, I'd say, 'There's nothing to tell you, and I'm not even thinking of anything.'

He'd become more obsessed and wanted answers. He'd upset me, and I'd retaliate and say that my mind was the only thing he couldn't take from me. I owned it, and I'd tell him: I refuse to give you my mind.

Some days, the feelings of desperation were so great, the unbearable loneliness and sadness, and the pretense

I lived in; I would feel as though I was going to die. It was like my life force was closing down on me. To drink water was difficult, and I suffered feelings of drowning. The house, myself, and my body, were like a prison I couldn't escape, or do anything about. I was trapped in these four walls, and all I could do was shrug it off, and do some work in the house to stop the intense feelings of being trapped. While occupying myself, I could keep my sanity, and with the occupation, the day soon was gone. There were times when things got so bad for me, that when Javier came home, he'd find me in tears. He'd demand that I tell him why I was crying and what was wrong with me, but there were no answers or reasons to give to him, other than I was lonely and sad.

I'd reply, 'Nothing.'

This upset him more, but I couldn't tell him my true feelings. I don't think I really knew why myself. I had never experienced these feelings on the farm, even with all the issues there. I couldn't tell anyone about my pain; it was too much, and so I had to bear it. Stupid thoughts began to enter my head, especially after Paco had placed that glass upside down on my table and moved it. Thoughts of selling my soul were entering my head, and this caused me to battle within with these stupid thoughts, and it was a fight to retain my own sanity.

I was twenty-five years old when these strange events were taking place in my life, and I couldn't understand what was going on. I had a strong fear of life in general. It was lonely, and Javier was working long hours. In one way, it was good to have him away from the house all day and well into the night, because this gave me some sense of freedom from him.

I was sensing death around me and feeling things in the house, and becoming more afraid in my house, especially in the shower. While showering, I couldn't close my eyes. If I did, fear gripped me, and I felt someone was watching me.

'Why am I so afraid?' I began to question.

I'd always waited up for Javier to serve him his dinner when he got in from work. He was always coming home late, around ten or eleven o'clock at night. Sometimes, I'd watch TV, or do some ironing. This night, I'd put my boys to bed, ironed the clothes, and I went into my bedroom to put them away.

I heard my name called: 'Christine.'

I froze. Fear overtook me, and I couldn't move. Gradually, I turned to look around the room, down the hallway, and into the kitchen. Slowly, I went to the kitchen. I checked the back door to make sure it was locked. It was. Fear enveloped me. There were too many strange things happening.

From the age of twenty-five, up until twenty-eight, I was always crying for no reason at all, and I began to hate Javier more and more. That was so strange, because on the farm, I never hated him to the degree I did then. I knew he was different, and he'd never understand me, but this was real hate towards him.

At this time, I was having many dreams, and I didn't understand them. There were two very significant dreams with Jesus. I wasn't a religious person, and never had any religious instruction or upbringing. I'd usually seen God as a scientist, a creator of life, and God, to me, had us all created in laboratories. I saw God as a man creating all of nature and life. Religious things never really interested or entered my mind.

These dreams were so clear, so vivid, and in them I saw myself walking with the *Christ in India*. He was instructing me and pointing out to me various things about the people, and he was giving me knowledge. In those days, I never kept a journal. Those days seemed so dark. In another dream with the *Christ*, I was walking through a tunnel with him that must have been where we go to after death, and in that tunnel, there was this most beautiful music playing. I felt so much peace and serenity.

'Why am I being shown these things?' I questioned. My life was full of questions, and there was no one to answer them. Outside my dreams, life seemed dark and full of hatred, but my dreams took me to places of love and peace. I was torn between two worlds and understood neither.

As time went on, I became more sensitive. The lady next door, Mrs Delmore, had her brother, Samuel, come to live with her. Samuel was a midget. She had never told me she had a brother, and when he came to live with her, she told me he worked in the circus. She told me, without his knowledge, that he drank quite a bit, and if he was drunk, not to worry. He wouldn't hurt me. But he did frighten me, and he bought up fears from my childhood that still lingered within me: fears of drunken people. I couldn't avoid Samuel, because I had to go to our laundry through our kitchen door, and as soon as I was outside, he would appear, and he'd start talking to me. He was creating very uneasy feelings in me, and it got to the point where I didn't want to go outside to the laundry, or into my yard. I had Jerod with me at home; he would cling to me when I spoke to Samuel. I didn't like some of Samuel's topics; his conversations held some sexual innuendo. He seemed drunk all the time, and his speech was very slurred. I tried to avoid him, or if he caught me outside, I'd talk out of politeness, and make an excuse to go inside to get away from him. I could see he had many problems; especially on a medical level with his sinuses, because he snorted. I felt he had tension in the sinus area, and that there was some type of pressure in his head. He'd told me he suffered from headaches, but I was so fearful of him, I didn't know what to do or say. He didn't seem stable, and I sensed it; this caused me to be wary of him.

One night, there was uneasiness around me. For the first time, I was sensing death was near to me, and that there was going to be a death. Our dog Laddie must have also sensed death, because he was howling at the side of the fence that was facing into Mrs Delmore's front yard, which was directly near my bedroom window. I couldn't see a thing, so I just shouted at Laddie to stop howling. He did for a moment but resumed his howling. I peered out of our front bedroom window at Laddie. I could see him looking into the neighbour's yard. I peered into the long grass and couldn't see what he was howling at. I wondered why Mrs Delmore hadn't come out and hushed Laddie herself, because she had done that on other occasions. Javier kept complaining to me about Laddie, and I told Javier I was sensing someone was dying. He stared at me as if I was insane.

I insisted. 'There's going to be a death.'

He looked at me strangely and seemed almost frightened of me. I couldn't understand my own intuition of upcoming deaths or situations back then.

Between me inferring there was going to be a death, and the dog howling, it was all too much for Javier. He ran outside the house and dragged the dog off into the laundry. I lay there waiting for him to return to our bed, thinking: Javier doesn't understand me. The feeling of death intensified.

The next day, I found out Samuel had died. He'd got to the front yard and fell into the very long grass and died. I felt so bad, but I never saw Samuel in the grass; it was so long, and he was so small. He was thirty-four years old. Due to his age, there was an autopsy, which revealed he'd had a brain tumour. Was that the pressure in his head I had picked up on? No one knew he had this tumour. He'd often complained of headaches, and he'd suffered with his sinuses. I felt so bad, realising Samuel must have lived an unbearable life within his tortured body. Due to my fears and my ignorance, I'd probably misinterpreted him. My ignorance caused my fears. This was to be the beginning of the many times I'd sense death.

I was very protective and possessive of Jerod while he was still at home. Sometimes Cody, from next door, wanted to play with Jerod. Both of the boys were four years old and getting on quite well. Often, I was mean, and when Cody called out to Jerod to come and play, I would hold Jerod and say to him, 'Stay with Mummy.' Jerod would stay with me, and we'd pretend we hadn't heard Cody. Other times, I'd let him out and the two boys would play together. Jerod had a lot of really lovely toys, and his toys were only played with inside the house, but Cody wasn't allowed in our house by Mrs Delmore, and Jerod wasn't allowed in his house, because to me they were too young. I wanted to be able to see my child. So, Jerod asked if he could take his robot outside to play with Cody. I agreed to let him take it, and they played down the backyard near a tree behind the garage. They'd been playing for quite a while, and suddenly, I heard a loud scream. I ran outside to the tree where Jerod was, and I saw him crying. I picked him up and comforted him, asking, 'Jerod, what happened?'

Cuddling me, he sobbed, and he turned and pointed to the ground. There was his lovely robot, lying smashed against the tree. He turned and looked at Cody, and said, 'He broke my robot.'

I just patted his back and said, 'Never mind, Je.'

Of course, Mrs Delmore had come to the fence, and she was calling out to Cody to come over to her.

I looked at Cody, and his little freckled, moon face stared up at me. I gently touched his shoulder and said, 'Come, let's go to your mummy. She's calling you.'

He ran off to her, and I picked up the toy, Jerod still cuddling into me. We walked to the fence to see her.

Knowing it wasn't her child's scream, she immediately enquired, 'What's wrong with Jerod?'

I said, 'Jerod's toy robot has been broken, and Jerod said Cody has broken it.'

She looked at Cody, who hadn't said a word, and she questioned him. 'Did you break it?'

'No, I didn't, Mummy.' This little boy was certain he didn't do it.

Jerod just clung to me and said no more.

Mrs Delmore finished the conversation with, 'Well, whoever isn't telling the truth, Jesus will punish him.'

I was shocked to hear such words said to a child. I said, 'No, don't worry, it's okay. It's only a toy.'

But no, she was strong in her convictions that the boy telling a lie would be punished. I put Jerod and the robot down, and lifted Cody over the fence to his mum. They said goodbye, and Jerod and I went inside. I took him to the bathroom and washed his little face and hands. As we played in the water, he rubbed his hands under the running water, and said, 'Mummy, Cody threw my robot on the tree.'

'Did he, Jerod?'

Looking at me, he nodded.

'Are you hungry?'

'Yes, Mummy.' He raised his arms to be lifted up. I swung him from side to side, and he laughed.

Later, Cody developed chickenpox. I had no desire to teach my children about religion, because I had no religious background, and no understanding of religion. Nonetheless, I never used religion as a scare tactic for children. I reasoned that God would not punish children or adults due to them being naughty or doing something wrong.

None of my family ever threatened me with the wrath of God. For me, man was the holder of his own heaven and hell, within the confines of his own deeds. We were responsible for our own misery. I knew that much, because I was doing this to myself in my loneliness. What happened to me was of my own doing, out of my own fear of standing up to those I feared, in case I lost their love.

Nonetheless, I did appreciate the religious education system.

Dad informed us that Star, our last remaining horse, had finally died. All our horses had lived long lifetimes. Now there was only one other life left that connected us to the farm: my Grandma.

# Chapter 53

# Married Life And Its Pressures

By 1978, both of my boys were attending school, and I really missed them. Javier had trained me well, or scared me enough, or maybe a bit of both. Because of this fear, I was a perfectionist in the house. Somehow, this kept me sane. Being busy stopped me from thinking about other things, like the loneliness I constantly felt. Regretfully, there was a downside; it made me into an obsessive cleaner. Javier expected the house to always be clean and immaculate, so this task filled in my days, and it all got done on time. I had no friends of my own age and the boys did make my life easier.

When I got Javier off to work in the morning, I'd go back to bed and wait for my boys' time to get up for school. Mostly I'd get up before them. That extra sleep-in gave me the feeling that all the people in the world had disappeared, and I was the only person left on the planet. That fear made me get up quickly, and I'd have to look out of the window to see if I was the only person in the world. As I looked outside, my breath felt like it was being taken away from me. It was so silent some days, and there weren't many cars on the road.

The boys woke up some mornings before me, and they'd jump into bed with me. We'd have a lovely time playing, cuddling, and we'd laugh. I really loved those moments with the boys; they were so special. Some days, I didn't want them to go to school. I wanted to keep them at home with me. To get them out of bed, I would say, 'The last one out of bed is a fairy princess.' Like little mice, they would scurry out of my bed laughing, point to me and say, 'Mum's the fairy princess.'

Jerod was tiny, and he had his problems when he first went to school. He was a target for the bus conductor, but I soon fixed that, when I found out the reason why he started to not want to go to school, and how the bus conductor was picking on him, and scaring him. I reported the incident to the principal, and she had the bus conductor removed. I must say, the Catholic school never put up with any nonsense when it came to their students. I was also very happy with the Catholic education system. I thought, I had better give some of my time to the school. When I offered to help out somehow, Mrs Armstrong, Julian's teacher, asked me if I could come to the school, and give the children eye exercises. I agreed to, and I ended up listening to the children read. I enjoyed doing those activities.

There was an incident that made me step back into my own past. There was one child I had an uneasy feeling around. He was a shy, thin boy, the tallest in the class. Julian was the second tallest, as well as having the biggest build.

This boy reminded me of my own abuse as a child. I had to face the fact that this lay dormant within me. I was sensing that this child may have been a victim of abuse too. Do those who have been abused sense another who is being abused? Was I sensitive to others who were suffering abuse? I couldn't ask the child if he was okay, and how would I tell the teachers that I was picking this up? This was a dilemma, and no one spoke of such things back then.

I continued doing the eye exercises and the book reading and closed my feelings down around the children. I didn't want to pick up on some of the children's fears.

I had a go on the tuck-shop, but I was never any good at that. I felt I didn't fit in with the other mothers; I felt inferior to them, preferring to help the students. I remained helping out at the school until both the boys went on to the higher classes at the third-class level, and they were transferred to Hastings Crossing Catholic School.

The Catholic education system was a good system, but my boys had to go to Mass. I'd had them both Christened in the Church of England, because I'd wanted them to go to a grammar school, but that was too far away in Dawson Hill, so the next best option was the Catholic school in our home town.

As they moved through the Catholic School system, we were advised to Christen the boys Catholics. To me, the church was not the issue, a good education was. Going to Mass was an ordeal for the boys, but it was an even harder ordeal for me, not having come from a religious background, or from a family that attended church. I took them to church so they wouldn't get into trouble from the older parish priest, Father Shamus. The boys really loved the younger priest, Father Liam, who was very modern and understanding that the boys sometimes didn't want to go to Mass.

My time with the boys was so precious, and I loved school holidays, even though Julian was a torment. Some days, he had me a nervous wreck, but I still loved him, and loved having them at home with me. I was very child-like myself, and I felt like a child with them. We'd all play games together. I was a torment as much as Julian, and I loved to scare them, not with inventing creatures, but by sneaking up on them and saying boo. I didn't like it if other people tormented them. I hated anyone else scaring them with creatures, such as the Bogeyman, and for my sons to form beliefs around a figure that could get you. If anyone brought up the Bogeyman, I'd jump on them and tell them not to do it, and not to scare my boys.

Living with a big family, it's hard to stop such behaviour from others. Javier's family often scared the boys, telling them that Coco would get them if they ventured out into the dark. They were getting older, so I just reasoned with them, telling them there was no such thing, and it was just used to scare them.

I think the boys loved me being able to play with them, and we had a good rapport, even though I was the biggest torment. As Julian got older, the things I was seeing in him were too close to my own traits, and this was why I found Julian the most irritating of my children. He was so much like me, and he was making me look within myself. At that time, I didn't know about such things as mirroring and reflecting.

The movie 'Planet of the Apes' was popular, and the boys had masks of the apes. I was in one of my devilish moods, and I went outside the dining room window where I'd left them, standing with the intent to scare them. I can still remember Jerod's face as he screamed and shivered, grabbing Julian for protection. Julian was laughing. But seeing his fear and how frightened he was, I pulled the mask off and rushed into the house. I had to calm him down, saying, 'It's me, Je.' Julian wasn't one bit frightened like Jerod was.

In spite of my playing and fooling around with the boys, I also had a serious side. At times, I was so mischievous, and other times, so serious, like I had someone else locked up inside, wanting to escape.

When Julian was seven, we'd taken him to Timothy, a reputable and well-known guitarist in our town, to teach Julian the guitar. Unfortunately, we had to stop the lessons after a couple of weeks, because Timothy told us Julian was too shy to teach, and to wait for another year.

That time came around, and this time he was ready, which brought through his amazing skills as a guitar player. At first, he learnt the electric guitar; Timothy had advised us it's better for young ones to start with the more fashionable music. He learnt very quickly. It was amazing; he only had to play the piece once or twice, and then he knew it.

Later on, we bought Julian a Spanish guitar. He learnt to play Spanish Flamenco music, and he was excellent at it. Practicing was his problem; I had to insist he practice.

During the winter period, my boys both joined the junior football club. We owned a four-wheel drive, and all these activities not only gave my boys an outlet, but me too. I became very busy taking them and their team mates to their training sessions. My new job was to go around the streets, picking up all the neighbour's children, piling them in the four-wheel drive with my boys, and we'd all head down to the football oval. Sometimes I'd sit in the car and watch them practice, or I'd drop them off, going home to prepare dinner. It all depended on Javier, if he was coming home early or late; or if I'd got in early that day and cooked dinner for later on.

I was starting to feel comfortable around people, and it was good to see other people, and to chat. I was still painfully shy, but gradually, by just standing around people, I became at ease with them. Later on, Javier made friends with Carol and Butch. I'd go and sit in their car with Carol, as we watched the boys playing. Carol must have felt safe around me or sensed she could open up to me. I didn't know who I was, and what I possessed within me. As far as knowledge was concerned, I had none. It wasn't general knowledge I possessed; it was knowledge and understanding of life.

One time, Carol was restless as we sat in the car. She seemed as if she wanted to say something, and she wasn't too sure how to start it off. Then she blurted out, 'Chris, I have to ask you something, and I feel you will understand.'

I said with caution, 'Yes, what is it?'

She looked around to see no one was in ear shot. 'Our son, Oscar, well...'

Her hesitation induced me to say, 'Yes, your littlest one.'

'Yes. He's three, you know.'

I smiled. 'I know.'

'Well, he said something strange to Butch and I the other night.' Again, she looked around.

I became intrigued and moved in closer to her, more interested in her every word. 'What did he say?'

Puzzled, she said, 'This may seem strange to you, but somehow I don't think it will.' She searched my eyes for clues. 'Oscar looked at his father and said, "You know who I am. I am your best mate, Glen. I died in Vietnam right next to you."'

As if a burden was lifted from her, we both paused. 'Wow, he's had a past life recall and he remembers,' I informed her.

'Chris, we've never talked about the war in Vietnam, so he couldn't have heard it from us. Butch never talks about his experiences in that war, and we're going mad from his comments.' She looked at me for clarification, as if I had the answers, and she asked, 'Do you believe, Chris, he was with Butch?'

Without hesitation I said, 'Yes, I do. He probably was with him that very day. However, don't worry; it will leave him as he gets older. The only thing is, it will bring up memories for Butch, and this will be hard on him.'

At that time, I had no idea how to handle such experiences, but I believed in past lives, and I knew they happened. Carol and Butch weren't the only family I was to meet who experienced the unknown; Trudy's family understood as well, especially her mum. For some reason, I was being exposed to these unusual events, and meeting lots of like-minded people who'd had unusual experiences. Trudy was fifteen, and we got on really well. Her brother, Andrew, who was Julian's age, was playing in the same football team as Julian. She'd come and sit with me during the game, and we'd talk. After a while, she introduced me to her parents, Janice and Morton. I was a bit fearful of what Trudy was expressing to me.

One day she asked me, 'Chris, do you believe in entities?'

Not knowing the names of things then, I asked, 'What are those?'

'You know: ghosts.'

I became tense and said, 'Yes, but I don't want to meet any.'

She laughed. 'Well, we have them in our house.'

Wide-eyed, I said, 'Really?'

'Yes. Some mornings, the books are all pulled off the bookcase shelves.'

I froze there and then.

'Do you want to see?' she asked me.

'No, Trudy, I don't want to see such things.'

She could tell I was scared and changed the subject.

Why are people dragging me into these experiences, I questioned.

We went to their house once or twice, and while there, I was very wary. As soon as I saw the bookcase, I wondered, but quickly dismissed it.

Many strange things were occurring. With the boys at school, I was more alone in the house. While sitting in the lounge room one day, a strange feeling came over me, as if I was not myself, and I began to rock within. It was not my physical body rocking, but a part of me from within, another part of me I never knew about, and it was as if this part of me wanted to get out and escape. I enjoyed the rocking feeling; it was so relaxing, but it was getting stronger and stronger. Fear grasped me; I froze and stopped it. I don't know how I knew, but I knew I couldn't leave my body, because if I did, something else - I don't know what or where from, but something else - would enter my body, and take it over. It was as if I'd experienced these experiences before in other lifetimes. This phenomenon happened to me a few times while I was in bed. I had to control it, and I did; it stopped. In my late forties, I would find out about astral travelling; I may have been on the edge of that experience. There were many unbearable times in my life, and I was so depressed. I seemed to go in and out of moods, and the loneliness was too much. I had no one to talk to or confide in about what was happening to me, and if I did, how far could I go with them? I was in so much fear of the unknown. I couldn't tell anyone about my thoughts and these strange experiences, not even Trudy, because I also had issues around trusting people.

A dream came to me of my sister and her family: Collin, Alex and Geoffrey. They were travelling in a four-wheel drive, and the dream was like a negative film. Suddenly, their vehicle rolled down an embankment. I woke up in a start. Weeks later, while out on a camping trip, on their return home they were in an accident, and they rolled their four-wheel drive over an embankment. Alex suffered the most; he had broken glass lodged in his back, and he had to have a few minor operations to remove the glass.

While I was out shopping for our weekly food, I was in the Morefood supermarket at Hastings Crossing, our very small community. I was at the delicatessen counter waiting to be served, and my attention was diverted to the people further along this counter. To my right,

I saw a girl standing, looking exactly like me. I looked at her and she was so solemn, like me. It can't be me, I thought, and I wanted to go over to her, but I couldn't move, and then I was served. My attention was taken away, and after I was served, I looked back over to my right, and she was gone.

Was I looking into a parallel world? In 1997, I would see that very same girl again, but this time in my house as I was reading.

So I ask myself, what is the truth of life? And I ask you, the reader, the same question.

# Chapter 54

# Financial Freedom

Fears seemed to restrain me. Or were they the fears of others? In time, I will discover life is a tangled web we each weave through the beliefs of ours, from others' beliefs of us. The mystery is to untangle ourselves from this web, and free the self from it.

All my life, I had seemed to be the victim of abusive people. Was it because I had been so abused from a very young age? I didn't know or understand the extent of this abuse: because, as children, we are so reliant on our role models and caretakers, they couldn't possibly be doing anything wrong to us, and what they said and did was right.

I was faced with feeling abused again, even sexually, because I felt no warmth from Javier during his lovemaking. He demanded sex, even if I wasn't in the mood. He overrode me, and he didn't respect my choice to say no. As a child, I was abused, and I'd drawn that in with this man I married. What could I do? I had my two boys. I had no education to assure me a good job to provide for them. That was my goal: to make sure they never suffered as I did, and to give them a good start in life.

Firstly, by providing them with love, and a safe environment; and a mother who would listen to them, play with them, and be able to step out of her adult role to join her children in their age group; to always remember how I felt at their ages, and to not do the same things to them, as was done to me. Guidance and a good education; that was all I could do.

My body was going through a lot of changes: the hair on my face had been darkening; I was taken off the hormonal pill I'd been on since giving birth to Jerod. I was placed on a non-hormonal pill; I'd lost a stone in weight, and my body shape was good, but I developed skin pigmentations, and I was getting too thin. The new gynaecologist, Dr Phillips, was an easygoing man, and he was willing to do things for you that many doctors wouldn't. I wanted to get my tubes cut and tied. He agreed that it was the woman's right. Javier wanted me off the pill, and he wouldn't have a vasectomy, so I decided to go ahead.

Dr Phillips was very understanding, but he asked me if I was certain I wanted this. I told him I didn't want any more children, and I was ready. On the day of the operation, the anaesthetist had given me a dose of anaesthetic, but I was still wide awake. I panicked and told him not to let the doctor start yet, because I was not asleep. He gave me another shot.

I woke as my sons approached my bed. I sat up.

A lady I'd befriended before my operation, looked shocked when I looked over at her as she said, 'I thought you were dead.'

I smiled at her and asked, 'Why did you think I was dead?'

'Do you know the time?'

'No,' I said.

'It's 7.30pm, and you went down at 4.30pm. I was told they couldn't wake you in recovery.'

I smiled, but it didn't sink in. I was just happy to see my family. When they left, I was violently ill for the rest of the night. I was up until 4am vomiting up bile. I must have had too much anaesthetic.

I needed an outlet now the boys weren't at home, so I started to go around my neighbourhood to visit the old people. Our street was full of old people. They brought me a lot of comfort, and in return, I did likewise for them, by chatting and keeping them company. I was still unhappy deep down, and unable to rid myself of it. It was so hard not to show my true feelings around my boys.

In late 1978, Karel, Javier's work companion for the past five years, died in a car accident. Javier was really devastated, causing him to quit working in the construction industry. I used to get annoyed with Karel, because he and Javier always went drinking to the pub after work. I was sad when he died. Many times, I was so angry with Javier because he had upset me, and I'd wished for Javier to die in an accident at work by falling off a building. Karel died instead, going to work alone without Javier. Javier had been away in Chester Hills when the accident occurred. He'd died instantly on his way to Dawson Hill. I had never seen Javier so sad and upset. This was the first and only time I'd seen him cry over someone's death. Javier had been working for various construction companies since we got married, and he was always chasing the best money.

I had tried to get Javier to form his own construction company with Karel, but Javier told me Karel was too scared. He said he'd never take a risk, so Javier always blamed Karel for them not forming their own business. Javier would say Karel had to hear the money jingle, or he'd not accept it as money, meaning he wouldn't ever accept a cheque, or trust a cheque. He would only work for cash, and Javier didn't want a business if Karel wasn't in it with him.

Not long after Karel's death, Maxine's husband suffered a loss. It was his older sister, Sophie. She was only twenty-seven and left three children under the age of ten. Maxine and Collin wanted to care for the children. Sophie's husband took them to his mother and father to be reared. This was a tragic time for Collin. He started to drink more, and he'd go away on more camping trips. Both my sister and I were left alone for longer periods of time by our spouses, but now I had my husband back, it wasn't always good.

Javier applied for a job at the foundry in our home town. The death of Karel changed his mind on travelling to Dawson Hill for work. He left the job at Chester Hills; he said it was all too much, and he needed a change. He was accepted by the foundry and started work there just before December. I noticed changes in our lives; it was a good change. He was now away from construction companies, and he didn't have to work long hours, or go away to another town to work. It changed him. He seemed happier to be with us at home, but it had its disadvantages. He was a shift worker and wasn't used to shift work. It meant he was at home more often, and he started to really torment me, and put me down in front of our boys, and virtually tried to make out I was mad.

The job at Harper's Foundry proved to be a good move financially. Javier got a personal loan from the company's credit union. We'd bought our house for ten thousand, seven hundred and seventy dollars in 1973; now the prices of houses were skyrocketing. They were triple the price we'd paid a few years before. Most people were getting personal loans for ten thousand dollars for a car, so we reasoned we should cut our twenty-five year mortgage to a four year personal loan timeframe. At the end of the four years, we would have paid off our house in nine years, and it would be ours. Financially, we were very lucky. We were like my parents, living rent-free; but the difference was we owned this house.

Because we were more financially sound, I could buy good quality clothes for us all. I shopped in boutiques for myself. Earlier in our marriage, I went without, but slow and steady wins the race. I really liked those old, wonderful phrases of encouragement, and me being a practical person paid off. I'm not a person who likes to hoard a lot of clothes, and I'm not a shopper. Actually, I disliked shopping, and I only bought what I needed. My mother made up for what I lacked in the shopping department, because she was a shopaholic, and she had wardrobes of new clothes. I'm not exaggerating when I say she had at least one hundreds pairs of shoes. Funny, though, she never wore them, or the new things she bought. What she did was choose one item and one pair of shoes from her massive wardrobes, and then she'd wear those items until they virtually died on her back.

# Chapter 55

# Awakening In Me

John and Lois lost a baby about six months after they got married. John began to show his angry side. Being domesticated got too much for him. I heard he had belted into Lois. Of course, her family protected her, ousting John, so he was back in town. He wasn't having any influence on us. John came and went, and no one questioned his whereabouts. Sometimes we'd see him at his mother's place, and other times we never saw him. Javier was settling into his new job at Harper's Foundry, and he met an old friend of my brother's and of my own family.

Lenny; Lenny used to come out to our farm to play with Barton, and all my family liked Lenny. We formed a new friendship with him and his wife, Celia. I liked them, and I was pleased to have Len around me again. Often, Len had us over to their house, because he loved to cook Chinese food, so it was a nice treat having them as friends. Knowing my parents, Len was like family; but one day at their house, Javier started running my family down as much as he possibly could, referring to my parents as the lowest of the low.

Standing up, I said, 'You can say all you like and criticise my family, Javier, as much as you like, but you will never make me hate them or stop me loving them.'

Everyone went silent, bowing their heads. Len knew my family well, and I guess he couldn't say anything in their defence. It must have been hard for him to listen to Javier, because often Len looked at me and lowered his head. I knew he actually liked my family.

Len and Celia were both in an awkward position, and it wasn't the place to air family matters, but Javier never had a kind word to say about my family.

The more I reacted to his torments, the happier he was, and I was so stupid to have reacted. I tried not to, but it got the better of me. I couldn't control it, and I had to lash out to say it was not true, in defence of me and my family. He delighted in the emotional games, and I was a good fish, taking the bait every time. I'd ask him, why are you doing this to me, why? He'd niggle me, hoping to score a laugh, but I did the opposite, flying at him in a rage, screaming and trying to defend myself or my family. He'd become upset with me, and it usually backfired on him. He'd be the one ending up angry, and then the bastard would turn the tables on me, accusing me of starting all the arguments. This was always done in front of our sons. He'd walk away from me and wouldn't talk to me for days. We'd have to live in silence, and the silent treatment was torture. It was a matter of waiting for one of our families to visit us to break the ice.

I hated his family coming all the time, but after one of these sessions, I appreciated them. Javier was so nice to everybody's face, with his sickly, evil smile and syrupy voice that had a definite undertow of malice and hatred, back then I didn't understand, this was what was happening in my own family between Mum, Dad and Grandma.

Strange things were coming out of me, and strange behaviours were surfacing from within me; I didn't know who, or what, I was. There was a time I was growling silently from within, making the facial gestures of an animal that was trapped, and this animal felt like a werewolf. I wanted to rip Javier's throat out, and I would have felt nothing in doing that. He sensed or heard nothing of this deep, primordial being trapped within me; it growled in silence. Somehow, that animal never scared me; I accepted it fully as part of me.

I was in the kitchen washing up, and the boys were outside playing. Javier came into the kitchen from outside. I turned and looked at him as he wiped his feet on a towel I kept at the door. I saw something in his face I didn't like, and he sneered at me and walked off. I cracked, dropping the dishes and, picking up a tea towel, wiped my hands and said, 'Javier.'

Turning, he said, 'Yeah, what?'

'Javier, I can't take this anymore. I want a divorce.' The words flowed comfortably from my mouth. I felt another stronger part of me express this, as I stood at the kitchen bench staring at him.

He looked at me dumbfounded. He didn't know what to say.

Again, I said, 'I want a divorce. I want to leave you and not be with you, and I will take the boys away with me.' As I spoke those words, I heard a scream of pain and stress. I rushed passed Javier, who was in shock.

Jerod was on the settee, screaming and throwing his head up against the back of it, crying out, 'No, no, Mummy, no.'

I cuddled him. 'Okay, Jerod, it's alright. Mummy won't go, and we'll stay.'

The child pushed me away and screamed uncontrollably, staring at me with fearful eyes, as if terror had entered his life. It took us a long time to calm him down. Eventually I could cuddle him. I decided I would stay until they were educated. Jerod clung to me and sobbed. Javier just stared at me, and, for once, I showed my own suppressed power: I showed him that he didn't totally scare me. I glared back at Javier as I held my child, who feared family separation more than all of us. Jerod must have come back into the house and I hadn't noticed him. He was probably in his room when I was telling Javier of my plans and heard me and went to pieces. If Jerod hadn't heard me, I could have gradually got the boys used to the idea and drummed up my own courage to leave Javier.

Later on that day, when the boys were out of earshot, I approached Javier and informed him, 'I will leave you when the boys are educated.'

He never answered me or raised his hand or commented, and, for the first time, I think he saw another side of me. He stood there staring at me in disbelief, and I saw Javier in his true light; he was an insecure and weak man. He also had a power within that I couldn't work out. It wasn't a power of good intent. I still didn't trust him, and I felt this person could snap and maybe hurt me.

As time went on, he joked about it, thinking I'd never leave him. Javier thought of me as basically a weak person, but he wasn't too sure. Javier was the type of person who quickly forgot things. I felt like a weak person around him and felt like my whole life had been stripped from me.

# Chapter 56

# I Am So Sensitive

Lorna and Barton had three children, their last baby a girl born in 1978 called Sarah. She was the only girl in our family, because we'd all had boys. Lorna was not the cleanest mum with her kids, and Barton didn't say anything to her about cleaning up the kids. Often, the children were so sticky you couldn't touch them, and this was terrible for us all, except my mum. She would pick them up, but complain to us later when they were not around. This stopped me from cuddling my niece and nephews, with their filled nappies or grubby faces and runny noses. It was so hard with my obsessions around cleanliness. This isolated the children and their mother from the rest of the family. I wasn't the only one affected. Lorna seemed to me to not display love towards her kids. She'd often scream at them, glaring at them more often than she talked to them. I also screamed at my boys, but loved them and cared for them in-between. There was no excuse, only ignorance on my part; it was my fear of germs that prevented me just loving them and washing myself later on. I should have known better, and not neglected my own niece and nephews, especially with me being misunderstood as a child and having to live with my own isolation.

Even though life dished out some not too successful times for Barton, he possessed one thing I seemed to lack: a generous heart. Not to his betterment, more to his detriment. My brother had a heart bigger than the universe; he was like an angel under all his bad luck and misery. He could always help others in their time of need, regardless of his own needs. His house was always full of down-and-out people. He fed them, helped them and their families until they could get on their own feet, but his own house was not so clean. Barton seemed to always have sores on his neck from constantly scratching himself, and his skin looked unclean. His friends looked the same, and they all seemed like riff-raff, but they weren't when you talked to them. Poverty and hard luck was what was in front of them, but they all seemed to be happy in their own lack; whereas me, in my clinically clean house, I lived in misery.

I felt young people needed good, understanding parents, and from those parents they needed to receive love, guidance, and most importantly, acceptance of who they were. As children grow up, they need that older adult role model for their security and safety. Good sound support must be given, as well as understanding, with an adequate education, to live in a happy environment. I felt children should feel safe to approach either of their parents, without fear of reprisal, and know they would be helped, and not shunned. Parents are leaders and role models of the future people of our nations.

I felt we didn't receive proper guidance as children. We all lacked in some way, due to poor guidance. I saw that there had to be change in my immediate family, and I wanted to do things differently. My determination and drive helped me to succeed in making these changes. I didn't realise to what extent I had that determination and ambition, but things changed. To change the familiar, first we have to learn about patterns; that is where we often find the familiar. Many of us will never even know we are following familiar patterns, behaviours and habits, passed down through the family.

Only awareness can tell us we are playing out the familiar. I was aware enough to know that how I was reared wasn't right.

Parents can be so destructive, especially mothers, because the mother's love is detrimental to the child, and her encouragement and support is crucial to the child's well-being.

My brother suffered greatly as a child, and I witnessed undue cruelty being dished out to him. Firstly, in his body, from birth to twelve months, he'd been trapped in a body through eczema. Later, through Dad's hatred of him, his life would be greatly affected, and it would affect me unconsciously, so much so that I was unaware how much it did affect me until late in my fifties.

# Chapter 57

# The Shotgun

L en and Celia were often coming to visit us, or we'd go to their house. Len was a nervous type of guy, always moving around; even when he sat in his seat, he couldn't sit still. I liked Len, and especially Celia, who was close to my age. Celia was a very homey type of girl with a warm heart; she never seemed to run anyone down. She only questioned her father's impatience with her. Celia was the complete opposite to Len. He was always on the move, and she was always sitting, and she seemed to have the patience of Job - as my Grandma would say of people who were quiet and easygoing, and never got their feathers ruffled. Although they were like chalk and cheese, you could see they loved each other. They lived in Denver Shire, about a twenty minute run in the car from our house.

Suddenly, they stopped visiting us, and they seemed to have disappeared. I never questioned it, and thought they'd had enough of us or were busy, so I shrugged it off; realising people come and go in your life. As suddenly as they'd disappeared, they reappeared out the front of our house after a long break. They came around the back door, and I ran out to greet them. Len asked me if Javier was home; I told him he was. I was so happy to see Celia again.

It was a strange day when this happened, not long after I'd told Javier I was leaving him. I ran back to the kitchen door, singing out to Javier to come and see Len and Celia. He sheepishly came to the door. Len asked him if he would go with him to the pub. Len seemed in a hurry, and Javier nodded. He went inside and changed. I asked them both to come in. Celia went into the house, but Len wouldn't come in. He seemed too anxious to get Javier out of the house and go to the pub. Javier came out dressed, and they went off.

I didn't think anything of the incident. Celia sat at the dining room table. I made us coffee and we talked. Celia said nothing as to why Len was behaving as he was. About three hours later, Javier and Len returned to the house. Javier was very drunk, and not in a sound mind.

Len told Celia, in a very sharp voice, but not to her in particular, 'We're going now.'

They left with no real goodbyes. I was startled by Len's unusual behaviour. We always saw our guests off at the front gate. I looked at Javier. I wasn't feeling safe; I could see Javier was in a strange mood. The boys were off playing with their cousins. The more I looked at Javier, the more his mind seemed to be twisted. I avoided his eyes, and to divert from him, I told him I had to go to the toilet. As I walked out of the kitchen and into the hallway, I felt him staring at me with ice-cold eyes. Moving up the hallway, he was behind me. I turned to see why he was following me. His eyes were glaring hard at me, as if I'd committed some mortal sin.

For the very first time, I felt terror with my husband. Was he going to bash me? I'd always feared being bashed to a pulp. He grabbed me without speaking and threw me up against the wall in the toilet, holding me at my throat, and he was pushing me into the corner of the toilet, cursing me and accusing me of sleeping around with other men.

I begged him to stop, protesting, 'Javier, that's not true, what are you saying, and why are you acting this way?'

His grip got so tight that I was struggling to get away. He must have come to his senses, releasing his grip on my throat.

I held my throat and coughed. 'Why are you saying these things? You know it's not true.'

He backed out of the toilet into the hallway. I moved out of the confined area of the toilet. We were both in the hallway, facing each other, which sparked him off. He grabbed my throat again, shook me, and threw me flat on my back, inches away from the tiled kitchen floor. I'd landed on the hallway carpet, in shock and confused. My mother and sister appeared at the back door.

They'd seen him throw me down, and they ran to my assistance.

Maxine screamed out, 'What are you doing to my sister?'

Mum was picking me up off the floor. Maxine helped to lift me up. Javier didn't answer, and walked off to the bedroom, slamming the door shut.

'Chris, are you alright? Has that bastard been hitting you?' questioned Maxine.

'No. I don't know what happened. He's not long come back from the pub with Len, and he just acted strange. I'm alright.'

Maxine and Mum looked at each other, and Mum asked, as she stared up from under me, watching my eyes, 'Has he done this before to you?'

'No, never. He's got drunk before and never been abusive to me, but this time he got angry for some unknown reason.'

Maxine warned me, 'If that bastard touches you, you tell me and he'll pay.'

I said, 'Don't worry, he won't do it again. He's probably had too much to drink this time. It will be alright.'

Mum made us a cup of tea.

Maxine and I talked. 'Chris, are you sure you're safe here? Are you telling me the truth? Has he done this before?'

I was in shock but reassured her he'd never done this ever before. Javier had surprised me; I didn't think he would do such a thing.

Her words still rang in my head as Mum placed a cup of tea on the table in front of me. I said, 'No, he's never physically hurt me,' it was as if I was consoling myself.

We had our tea and chatted.

Maxine was so irritated and said, 'I am glad we came here, Mum.' Mum nodded, as if to agree, and Maxine continued. 'I said to Mum, let's go and surprise Chris.'

I smiled. 'I'm glad you came to see me, and I am sorry for what you saw, but it's not usually Javier's behaviour.'

They looked at each other and Maxine said, 'If Collin ever laid a hand on me, he'd pay for it.'

'It's okay,' I told them about Len and Celia leaving in a hurry and speculated that maybe Javier and Len had had an argument.

Maxine smirked. 'I don't blame Len, and Javier is so thick…'

I said, 'Shh!' putting my fingers to my lips. 'He might hear you.'

'Well, he is. No one can speak their mind or give their opinions around him, and he's the only one that's right, and what he says, goes. I don't know how you stand him, Chris. Half an hour with Javier is all I can tolerate.'

Quickly, I whispered, 'He's not that bad.'

She sniggered. 'He is, Chris.' She raised her eyebrows.

I knew she was right, but I had to stay because of Jerod. I didn't want him to ever be that hysterical again. What could I do? I could only wait it all out.

The evening was well upon us. All four boys were standing at our front gate, returning from their day out. Julian was opening the gate and letting them through. The boys rode their bikes up the driveway and around to our back door.

I got up as I heard Alex ask, 'Aunty Chris? Is Mum there?'

'Yes, Alex, she's here.'

My boys were putting their bikes in the garage. Mum and Maxine came to the kitchen window.

Her children smiled and asked, 'Mum, are you coming home now?'

'Yes, I'm coming now,' she replied.

The boys talked amongst themselves outside, and I asked Maxine and Mum not to say anything to my boys about what had happened. They agreed, but I had to agree to tell Maxine if I was in any trouble.

As we all walked to our front gate to see them off, Maxine asked one more time, 'We are going now, Chris. Are you sure you're alright?'

'Yes, don't worry. I don't know what happened, but it will be alright.'

The boys were in a buzz from their day's outing, and hungry at the same time. My sister glanced at me as she and Mum walked off with her two boys. I smiled back and listened to my boys as they talked about their day's adventures.

'Shh! Dad's sleeping,' I said, so they lowered their voices. I cuddled them both as we walked back into the house. I got them to go and bathe, and I prepared our dinner. I dreaded Javier getting up, and hoped he'd sleep it off until tomorrow. I knew tomorrow he'd be all apologies.

About 8.30pm, I put the boys to bed. I watched TV, dreading going to the bedroom as it approached midnight. I tiptoed into our room, and he woke as I sat on the bed's edge to slip in between the sheets. Suddenly, he became deranged again, and verbally attacked me and accused me of having many men in my life.

I said, 'I have no one, only you,' and I knew no other men to have other men in my life. 'I'm not interested in other men, Javier, you know that. I'd never play up on you.'

I tried to reason with him as I got up off the bed and stood over near the window. He sat up on his haunches, moved towards me and pushed me towards the bedroom door. I got scared. He was in a stupor. Then he did the unthinkable. He reached up onto our wardrobe, grabbed his father's double-barreled shotgun, took it out of the case and pointed the barrel at me.

I ran from the bedroom, not looking behind me. I ran to the front door and he was behind me. I flew out of the house and up the side passage on my neighbour Mrs

Delmore's side. He was behind me. I'd never known Javier to be violent, but now he was, I did not know where to go. I was scared for my life. I looked behind me, and he was drawing the gun up to his face slowly, pointing it at me, aiming, and next I felt myself hurdle the four-foot fence. I ran barefooted into the neighbour's property. At her back door, which was open, I ran in, looking behind me.

I heard, 'Chris?'

Dazed and in shock, I looked at her and the back door. I couldn't speak.

'Chris! Chris! What's wrong?' She came in closer to me.

I turned, dazed at the voice. I was bewildered and stared at her, saying, 'I can't believe what's just happened.' I paced in her kitchen, and she tried to calm me down and got me to talk. Reality hit me, and I said in a frightened voice, 'My children. Mrs Delmore, Javier's just tried to shoot me. I am worried for my boys.'

'That bastard, I knew he was no good.'

I couldn't answer. 'Mrs Delmore, my children.'

She reassured me. 'They will be alright, Chris, he won't hurt your boys; he loves them too much.'

I was ashamed for running out of the house and leaving them. I asked her again, 'Mrs Delmore, my boys, will he hurt them?'

'No, Chris.'

Cody entered the room. I heard her tell him to go back to bed.

'What's wrong?' His little face was distorted with worry, but she ushered him to his room. He refused to go, pulling away from her. She returned and calmed me. For the first time, I started to feel the cold of the night. I only had on a thin nightie, no shoes on my feet.

I heard her talking to Cody. I was incoherent. Cody was seven, a few months older than Jerod. I heard her voice.

'Chris, come and sit down.'

I can't sit down, I thought, as I gathered my senses as to where I was. I was so fearful of germs, and for my boys. I knew I must return to the house. I heard her telling Cody to go and get me a coat, because I'd begun to shiver. I quickly said, 'No, I am alright. I don't want a coat.' I was still aware Mrs Delmore's house wasn't clean. I diverted my eyes to the room, and saw their house was dirty. I couldn't sit; my phobia with germs prevented me.

Again, I asked her about my boys, and again, she reassured me. I looked through her lounge room window over to my house and into Jerod's bedroom, but I couldn't see a thing, because the window was well-covered with curtains. She witnessed my distress, repeated my need for reassurance, and said, 'Come and sit.' I had to eventually succumb to sitting, and when I did, I relaxed with her. I looked down at myself and clasped my hands, staring into my nightie. I must have been in shock.

I calmed down. She patiently waited for me to talk.

I said, 'I can't understand what I've done to Javier to cause this outburst.'

'Chris, what happened?' I told her of the night's terrible events.

She nodded, and then asked, 'Is he very drunk?'

'Yes.' I nodded, ashamed, and then stated, 'But no, no more than usual, and he's been drunk before, and he's never acted like this.'

Telling her my story had made me feel better, and I could look her in the face. She was so old-looking, older then her age. She had also lived with a husband that drank. You could tell by looking around her house, and at her prematurely aged body, life hadn't been kind or easy for her. I came to my senses more and more and added to my description of events.

She asked, 'Do you want to call the police and press charges?'

My eyes widened in horror. 'No! Please don't do that. Javier won't do this again. Something has triggered him. It's not him to do this. No, please, no police.'

She could see my fears. 'Alright, but if I hear you upset or screaming out, I'll call the police.'

I nodded and let it go. 'Mrs Delmore, I have to go back into the house.' My mind had carried me back to my boys. 'Mrs Delmore, I must go.'

'Will he be asleep by now?'

'Yes, he should be.' I thanked Mrs. Delmore, and apologised for involving her.

She said, 'If he ever lays a hand on you, call me, and I'll call the police next time.'

'He won't do it again. I don't know why he did it this time. I can't understand why.' I thanked her again, walked down her front steps to her footpath, across my front footpath, and to our front gate. Gently, I opened the gate and stepped onto our driveway. I headed for the back door and went into the laundry, where a spare key was kept. I quietly opened the back door and sneaked into the house.

It was in darkness, and I reasoned he must have gone back to bed and fallen into a deep sleep. There was no way I could go to our bedroom. I checked the boys. They were sleeping, and all was quiet. I went into Jerod's room and crawled under his bed, near the window side, and I hid there, shivering and crying to myself, questioning why this had happened. What did I do that was so wrong? I couldn't sleep. I was too terrified, and more terrified to get out from under Jerod's bed. I knew, when the drink wore off, he'd be okay. He always was sheepish the next day after a heavy drinking bout. I'd learnt it was best to say my bit about his drinking the following day, not that what I said would ever stop him from drinking.

The morning was approaching, and I didn't want to be under Jerod's bed when he woke up, so I got out. I looked at Jerod and thought, the children will never know what happened last night. I was so upset with Javier, and I was still questioning why he did this. I went into our bedroom. He was asleep. I looked at him with hate. I felt no respect for him at all. He was just so dangerous, and he could easily snap at any time. Really, this wasn't the first time I'd seen him have these bouts, where something was triggered in his brain and he became uncontrollable, but last night was the worst I'd ever witnessed.

Later on that day, when he got up, I could tell he was remorseful. I asked him, 'Javier, what happened?'

He lowered his head like a scorned child. 'Chris, I'm sorry. I don't know why I did it. I promise it will never happen again.' He lifted his eyes and looked at me for forgiveness.

I looked away. I was tired of our life. 'Javier, I don't want that gun in our house any more. It's got to go.'

He immediately agreed. 'I will give it back to my father today.' He came near me, and I shuddered at his touch and walked away. I was cold towards him and his touch. Today, I could see who he was. He was an intimidator, but I could also see he was weak. My time would come when I'd take charge and control of my own life.

He must have felt so bad, and so happy that I didn't leave him. He knew I had grounds to, and he played happily with the boys in a different way. I felt he saw his mistakes. The gun was returned to his father that day, but it was not the complete end to his aggression. He also quickly forgot his deeds. He actually started to become worse when he was drunk, in his mental, abusive, tormenting behaviour, which caused us many fights and arguments. Many times, Mrs Delmore would sing out from her lounge room window to warn Javier off, or if she caught him being abusive to me in our backyard, but that never stopped him, and I never wanted the police to become involved. I could work it out for myself.

In 1995, the story behind Len and Celia would be revealed, through my dad meeting up with them while out shopping. The puzzle would be gradually put together. The truth always comes through.

# Chapter 58

# More Secrets Revealed

Gema was still coming to stay with me at my house. Now she was older, I don't think she wanted to be there with me. Having to come and stay with me made her resentful. She started to take it out on the boys, by tormenting the hell out of them, and me too, with her neurotic behaviour. She was twenty-one. Regardless of her behaviour, I still loved her, and understood she needed her own life. I'd never asked her to come and stay with me, so I reasoned she must've wanted to come herself, but, of course, Javier was probably forcing his parents to make her come and stay with us.

She had her own issues. She had to bribe her father to let her go out at night, to get away from her family house. She'd confided in me that she had a boyfriend but couldn't tell her family, because she wouldn't be allowed to go out with him. The only two in her family who knew about the boyfriend were her brothers, Alexandre and Paco. Gema felt it was time I knew more about the family secrets.

Gema and I were more like best friends than sisters-in-law. When she was little, she'd stuck close by me like glue. Gema felt comfortable with me and trusted me, because I never divulged any of her secrets. She felt safe with me, and in that safety, she accepted me. She hated me being kept in the dark about her family. That was an injustice, seeing as I was married to Javier; plus, she'd become fed up with the attitudes of her own family.

We'd got the boys off to school and sat down with a cup of coffee at the dining room table.

She started, 'Chris, I want to tell you some more secrets. You're kept in the dark all the time, and I don't think you should be.'

Puzzled, I looked at her and said, 'Alright, tell me.'

'Be prepared.'

I smiled. 'I am.'

'Chris, the family is hiding many lies. Bianca's son, Leonard, isn't Henry's child,' she confessed. Her large, brown, almond-shaped eyes looked at me seriously.

Shocked, I said, 'What?'

'Yes, he's Nick's son.'

'What you're saying is, Pia's husband is Leonard's dad,' I repeated in disbelief.

'Chris, it's true, and I wanted to tell you.'

I shook my head, and said, 'That bastard Javier condemns my family all the time, and says terrible things about my mother's family, and all the time his sisters are…' I stopped.

Gema said, 'Yes, Chris, I know, and there are lots of things that go on in our family you have no idea of.' Her small, impish, dark-skinned face was solemn and concerned as she reminded me, 'Our father also molested Pia, I told you that.'

'Yes, I remember.' I paused and thought of my own children, and how he'd taken Julian to bed with him for an afternoon siesta. I wondered if he had touched Julian. I asked if he'd touched other family members, to assess if it was possible he'd touched Julian. 'Gema, did he touch Bianca?'

'No, he didn't touch her.'

My children concerned me and they'd slept with him. Panic grabbed me, and the memories flooded in of my own abuse. I brushed them away. 'Gema, he slept with Julian and Jerod sometimes. Do you think he…?'

Her face softened, and she sipped her coffee. 'No, Chris, he'd never do that with Javier's kids. He knows Javier would kill him.'

I wondered if he had, and I remembered Julian sometimes pushing him away and saying no to him. Most of the time he didn't want to go to bed with him. I'd defended Julian by saying he didn't have to go to bed if he didn't want to. Now I knew this, how was I going to stop him sleeping with my boys when he came to our place? Again, I asked, 'Gema, are you sure he wouldn't touch my children?'

She smiled. 'Yes, Chris. He did it years ago when Pia was young. I told you that, and how he slept with her because Mum refused him, and he slept with Mum's niece as well.'

Concerned, I said, 'I know; you told me that last time.'

My mind was overwrought and I was floundering. I was appreciating her telling me and was afraid of this knowledge. Near to tears for my children, and afraid for them if they were exposed to any molestation, I heard, 'It was terrible, Chris, when we were young. The old man wanted sex, and Mum hated it. You can't blame her; she'd had eleven kids.'

I said, 'But she really had sixteen kids, and some died.'

'Yes, Pia said Mum had about sixteen children, all told, but they were lost mainly through miscarriage. One died at two, and he was born after Javier,' Gema reaffirmed. 'Yes, and Mum and Dad never got over the loss of that baby, because he was two years old, and it had a name: Paulo.'

'Your mum said to me that Javier punched him on his death bed, when they took him in to see the baby laid out,' I said.

'He did.'

'I guess he didn't understand what was happening.' I empathised with the child part of Javier.

Gema said, 'The other children were miscarriages, and you can't blame Mum not wanting sex. There was no pill back then, and she was having a kid every year.'

I was in shock but understood what she was relaying to me.

'Chris, don't let them know I told you, will you?' she pleaded.

'I won't,' I reassured her.

The day was too much for me, as well as the worry over my own children's safety, which I'd tried so hard to protect. All those times Javier condemned my family, he was accusing my family of gross behaviour, and it was also happening in his own family. I didn't know what to do. I couldn't talk to Javier, or even my own parents. There was no one, only Gema.

# Chapter 59

# Cruelty Runs Through Them All

I was approaching twenty-eight years old, and life had little meaning for me. It was mundane and unrewarding. My only solace was my children. We were going to his mother's house. I dreaded it, wondering what I would face there. I hoped Pia wasn't visiting. My mood was very low. I leant my head on the window and stared out, watching the road whizz under the car. Javier went right into town, because he wanted to have a look at the beaches before we went to his mum's. We had a nice scenic drive around the Dawson Hill beaches, then he made his way down Queens Street, and I saw a tramp. This tramp hit my heart; I'm very sensitive to others' situations. I started to cry. Javier noticed me crying and demanded that I tell him why.

I said, 'Did you see that man back there. He was so poor, and only had rags on his back. I have never seen anyone so poor.'

He laughed at me. 'You're stupid. He's a tramp, and he isn't worth crying over.'

In defense I said, 'But he looked really poor, Javier.'

Javier was disgusted that I could have such sadness for a person like that. He directed his cutting hurt towards my boys, saying, 'Look at your silly mother, Julian and Jerod; she's crying for a man who has no money.'

The boys laughed, not understanding their cruel father. I couldn't look at the boys. I wiped the tears from my face and wondered why Javier couldn't see someone else's tragedy and suffering.

When we arrived at his mother's house and he had everyone's attention, he told them what I did, and how I was crying for some street tramp. They laughed and thought it was funny, but I'd never seen anyone that poor in my country. Even the tramps that came to our farm as kids didn't look that poor or miserable.

The biggest danger in the family was Pia. She could be so nice, like a sweet-smelling rose, but roses have thorns, and her thorns were sharp. Her life was so upside-down; she had a broken marriage and financial problems. Her intent was to bring everyone down to her level. She was a bitch and a witch, and when Bianca and the others were into séances, Pia was the one to cause most of the family problems between her parents and her siblings. She'd tell on them. What amazed me was everyone was old enough to tell her to butt out of their lives, but no one backchatted Pia, and no one was game enough to tell her off.

Bernat was the one she had the most control over. Also, his mother had control over him. On paydays, he'd come home with his sealed pay packet and hand it over to his mother. As he did, he'd stand there waiting for some type of approval or something. I'd watch them, and she'd open the packet and count the money. He'd then ask her for some money. She'd look at him with narrowed eyes and take out two dollars and give it to him. I was astonished the first time I witnessed that, and thought, out of a two hundred dollar pay packet, he's given two dollars? If he asked for more, he was smacked or pushed away. I saw it with my own eyes. This was how it was with them. The children worked for the parents, and no one could say anything about it.

I thought, no way will that happen in my family, and no way will our children be handing over their pay cheques to us, and they won't be even paying board, as far as I am concerned. My parents never took a cent from us, and we wouldn't be taking our sons' pay either.

I asked Bernat why he allowed it. He shrugged and said, 'That's the way it is.'

Pia had her own sisters fighting against each other, and she kept the one she favoured on her side, and if she fell out of favour with her, she'd bring the other sister in to her favour. It was a real game of chance, living among these people. Pearls are produced through mass irritation by sand, and she was the sand and she irritated the lovely ones, including me. She didn't realise that pearls are a sign of wisdom. Nor did I know that she was a gift to help me to uncover myself, and to understand people and life.

Pia was not like her sisters. She was short and she definitely had a masculine side. Her voice wasn't soft and feminine; it was quite husky. She considered herself a beauty, and she was always right. Pia was the overseer of the family. She had little tolerance and she was constantly running down other people's children.

I used to say to her, 'Be careful what you say about others, because it can all come back to you and your own.' I didn't understand my own words, but deep down I knew we shouldn't rubbish other people. I knew it could come back onto our own loved ones, and it did. Her children developed many problems with life and drugs.

Thanks to Gema, I knew about Pia's life and about Bianca's, and Pia's ex-husband, Nick, being the father of Bianca's son, Leonard, and Bianca's husband, Henry, also knew about it. Now I knew why he'd looked at me strangely on our first meeting. He must have wondered what was going on back then.

Bianca had a son to Henry, but their marriage was turbulent. They'd had many problems, but with all the stuff they were getting into, no wonder. No one should interfere with the other side.

Admittedly, Pia had a terrible life and an abusive childhood. I felt she didn't like to see anyone happy or having a good life. Pia betrayed my trust a few times. I soon learnt not to tell her anything. She not only told on you, but she twisted the story to suit herself, and make it more than what it was. Her mind was sharp, and her feelings for others were cold. She was a spider in a web; she could trap you in her web, and pounce on you before you knew it. She had told me she didn't have a childhood and was the real mother to all the younger siblings under her, and she was still playing that role. She was like flood waters; she could seep into every nook and cranny of everyone's lives.

I started to defend myself against Pia's torments, and one day I turned on her, much to her surprise and the surprise of the rest of the family. I'm like that; I will take and take, but I will eventually erupt. The younger family members were laughing after one of her remarks about me. She'd begun to criticise my nose size, saying I had a big nose. I was hurt, but let it go, not say anything in my defence. I wasn't a nasty person, but Pia and Javier were bringing out another side of me.

She was delighting in telling everybody about my supposedly big nose.

I snapped and lashed out. 'I may have a big nose, but at least I don't have tombstones for teeth.'

You could have heard a pin drop. They all looked at me and at her. I held my pose and dared them to say anything different. In my eyes, they had seen something my boys told me scared them. No one lashed out at me or drowned me out, as I stood firm. I hadn't liked saying what I said, because she was going through a hard time with her illnesses, and her teeth and gums had been badly affected by her medication. However, enough was enough.

From that day on, they refused to upset me, and if they did, they'd make a joke of it. If they got too nasty, I'd tell them how I felt. There were many incidents in that strange family that I was uncertain about, and I knew there were secrets I hadn't been told about as yet, but Gema would eventually tell me all. Because I couldn't understand the language, I had no idea what was going on. They truly had safety in their language, as far as I was concerned. From then on, Pia was sometimes kind and other times not - it depended on her mood - but she never criticised my looks again.

# Chapter 60

# Fear Leaves Me

Sometimes Pia, Bianca, Gema and I would go out together with our children. The circus was in town, so it was arranged that I'd go and pick them up, and we'd take our children to it. Javier had to do some concreting around our house, and it was a good excuse for us to leave while he and his friends worked. I got dressed up really pretty and decided to put on some make-up. Sometimes I wore it, and other days I didn't. I put on some eye shadow, mascara and lipstick. Even though we fought, Javier always complimented me, and he'd always tell me I was very beautiful, even though I couldn't see it.

I'd got us all dressed, and it was time to say goodbye. I sang out to him at the back door, 'Javier, we're going now.'

He came to the back door.

I said, 'We're off now; kiss Daddy goodbye, boys.'

They excitedly kissed their dad and ran to the front door, and out to the car parked in the front of the driveway. I kissed Javier and smiled at him. He stared at me.

I looked at him, shrugged, and asked, 'What's wrong?'

He said, 'Make this the last time you wear make-up when I'm not with you.' He looked across at his mates to make sure no one heard him, and back at me.

'But Javier...'

He said as he turned and left me, 'Don't do it again.'

I was so deflated, because I had been feeling pretty, and now I was put down. Of course, I did as he said, and only wore make-up in his presence.

There was a party on at Javier's mother's house. They often had parties. They had bought a big order of sardines from Rosemont and decided to barbecue them for their guests. I'd been outside and got sick of the effects of drinking on Javier. I was in the lounge room with Jerod, and I heard Julian screaming. I ran to him in the laundry, and Bernat came out with Julian.

Julian ran to me. 'Mummy, he put me up against the wall.'

I grabbed Julian, cuddled him, and looked at Bernat. 'What did you do to him?' I could see Julian was so scared; he was shaking and clinging to me. He'd been terrorised.

Julian's lip was cut. I noticed, on looking at it, it was bleeding. 'You've cut his lip. I will tell Javier what you did,' I threatened.

He begged me, 'No, Chris, don't.' He started to smile and told me he was only playing with Julian, and that it got out of hand. He said to Julian, 'Wasn't I, Julian?'

Julian was still scared and was clutching at my clothes. I had Jerod in my arms, and he was cuddling me more tightly. Bernat insisted it was an accident.

I stared at him sternly, and said, 'I will tell Javier on you if this ever happens again.' When I turned from him, Pia and Gema were behind me, and Pia said something to him in Spanish.

He said, 'Nothing happened.' He lowered his head, but I had my suspicions. I walked past them, and took my children into the lounge room, leaving them to squabble amongst themselves.

That night, Julian clung to me and stayed close by me. Bernat had been drinking heavily all day. Later on, he apologised. Bernat was my age. He'd never married. He wasn't very good looking, but thought he was, and he wore very thick glasses, like the bottom of a Coke bottle. Javier, Bernat and Vince also had very thick glasses, but not as bad as Bernat's. Alexandre and Paco also had to wear glasses, but normal glasses. Out of all the family members, Bernat was the most troubled person. Years later, secrets would unfold that would horrify me in regard to Bernat.

# Chapter 61

# Gema

On one of Gema's stays with me, she told me about Alexandre. I really liked Alexandre so much. I loved having a conversation with him, if I could, when Javier was not around. Javier didn't seem to go too far those days when we visited his mum's place. He always seemed to be close by.

Gema shocked me by saying, 'Chris, you know the old man won't let me go out without Alexandre.' She paused. 'And I have to pay him ten dollars.'

I was puzzled by her reminding me, but more puzzled by her having to pay him ten dollars. I answered, 'Yes, Gema, but why should you have to pay him. If anything, he should be giving you extra money to go out with,'

She laughed. 'No way will he give me money. If I don't pay him, he won't let me go out.'

I couldn't get her to change her thoughts. 'Well, you're working; you can pay your own way.'

'But I have to give my money to Mum, Chris.'

I shook my head and said, 'Really, Gema, you worked for your money; it should be yours, and not theirs. I will never understand such behaviour around giving your parents your money.'

These people had a strange mentality that I didn't agree with, where wages were concerned. I agreed, being a big family, they should pay board, but not all of their wages. Where was their incentive to save? Actually, there were no incentives; only work, with no rewards at the end of the week. It was terrible.

Once, Bernat asked his mother for extra money, and she said no to the extra money. He walked off, and accepted her no. No wonder they couldn't get anywhere in life. How could they, when their parents used them and controlled them. None of them ever stuck up for themselves. Javier told me it was the way they were, and he'd had to give them his wages. That's why he decided to leave home and travel around different jobs.

I told him no way would our children hand over any of their wages to us. Javier was manageable, and he agreed with me as far as the wellbeing of our boys was concerned.

Our boys started to get pocket money at a young age, and for a while, they spent it, until I taught them to save some of it. I started a bank account for both of them, and they would take their money boxes in and add some of their savings to their bank accounts. They actually liked to see the figures growing in their bank books.

In addition to their pocket money, they were always given extra money for any other reason, such as sport, excursions, movies, and show days. My sons weren't expected to use their pocket money on things other than themselves, because we, as parents, had that responsibility, so additional expenses were paid for by us. In the future, both my two sons would be very good with money and be able to create good futures.

Gema was very edgy; it was like she was bursting to tell me something.

'Gema, come sit down. What's up?' Taking a chair each, I sensed she needed to get something off her chest that was bothering her.

'Chris, I have told you many things gradually about my family, but there's something else I need to tell you.'

Dreading this news, I braced myself, and asked, 'What is it this time, Gema?' Looking at her face, I reasoned that I was ready for anything by now.

'You know when Alexandre and I go out, we go to gay bars.'

Thinking that was all, I said, 'Yes, you told me that, and you have great fun with the fags, as you call them.'

She giggled. 'Yes, especially with Stephanie. I wish you could come out with us, Chris. I know you'd have a ball.'

We both giggled.

I said, 'I don't think Javier would agree to that, Gema, even though I'd love to come just once to see your world.'

She was getting more restless. I asked, 'Gema, what is it? Tell me.' She had my full attention.

'Chris, Alexandre is gay,' she blurted out.

My mouth gasped. I was shocked. I hadn't expected to hear that. I leaned back into my chair. 'Gema.'

She reaffirmed it, saying, 'Yes, Chris, he's always been that way, and he's had problems with girls, because he's bisexual. But now he knows for sure he's gay and…'

I couldn't cope with what I was hearing. I'd never had contact with gay people. I knew nothing about gay people. I only remembered seeing the men dressed as women when Javier was taking me to the Capricorn Bar in Dawson Hill, and reading about gays in Dad's magazines. I didn't fully understand what was meant by being gay until recently.

I was not prepared for that news. As Gema continued to speak, I switched off. I don't know why I reacted like that.

'Chris,' I heard, 'its okay he's like this, and I wanted to tell you because no one will tell you anything.'

I was quiet, reasoning it all out in my mind. Alexandre was so effeminate. When I saw him the first time after this news, I said under my breath, 'You're no virgin.' I don't know why I said that. He's a boy, but I was disturbed by him being gay. I could really see his feminine self, and the girl within. I noticed it in his walk, and in his speech. Time erased the initial shock, and, gradually, I accepted him as gay. It was his choice to be what he wanted to be. Being with Alexandre was like being with another girl. This news made me look at him differently for a while. I adjusted and loved him the same as I did before. He and Paco were the only ones with intelligence and determination to better themselves.

Even though I had these people around me, I was not allowed to be alone in my own house. I constantly had someone staying with me, but they weren't meeting my needs. Their conversations were limited, and mainly on bitching about each other. Javier would leave me with them and go to the football.

I knew our marriage was breaking down. I'd got fed up with the fighting and arguments, and then the no talking for days drove me nearly insane. When we argued, I'd threaten him by saying, 'I'll leave you.'

He'd just glare at me, saying, 'If you do, you'll be sorry.' He also knew I had standards, and he knew I needed him to keep those standards. He knew I couldn't live below those standards. He was sure I'd never leave him, so he continued to harass me.

No way was I able to support my boys alone and give them what I wanted for them. Most of all, I wanted to break the cycles of both our families. My boys were going to be university educated, so I had to bear with his behaviour. I saw in his family the results of broken families. Pia was a good example. She was living in a housing commission area and struggled. I could see a difference between her children and mine. I could see the importance of a child having a father. I didn't want my boys to struggle, and I knew Javier wouldn't provide for us if I left him.

It was too much to bear at times, and I was going mad with hate and depression. I was wishing him dead way too often, which wasn't a healthy thing. When he left for work each morning, I'd just stare at him and silently wish it. Other times, I'd voice it to him. The hate was eating at me. He must have felt my hate, but he never commented on it.

# Chapter 62

# Mum

Mum was very negative, and so was Dad. No, he was more of a pessimist. They were chalk and cheese. Mum would get upset over the smallest thing and cry over other people's pains or tragedies she'd seen on TV. If someone had died in a car crash or had died of a disease, Mum was off crying. I used to get cranky with her, because she was crying for strangers, and not her own family. She couldn't feel for her own family members. Mum had her other side. If there was a comedy show on TV, she'd laugh hysterically and uncontrollably at the silliest of things. That irritated Dad to no end. He'd tell her to wake up to her stupid self, which resulted in Mum going into her shell, as she tried to hold back her emotions. It was so hard for Mum; she was full of emotions. Dad had buried his so deep, he'd lost touch with them. He definitely had no sense of humour and could only see the bad in everything. He'd rejoice in telling us that next year our economy would get worse, and life would be very hard for everyone. The more doom, the happier Dad was.

Dad felt he had all the answers, and that he knew which political party was the best. God help you if you went against him. Should you decide to follow the opposition party, he'd tell you all their faults, and run them down. This happened to me when I turned eighteen, and I was able to vote. I really didn't care for any political party. However, at this age, I was considered old enough to make a choice, and my choice, from listening to the political speeches, was for the Liberal Party; Dad's was opposite. Well, did Dad go off, to the point where I thought he might have even hit me. He was really angry.

To me, it was irrelevant what party led the country, as long as they did the right thing by the people, and they tried to incorporate some level of honesty and truth into their term of office to help our country flourish. I wasn't interested in the politics of the day, and I voted because it was compulsory to vote. If I didn't vote, I'd be fined; so much for democracy, when a fine insured a vote. Dad hated to see people happy. Only when he was happy, could you be happy. Mum was always searching for happiness, but she was too bogged down with self-misery to find any happiness. Grief and misery seemed to follow her everywhere.

Deep down I knew I was here to make changes. I caught myself out playing out their behaviour, but I had no idea of patterns and role models. I didn't know those words existed to describe family situations. I didn't know of the word 'peers'. I learnt that word at my children's primary school. I felt so inadequate in this world. How would I ever catch up to everyone else and their knowledge? Words weren't my forté. I feared words, and their meanings. My mind blocked me against words. If I read anything, which I rarely did, I'd be skipping big words, because I had no idea of how to pronounce them, or what they meant. So, I just made sense of the remaining part of the sentence to work out its meaning. Nothing was ever taught to us, and nothing was ever learnt, so I just glided through life, skipping sections of it.

I guess my parents were their happiest when they were going out to the club. When I was in my teens, I remember them both dressing up to go out. Dad would be whistling, and Mum would be adorning her cute little body, which she had back then, and putting one of her favourite ball gowns on, and one of her many pieces of beautiful jewellery Dad had bought her. One of us would clean Dad's shoes to a near-perfect shine. We'd get sixpence, or a shilling if he was extra happy. All dolled up, they'd head off to the local club. My scallywag Uncle Mitch was president of the club. They all enjoyed themselves.

Dad couldn't dance; Mum had other partners to enter in all the competitions. Mum was a very good dancer and won many prizes. Mitch was also on the Board, and Dad loved a drink and Mum loved to dance, so they were both in their element. The changes came for them after Dad and I were caught together. I guess it was his way of making amends, and to mend some of the wounds.

After the ball period stopped, both of them continued to go out to regular dances, because Dad liked a drink so much. 1968 to 1974, things were tough on Mum, and Dad wasn't at all fair to her, off-loading his mother onto Mum, staying out to all hours of the night, and probably having a fling. Mum could have refused to look after Grandma, but I guess she dared not suggest it, what with his hair-trigger temper. Time catches up on those who wield control over the less fortunate. The misery backfired and turned on him. Dad suffered his first heart attack around the age of forty-five, not long after they'd moved into Hastings Crossing. He stopped everything, because he wasn't allowed to drink alcohol or smoke, and he couldn't eat all the wrong foods he liked eating. Who did he take it all out on? Mum.

So, Mum suffered for his ill-treatment of himself, and he blamed Mum's cooking, and the way she looked after him. We all actually got to see just how extremely selfish this man was. He stopped going out to the clubs, where Mum got her only small relief from the dreary life she led. His excuse was that he couldn't sit in a club and watch others smoking or drinking, when he couldn't do it himself. This stopped them meeting up with other friends who smoked, but Dad couldn't restrain himself from his bad habits. Eventually, he went back to his former life, eating all the wrong foods, drinking and smoking, but their club days were limited to afternoons, not night-time events.

Bad treatment of the self eventually catches up to one, and it did to Dad. At the age of forty-seven, he had to go to Rosemont to the heart hospital for major open-heart surgery. The demon was really released within him. His selfishness grew to extremes, and Mum suffered the brunt of it. Mum was always at his side, and she was always condemned by Dad. He never said thank you to her. She let him wipe his feet on her. The more he whipped her, the more devoted she became. She whined to us, her daughters, but never to the perpetrator of her misery. Mum had a new complaint, and I mostly copped it. I had to face her and deal with this, so she moved from Dad's infidelities, to his intolerable behaviour as a heart-attack victim. I was constantly bombarded with their illnesses, and her woes.

Barton still helped by taking them down to the hospital, much to Dad's displeasure, because Barton smoked, and this caused Dad some irritation. His jealousy of my brother over Mum was still evident, but Barton supported Mum, and she needed that badly. When Dad came home, Barton was the one to always help him. Barton could never do anything right in Dad's eyes. He constantly put Barton down, so Barton's help never changed Dad's mind towards him. He had little tolerance, acceptance or love for my brother, and he still called him an idiot.

The one that's least appreciated, is put down, and kicked from pillar to post, is the one that does the most, and doesn't hold any grudges towards their abuser. Both Barton and Mum wouldn't have anything said about Dad, especially Barton, and I don't think I ever heard a bad word about our father from him. Of course, Mum whined about Dad, but it was only okay if she did it, and if you got too critical of Dad, she'd turn the cards on you. Barton did what he could, with love, and with no expectations of Dad. I believe my brother really loved Dad, and Dad just didn't see it.

Mum and Barton were both punished for Dad's health problems, and he punished them for his mixed-up life as well; but they couldn't see what he was doing to them both, or maybe their love for Dad was stronger than my understanding of my father. When Mum told me Dad was blaming her for his health problems. I couldn't understand her accepting his hurtful words, and not telling him he was wrong, and that he caused his own health problems. She told me she couldn't throw it back in his face, because he'd never accept his own mistakes. So, Mum became more negative in her conversations around both of their illnesses. Now they had a common issue: illness. Mum was always a hypochondriac; now she could take Dad down that road as well, so he could at least have some understanding of her need for pills to cure her. Pills were always better to hide behind, to keep one's self semi-comatose, and to suppress old memories; better than letting out the truth of the self.

At fifty-three, Dad would suffer another heart attack. Before he died, he would undergo three heart bypass operations. At the age of fifty-three, he had to retire from work, and then he became more difficult, because he couldn't eat what he liked, and he couldn't have a drink or smoke. Of course, that didn't stop him. He'd do what he wanted, and he threw all the surgeon's good work out the window, so to speak.

# Chapter 63

## Javier's New Friends Enter Our Lives

Life was quiet, and we were on our own for a while, after mysteriously losing Celia and Len as friends. They never returned. If I asked Javier about Len, he'd say he had left Harper's Foundry. We'd go and visit Javier's mother, or go to my parents' house.

Excitedly, Javier told me, 'Chris, I met this man called Lenard, who we'll call Len, and he's a good, religious man, a Catholic, and he wants to come and visit us. I've been meeting him at the football.'

'Okay then. When will he come?' I asked.

'I told him to come tomorrow after work,' he announced.

I smiled, and I was happy. Javier being happy was great for me. I said, 'Sounds good.'

It was rare that Javier ever brought strange people into our home; he wasn't the type of person to do that. I thought this Len must be a good guy. Outsiders weren't usually allowed in our lives, only family, unless you had the right credentials that impressed Javier. I was never allowed to form friendships with strangers outside our family circle. Only Javier decided who would be our friends.

The following day came, and Javier sat in the lounge room watching TV as I busied myself. All morning I'd been a perfectionist, cleaning and tidying the house. I had to have everything in order, and it had to be spotless to meet our new guest in the afternoon. I cooked cakes, and prepared sandwiches for our afternoon tea. Later in the afternoon, as I was doing my last minute tidying up, Javier came to the kitchen and said, 'They're here.'

'Okay, will you go and greet them?' I asked. 'I'll just finish this off.'

I quickly wiped over the sink from the last lot of dishes. I could hear voices coming around the back of the house. The man's voice sounded familiar. Javier walked in all smiles, and a short, stocky man followed him through the door.

Javier said, 'Chris, this is Len, and his wife, Naomi.'

I looked at them, and said in an astonished voice, 'I know you.'

Len looked at me quizzically. 'My God; the lady with the broccoli.'

'Yes,' I announced sarcastically.

His wife Naomi turned light pink with embarrassment. Javier was looking bewildered.

Len started giving me a long spiel. 'You were right about the broccoli. We should cut the stems and leaves off it.'

I smiled, and said, 'Yes, you should.'

Len and Naomi owned a fruit market in Hastings Crossing. They were selling good quality fruit and vegetables, regardless of them being quite expensive. One day, I'd had to complain, because he was selling the broccoli with the stems and leaves, and this was weighed, and I was paying for that weight and then cutting them off and throwing them in the bin. I was getting too much of that part of the vegetable, and not enough of the edible part.

Naturally, they didn't agree with me back then. Funny he did in our house. Personally, I didn't really like Len from the fruit-shop days, and I thought he was only interested in making quick money, not in the customer, and there always seemed to be something sneaky about him. He could never look you straight in the eyes. To me, that was a no-no. Javier later told me Len was like a Jew. So, a friendship was formed with them. They had six children in all, four from Len's first marriage that he never got over. He apparently lost his first wife while she was giving birth to the youngest of his first four children. There were two other children with Naomi, and they were the same ages as Julian and Jerod.

Len actually opened a door for me, and Javier allowed me to go and visit Naomi, so I would often go into their house. Naomi actually gave me the rundown on Len's life, telling me all about his first marriage, and how Len was devastated over the loss of Doreen. He never got over her death, so much so that he still wore her wedding band, but was married to Naomi. I asked Naomi how she felt about that, and she just shrugged, and never said anything. I felt for Naomi, and could see that it gave her pain, and even in our company, Len constantly talked about Doreen and about how good she was, a perfect mother and an angel of a woman, and that there was no other woman like her. As he praised her, you could see he was still in love with the dead wife. I could see Naomi's anguish in this situation. She had no chance of competing with a dead saint. That was what Doreen was in Len's eyes. During our group conversations, when Len reminisced, I would look at Naomi, and she'd look away. I felt she was just there to rear his children. Naomi was under a lot of pressures with this man, and I felt he was no saint. He had a bad temper under that jovial laugh and smile. He'd smile with his eyes closed or squinted, or with his eyes darting in all directions. To me, he seemed worse than Javier, because he used his religion to profess to be a good man, and being a good man has nothing to do with religion. Good men are born and bred good men; however, some hide behind a mask, and claim that virtue through a faith.

Naomi was a nervous, edgy woman, and she smoked excessively, chewing her nails down further than I chewed mine. Her hands trembled as she smoked. She told me there were many problems between them, but Len always seemed happy, and made out they had a great marriage. There was no fooling me, even though I was very naïve. I sensed things happening to other people, but alas, never for myself - or rarely.

On many of my visits to see Naomi, she told me that Len had two faces, and she honestly thought Len was seeing other women. I couldn't relate to that. I didn't feel it, so I just listened to her. I had my own issues around freedom with Javier, and my mind seemed to close off to other people's emotional issues those days. With Naomi, the more I saw her, the more familiar she was becoming to me. Mum was forever ringing me, complaining on the phone to me about Dad, and crying to me. Unfortunately, I couldn't solve Mum's problems or Naomi's problems, and I wanted a friend who was problem-free, as far as infidelities were concerned; but, for some reason, infidelities were bombarding me to solve.

I learnt to switch off. I learnt to be with the person and let whatever they said just slide over me, like water off a duck's back, and in doing this, I survived better, and coped better listening to their repeated problems. I switched off.

Javier and I ended up going out at night to the club with Len and Naomi, and it was good to go out. I didn't mind going to the clubs, but I much preferred to go to a classy restaurant. This brought up lots of issues around my mother, because now Mum lived in Hastings Crossing, closer to us, I much preferred her to look after my children. If we were going out of town, I'd drop the boys off at Javier's mum's house. This put Mum into a panic, because of my brother's wife, Lorna. Her children weren't the cleanest, and Mum didn't want to have to look after their children and put them in her bed. Because of that, my children and Maxine's children were penalised. Her reasoning was that if Barton saw our children at her house, how would she explain it to him why she was minding our children, and never offering to look after his children. She couldn't tell him to wash and clean his kids up. Her fears around hurting Barton just frustrated both Javier and I, and also my boys were caught up in her drama as well.

Then it became a secret squirrel venture. We had to either sneak our kids into their house, or if Barton was there visiting her, we had to wait for him to leave her house. That was painful, because Barton had no concept of time, and he was never in a hurry to go home, or anywhere. The escapade caused more friction between Javier and I. After all the waiting or complaining or yes and no, if it wasn't possible to leave the boys with Mum and Dad, we'd then have to drive the boys to Dawson Hill to stay with his parents.

Len's marriage was on the rocks, so Len and Javier started to spend more time together. Javier seemed to be away from home more often again, and they either went to the football, or for a drink at the local club. Many times, Javier came home late after the football finished at 5pm. On their first late morning return, I was still up waiting for Javier, and he wisely brought Len in to support him. Len had the gift of the gab. He was good at creating stories, which I believed. One incident when they returned home at 4am in the morning, I was really worried. Javier must have seen our house light on and got Len to come in with him.

Len straight away spoke up on entering the house, his eyes flying all over the room. 'Sorry, Chris, we were very drunk, and fell asleep in the car, and just woke up. It was so strange. We went to the football and followed the players to the club to celebrate their victory. We left the club to come home, and I said to Javier, 'Mate, I need to rest before I drive home. I've had too much to drink.'

I darted my eyes over to Javier to catch his expression, and he was looking pretty sheepish, not saying anything and letting Len tell the story.

Len caught my suspicious glance at Javier. 'And Javier told me you know that you have to be careful drinking and driving. You know that, Chris. And Javier's a good guy, Chris.'

I looked quickly at Len's eyes, and they were squinting and moving all over the place. I knew nothing of body language back then. If I had, I would have thrown him out the door. He was so convincing, and, gradually, he won me over, and swayed me to believe his story. Calmly, I said, 'Is that what happened?' Oddly enough, I never suspected any wrongdoing, or infidelity, from my husband. I was just annoyed they'd been out enjoying each other's company, and I'd been at home with the boys.

Len said, 'I'd better go. Naomi will be wondering where I am.'

'Yes, you better,' I suggested.

He left, and we went to bed, and nothing more was said of the incident.

I still had my ingrained conditioning that I was unconsciously forcing on my boys. I was expecting perfection from them, and if they didn't give it to me, I became nasty. I'd learned that from my father. Even though I tried not to be like my parents, I did slip up in many areas. My parents didn't care if we got an education; this wasn't my father's issue. It was mine, and I made the boys study and do their homework to perfection.

The perfection bit was Dad's, and if it was not perfect, I would rip it up in front of them, and make them do it again. I also started to swear at them and call them stupid. This I was aware of, and I had to stop it. I hated that trait surfacing in me. This insisting on perfect handwriting caused my boys lots of problems with their handwriting. Like my handwriting, it was hard to read. I was just as bad with myself; everything had to be perfect. I screamed at them, and called them names. I was starting to demand silence in the house, and if they weren't quiet, I'd scream at them for the littlest, silliest things, just like my father did. I caused them lots of damage, I am sure. My depressed state of mind was getting worse. I hid it well from everyone. I was so perfect to the outside world, even Len noticed my perfection.

Javier said to me, 'Chris, Len says when you're in church, you look so perfect; he says you're like an angel.'

Yes, I was perfect, but dead.

Funny Len mentioned that at home in front of Javier, much to Javier's delight. He loved it if his wife was perfect. When Len said I was an angel, I felt a shift within. I knew a beast resided within as well, waiting to rant its fury of suppressed anger and rage.

Len was a strange man. He never talked to me at church; he seemed to ignore me. He nodded, but kept his distance. I felt he thought I wasn't good enough to talk to in front of the church people. He was such a hypocrite, because I knew he drank, gambled, and gave his wife a hard time, and in the eyes of the Catholic Church, you shouldn't do any of those things. He'd often go to Confession to rid himself of his sins, and then redo them the following day. I didn't particularly like Len, but I had to take the boys to Mass because it was a school requirement, and also to keep the old priest off the boy's backs, so he wouldn't give them a hard time at school on Monday morning. We went to save face, not because we wanted to. It was hard for the boys and I to go to Mass; we were not church-going people. I did like the hymns, especially *The Lord's Prayer,* and the *23rd Psalm.*

# Chapter 64

# Javier Drifts Further Away

The relationship between Javier and Len grew stronger. They'd go to the football every weekend. After the football, they'd be out to all hours in the pub or club. Because I was so depressed, I just didn't care.

Janice, Len's eldest, who was about twenty, was always chatting up Javier. I think she was secretly in love with him. I could see it in her eyes, but I dismissed it. She was only a child, and she was also Len's daughter. Javier was always accusing me of cheating. I knew nothing about projections, mirrors and reflection. Now I know why he would never let me out: because he knew what he was doing. He was afraid I'd do the same thing. During our marriage, I had contracted some infections, but I never questioned him about them. I never suspected him of cheating on me. Those infections must have been minor, because they came and went. I was always wishing some woman would come into his life and take him from me. I hated him so much.

We had major fights, which made me hate Javier, but as quickly as I hated him, as quickly I forgave him. I had fallen out of love with him years before, and maybe

I never loved him; maybe I was only infatuated with him, and that lasted for our first six years of marriage. That's if I was ever in love with him at all. He was different because of his dark, handsome looks, and he was ethnic, but it was all questionable. Fortunately, I was a very adaptable person. I knew I had to stay where I was because of my boys, so I learnt to recover quickly after a bad fight or upset. I learnt to make the most of life, and the situations that faced me.

Before Javier and I got married, I was once a bit jealous of him. That was at Camilla and Pepe's wedding; a girlfriend of Camilla's was eyeing him off. She'd raised jealousy in me that I'd never felt before. He was also flirting with the girl, but it was quickly resolved, because I walked out of the wedding reception. I was going home. If I'd gone home, he would never have seen me again. He followed me out of the reception, apologising and taking me back into the reception, and from then on, he behaved.

Another time, I'd come home from hospital after having Julian. I'd become ridiculously jealous of my own mother. I reasoned that out quickly and got over it. There wasn't much of an age difference between Mum and Javier, but it was my mind playing tricks on me, and I stopped it. After these two incidents, I never felt jealousy with Javier again. There was no need to. I'd often question myself as to why I married this person. I didn't want to marry until I was at least twenty-eight. He came in, and I married him. Why?

Later on, Javier made more friends at Harper's Foundry. These people were so different to people I'd known, and we started to go out as a group: Nancy and Morton, Len and Naomi, Javier and me. We were having lots of fun, especially with Morton. He was a real character. He looked a bit like Paul Hogan and was just as funny. I loved these outings, and we started to go out again to really good restaurants. We'd always done that when we were going out with Javier's brother, Dante.

I didn't realise how beautiful I was. Javier was always complimenting me, but my hatred of him squashed any belief that I was beautiful. We were out at a plush restaurant, where the waiters wore white shirts with a bow tie.

I was laughing at one of Morton's many jokes, and Len's back-up to his joke, when it came time to order.

This young waiter wasn't able to contain his feelings, saying in front of everyone, 'What would you like to order, you beautiful doll.'

I froze, looking at Javier immediately.

Everyone went silent and they looked at Javier. His eyes glared in anger. The waiter was oblivious to Javier, and kept smiling at me, not caring what the others thought.

Len broke the silence. 'Chris, what did you say you wanted?'

'Oh, I'll have the lobster mornay, thank you,' I smiled at the waiter, then gradually lowered my eyes, looked at Javier and smiled. Javier smiled back. All through the night, the young man made sure he had every opportunity to serve me, leaning in really close, brushing pass me as often as he could to try and get my attention and to look into my eyes. He was so young. I couldn't understand him finding me attractive.

With our new friends and going out, I was happier. Sometimes, I wanted to cuddle Javier and hold his hand, but he'd never let me. I asked him why he didn't allow me to touch him, and he told me that I aroused him too much. I questioned him on what he meant by that. He said I was sexually arousing him, and he couldn't touch me in public. I didn't understand my magnetism; instead, I was upset, because he was rejecting me. He was too highly sexed.

I noticed changes in Javier around the wives of these men from Harper's Foundry. I turned a blind eye to a lot of things, not even questioning Javier in regard to these women. I thought, well, they're married, and no one would cheat on their partners. They all seemed so happy in their marriages. I had enough problems questioning Javier over his drinking issues, which I learnt to question the next day.

There was a strange incident between Javier and Nancy, Morton's wife. I never questioned Javier over it. Nancy came to visit us on her own. Morton was one of Javier's newest and closest friends. Nancy and I were talking in the kitchen, and then she left me and went off. I didn't take any notice of where she'd gone, maybe to the toilet, or to check on her children. They were playing in the lounge room with my boys. I started to wonder where she'd gone. I couldn't hear her in the lounge room. I went looking, and eventually found her in our bedroom. She and Javier were in the dark when I entered and switched on the light. She was sitting on the bed talking to him. They both acted as though I did not exist. It was okay for them to be talking to each other, as far as I was concerned.

I said, 'Oh, there you are. I wondered where you went.'

Nancy said, 'I just came in to talk to Javier.'

I said okay and left them. I really didn't care.

More and more, Javier started to accuse me of many infidelities. He became more abusive, telling me I had loads of boyfriends that he'd question me about, asking me how many I had. As usual, I pleaded with him, saying I had none, and that I didn't go anywhere to meet people.

'You're a slut; you've got a string of boyfriends,' he'd scream.

I'd stare at him as if he was a madman to even think such nonsense, and react angrily, saying, 'Javier, I have no one. I am always home here. How could you even think such a thing of me?'

A fight would break out between us, and we'd both be screaming at each other. I was the biggest slut in the world, yet I never walked out of my front yard, and never knew anyone to be a slut with. It never dawned on me he was cheating on me.

I must have been totally stupid. I was under constant accusation by him, and surveillance by his parents. Again, we gradually started to lose our friends. Into the 1980s, we only had Len and Naomi left as friends. Morton, Nancy, and our other married friends disappeared. I often wondered why.

# Chapter 65

# Life And I Want Answers

At thirty I was questioning life more often, and I wanted books to answer my questions, but how to get them? Javier would never allow me to read books. When I asked him for some books, he told me no, I couldn't have any books, because of John's wife, Sarah. He told me a big story about how lazy she was, and how she never cared for her children, and how their house was like a pigsty, because all she did was read all day.

Javier had all the rules laid out, and I just had to obey them. There was no going against those rules. Well, not yet anyway. We had updated the boys' encyclopaedias from the *World Book Encyclopaedia* to the *Encyclopaedia Britannica*, and that was a start. These new encyclopaedias were good, but we kept both sets, so the boys could gradually work through both, and adjust from a children's edition to a more adult encyclopaedia.

Later on, it was as if the universe had granted me my wish. I received a pamphlet in the mail from Reader's Digest, offering books on the unexplained, and mysteries of the world and the unknown. This was what I wanted, to understand life, and life had presented the information and the opportunity to learn this knowledge. All I needed was his permission. These books weren't romantic stories like Sarah read. These were books on mysteries and strange happenings.

I used my talent in conning, which I was able to do now and then, and I was allowed to buy those books. I was so thirsty for knowledge. As soon as the housework was done, I'd sit and read those books, but I needed other books. Slowly and steadily, I'd work on him to achieve what I needed. In the meantime, I was learning many things, things I knew. There was more to life than meets the eye.

I was very resourceful, and I worked out how I could achieve things I wanted and needed. I was mowing our lawns and being paid for it, so I mowed our lawn, the whole lot: the twenty-foot frontage, and the one-hundred-and-twenty-foot backyard by fifty feet wide. Javier was paying me to do this, so he could be free of the mowing on his days off. I bought myself books, and him new clothes.

In some of those books, I couldn't read certain parts. If I saw the word 'occult' or 'devil', I would fling the book shut, as if the very word had life. I could never see any badness in the world. To me, there was only good in the world, and mischievous and naughty.

My thirst for knowledge got stronger, and so did my need for newer books, and in this need, my wishes were answered by my brother-in-law, Alexandre. He was also into reading lots of books. He'd bought the Virginia Andrews' book, '*Flowers in the Attic*,'and he also had '*The Godfather*' and a book called '*The Cell*.' Alexandre gave me these books to read. Javier agreed to me reading them, because Alexandre said there was no romance in those books. I was very careful not to read them in front of Javier, because he'd only get upset, and accuse me of not doing my housework and being neglectful of our children.

I became very tactful and read if he was in the garage, or when he was away at work. Sometimes, I couldn't help myself; I'd have the books in the kitchen cupboard, and when he was watching TV with the boys, I'd read a few pages. There were many secrets between us: between me and books and him.

What I had in books was opening me up. I was starting to question the origin of man, and why man was as he was. Questions were entering my head: what are we here for, and where do we go to after death? How did life all start? Why is man as he is? I was an atheist; in my mind, I hadn't met God, and I felt I knew nothing about God. Issues around God were rising in me. It wasn't that I didn't believe in a God; I just didn't know God. My concept of God wasn't like that of the churches, which I'd heard of at the boy's Catholic mass. I started to see God as a scientist, and a council of men determined our lives. God was a superhuman that lived in other galaxies and on another planet, and we were the result of this God, or the experiments of this scientist.

I was compelled to look at the concepts of Darwin's survival of the fittest and man evolving from primates. This concept haunted me, and I wanted more answers. I questioned how we could be evolved from monkeys; that was all I had to go on. Somehow, it didn't ring true, us as monkeys. No, it wasn't possible.

I read in the encyclopaedias we had about Darwin's theory. It still wasn't ringing true. I studied the cave men; I couldn't see monkeys involved. This was all the books could tell me, until the Jehovah's Witnesses knocked on my door.

They were visiting our neighborhood, and I needed answers, so I allowed these ladies into my home. I found out that Marsha was the mother of my school friends, the Burski twins, Adela and Nadia. These ladies couldn't satisfy my hunger to know either.

Len and Naomi eventually separated, and Len quickly found Vera. Amazing how they were so close so quickly, but I dismissed it all as usual. I had more pressing questions to be answered in my life. Marital issues were the furthest thing from my mind, so I invited them to dinner at our house where we could meet his new girlfriend.

Meeting Vera for the first time, I felt she wasn't a very pretty girl. She was about five six with blonde hair and seemed to be confident. She acted like she knew Len really well. Her son, Neil, was also very easygoing with Len, and they all got on like a house on fire. We sat down to a wonderful dinner I'd cooked; in those days, I was a very good cook. As the night progressed, I felt that Javier and Len were settled, and I could ask the questions that were burning inside me.

Even though Len was a very religious man, I was hoping to get some answers from him. 'Len, can you answer some questions for me?'

Nodding, with his eyes that continually blinked, he said, 'Sure, mate, how can I help you?' He winked at Javier.

'Well, I'm wondering about the origin of man. I know of the Darwin concept, but can you help me to understand where the missing link between primitive man and modern man starts and ends?'

A bit flabbergasted, he stated, 'Well, Chris, our Lord created Adam and Eve, and he said that all men and women came from them.'

Not happy with that answer, I said, 'Yes, I've heard that, but what about primitive man, and the findings of primitive man many years prior to the Adam and Eve story. How do you explain that?'

Javier stared at me with daggers in his eyes, but his looks didn't worry me. I was beyond caring what he thought. I wanted some answers.

Len sounded like a preacher giving me a sermon. He stated, 'Chris, *The Bible* says that there was only Adam and Eve, and they were our first father and mother.'

*But how?* ran through my mind. I thought, there's evidence of other races. And the cave men, how did they come into the picture? I felt man was billions of years old, older than the cave man.

I couldn't get the answers I needed, and he was too much into religious explanations. I realised he couldn't help me. As we sat and listened to Len telling us the Jews will be the downfall of the world, my thoughts escaped, and I wondered if *The Bible* was man-made. If it was, then we were being ruled by men's rules, and not by God's rules, because men actually wrote the book. There were too many questions, and no one in my life that could help me to understand.

After Len and Vera left the house, Javier snapped, 'Don't ask him questions like that again. You looked stupid, and he doesn't want to be bothered with your thoughts.'

I just looked at him, and knew he wasn't on my level, and nor was Len. I'd have to seek my answers elsewhere; but where? Javier was put out, because he couldn't think beyond his own physical needs, and his next pay cheque. That was Javier's world: his food, sex, beer, shelter, and his pay cheque.

He was constantly worrying about money, and I used to tell him all the time, don't worry, it will all work out in the end, and it always did. Everything got paid, we lived very comfortably, and I couldn't understand why he worried so much about money. He even had his next pay cheque worked out, while we were spending the current one. I couldn't care less about money or such worries.

Knowledge was knocking on my door, and I needed answers. My questions got bigger, and the need to know got stronger and stronger. I wanted answers - now. I knew about life after death, that wasn't an issue. As a child, I knew that we never died; we came back. I didn't fear death, and from my childhood, I knew about other worlds, and how people lived on other planets. For me, that wasn't a mystery.

I had inner knowledge. I didn't realise we had inner knowledge. But how does life begin, and how did it begin on Earth? What happened to bring life to this world? Why do we live and die and come back? I believe there's life on other planets. I feel spirits exist, but I fear to see them, yet I know of them. How did man develop? From what did he develop? I wanted to know of the origin of man. There was the missing link theory, and I questioned it.

I felt there was a massive nuclear war back in ancient times and we destroyed ourselves. Man had to go into the caves, and the nuclear explosion caused disfiguration, so cavemen had to evolve again to what we are now. I just don't believe our planet is the only planet in the whole of the universe with life: all those planets and no one on them. Really? And the planet is way older than they claim it is. I think it's billions of years old, and life has come and gone on Earth over that period of time. Civilisations have developed and died off. So, what happened each time to each civilization that came and went? Are we the by-product of a distant human life not found yet, that may have even left this planet? In my mind, I felt mankind of ancient times had far exceeded beyond our discoveries and had developed to a powerful level, and to the point of self-destruction.

After that mass destruction by chemicals they'd invented, they caused some genetic interference, a defect that produced a variety of cave dwellers, like Cro-Magnon and Neanderthal man. Even if it was from natural chemicals, if it was an earthly catastrophe, chemicals would have been released into the atmosphere. After either one of these events, outside help came in. I felt outside help came to rectify our mistakes, or maybe even it was done on our own planet by our own people that escaped the catastrophe and remained as modern man. Gradually, they brought back modern man from the Neanderthal by regaining his original genes through genetic work, and so modern man reappeared out of nowhere.

During this process, man would have had to have gone through many stages of re-breeding until he could reclaim his true genes. Does mankind reach a point in evolution, and then is he taken back to basics, to rebuild intelligence through struggle? Did mutation occur from others visiting us from other worlds to help mankind right its wrongs? Or was this a breeding ground?

Was Atlantis a way station, a place where mass experimentations took place? Then came the time when that race had to leave us to allow us to evolve again, to further evolve through our own genetic memory. I had so many questions. The books weren't enough, so I tried to work it all out with the little knowledge I had, and with my own mind.

I found some books on Atlantis, but I couldn't get the right information I was seeking. There was this inner voice, and it was telling me that this is the way it was. How could I tell people those things? There was no one in my group that would understand this, only Alexandre, so he and I chatted sometimes about these thoughts. It still wasn't enough for my mind.

Javier's father was starting to tell me about the history of Spain. He told me about the Moors of Africa. I'd never heard of such people. Through Gema, he told me how, when he was in the Spanish Civil War era, he was assigned to a job where work was being done between a monastery and a convent, and he told me there was a tunnel found that ran between the two borders, and in that tunnel, they'd found the bodies of dead babies. I gasped. It shocked me. He said the priests were always telling them to do the right thing, but they weren't. My world was so sheltered, and I couldn't put it in my mind, but I was so hungry for any knowledge.

I began to have more vivid dreams, and I felt they were trying to show me what I was thinking and trying to help me to put it all into perspective. I never wrote down or recorded my dreams, yet there were a few dreams that stayed with me, especially the ones with the *Christ*, when we were walking together in India. There was another dream of an aquatic race; they had gills and swam under water, and I was one of them. They must have been related to the Atlanteans.

What was I seeking? There was an urgency to know. There was that vision I'd seen at sixteen, and the message from that vision was that I wasn't grasping life and its experiences. On that night, I'd felt unbearable terror and anguish that no one could conceive. Others would have screamed at that point, but no. I feared, but at the same time I knew there was something beyond me, even though I didn't know what it was.

My mind was turning to death, and I had my own ideas on death. Reincarnation was resurfacing for me to question, because I knew about that as a child. My own death became important to me, and I started to tell Javier what I wanted after I died: the death of my body. I told him how I wanted my body disposed of. Don't bury me in the ground or burn me. Put me out to sea in a glass coffin, I told him, and don't violate my body after death, and definitely no autopsies. This was so important to me, that the body, which was my vehicle for the time I journeyed on this earth, was to be respected for its support of me in this journey.

I was starting to know the power of the mind, without knowing, and realised the mind could make us or break us, and that there was a thin line between sane and insane. Life is a puzzle of clues that we have to be brave enough to seek out, but first, we have to become aware that such a thing exists. Most of us are asleep. I was coming out of a big sleeping period.

A program came on the TV, '*The Chariots of the Gods*' by Erich Von Daniken, and after watching his program, I became inspired that there were others in the world with like minds, questioning life and its beginnings. This man excited me to try in my limited life and in my marriage: to seek out the truth.

I got his book and I read it. It seemed to answer a lot of my questions. The local Community Centre started to offer films on the ancient world, and I got to see a film on Egypt and the ancient worlds. As I watched, something told me, no, it's not this way. It's another way. I took from the films what I needed and went away hungering for more information. There was still a lot missing. They weren't telling the complete truth.

In those days I had lots of questions and searched for answers in the only place I could, in my own mind, and I tried to work it out. My enthusiasm was so high, but I feared the unknown, the other side, the invisible side to our world that resides within our world. How do I know of these things?

To be continued…

# About The Author

I was born in the Hunter Valley in New South Wales, Australia, and am one of three siblings. I've had quite an interesting life, venturing outside of my own country, where I found the inspiration to write books. My greatest love is writing.

My favourite pastimes include reading, travelling and meeting people, and capturing these moments through photography.

My other passion is life coaching, helping other people; my life experiences have enabled me to understand others.

My website contains my Bio, links to purchase my books and reviews:
Website: www.christineucowinwriter.com
Email address: christine@christineucowinwriter.com
Amazon Central Authors Page:
www.amazon.com/author/christineucowinwriter

www.ingramcontent.com/pod-product-compliance
Lightning Source LLC
Chambersburg PA
CBHW021214090426
42740CB00006B/223